OXFORD TO CAMBRIDGE RAILWAY

Against a silvan background, Bletchley depot was not unpleasantly situated. A Webb compound goods engine is apparently ready for its duty rota, which could easily be one of the heavy brick trains between Bletchley and Bedford. A Class E, this 4 cylinder 2-8-0 engine was a progenitor of the 8 coupled breed of heavy goods engine that became an architype of the LNWR from the latter years of the nineteenth century culminating in the G2 'Super D' types lasting until the early 1960s. Stone blocks in the retaining wall behind are said to be those originally used as sleepers on the London & Birmingham Railway.

L&GRP/Courtesy David & Charles

OXFORD TO CAMBRIDGE RAILWAY

Volume Two: Bletchley to Cambridge

Bill Simpson

The seal of the Bedford & Cambridge Railway, quartered with the arms of Oxford, Bedford and Cambridge with Britannia from the crest of the LNWR.

Crown Copyright (NRM)

The seal of the Bedford Railway, with the town crest superimposed on the crest of the London & Birmingham Railway.

Crown Copyright (NRM)

Oxford Publishing Co.

ISBN 0–86093–121–8

ACKNOWLEDGEMENTS

The author would like to record his sincere gratitude to the following institutions for their help in placing essential material at the disposal of researchers, and to all the people that have so unselfishly given of their time and effort to help make this history possible, especially the men of Bletchley who have supported not only this volume but previous work with valuable first hand accounts. To the memory of those that, sadly, are no longer able to enrich our interest with their experiences of the great days of steam, and also the following:
The Oxford City Libraries; Buckinghamshire County Council Local History Collection; Bedford Record Office and Libraries; Bedford Model Railway Club; The Bodleian Library, Oxford; The London Brick Company; The Bedford Times; The Railway Magazine; Railway & Travel Monthly and Herpaths Railway Journal.

To Messrs F. Bateman (British Rail); M. Christensen (Signalling Records Society); F. G. Cockman, R. Crane (Bedford & Bletchley Rail Users' Association); T. J. Edgington (National Railway Museum); B. V. Garland, C. Gibbins, I. Hall, Lt. Col. R. Harvey (PRO London Brick Company Limited); G. Howe, C. Judge, P. A. Millard, R. Powell, J. Pritchett, S. Sellers, J. Spencer, S. Stollery, J. A. Turner, G. Webb, P. R. H. Webber and W. K. Williams (Industrial Railway Society). Finally to my wife De, who helped with the research and typed my heavily annotated manuscript, a feat of cryptology in itself.

Typesetting by:
Aquarius Typesetting Services, New Milton, Hants.

Printed in Great Britain by:
Balding & Mansell Limited, Wisbech, Cambs.

Published by:
Oxford Publishing Co.
Link House
West Street
POOLE, Dorset

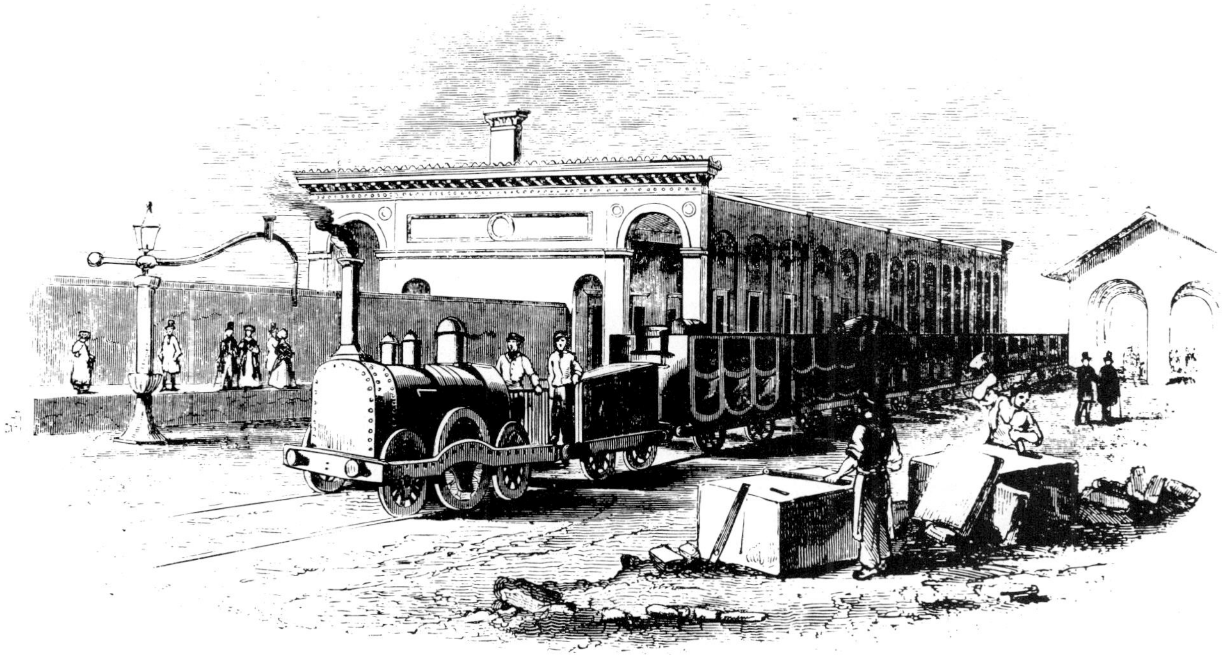

An early view of Cambridge Station.

In this second part of the history of the railway from Oxford to Cambridge, the story continues from Bletchley along a section of line that retains a strong visual contrast from the rural vistas of Oxfordshire and north Buckinghamshire. As the line passes into Bedfordshire it also enters into the heart of the industrious brickfields with many plants identified by the groups of chimneys like giant skittles on the flat clay plain, each trailing smoke along the wind's direction from the furnaces below. Brickworks passed on the Oxfordshire side at Calvert, Newton Longville and Bletchley are but a prelude to the capacious plants of Ridgmont, Lidlington, Millbrook, Marston, Stewartby and Kempston, all springing from the unique property of Oxford clay, its friable and combustible qualities becoming the catalyst for mass production. For along the line to Bedford, there developed a concentration of the world's largest brick plants, moving millions of tons for the generative building demand in all parts of Britain.

The short Bedford part of the railway, some sixteen miles, is significant insomuch as this was the original section of the line to be opened on the route in 1846. The Buckinghamshire Railway, to Oxford from Bletchley, was opened in 1851, whilst the Bedford & Cambridge Railway opened in 1862. This third and final section was also an essential aid in the development of the extensive market gardening holdings along much of its course. Sandy and Potton, in particular, played a large part with Sandy being on the Great Northern Railway's line giving direct access to the London Markets, which made high demands.

After 77 miles, a train from Oxford would weave into a confluence of other lines at Cambridge Station. As an emissary from rival academic lands, it would steal into the southern bay of the station where it transgressed into another destination – to Oxford by return! For 106 years, the territorial exchanges continued for 77 years under the neutral managership of the LNWR with their shiny imperious black engines with purple lake and 'spilt milk' coaches. With the grouping of the railways in 1923, this faded under the more sanguine crimson lake of the LMS, a progenitor of various shades and styles passing into the early days of British Railways.

The 'varsity' link was broken with the closure of the Bedford to Cambridge line on the last day of 1967, followed by the track being lifted. It was a tridimensional decline, as the Oxford to Bletchley line remained as goods only, while the short Bedford to Bletchley section remained open for passengers as well as goods.

As the prospect of a rail link being reopened between the two cities is remote beyond the wildest prophecy, indeed the surviving section has been embattled on several occasions. This record, both written and visual, is intended to retain the memory of this unique line with all its cross-country connections. Memories remain of fine trains calling at neat businesslike stations and, to the chagrin of increasing road users, over many white-gated crossings. However, as the line meandered on its way, it did, for a time, provide not only a very useful connection, but also the appealing sight of fields fresh with new growth – the market gardener's road to Cambridge.

Bill Simpson
Banbury 1983

The Oxford to Cambridge route, with all stations, in 1909. Bletchley, at the centre, was once a small village station on the London & Birmingham Railway that developed into an important railway centre. The extent of the Bletchley operating district stretched from immediately north of Tring Station to a point just south of Roade, a distance of 28 miles, to which was added branch lines totalling 114 miles.

R. Havard Collection

CONTENTS

CHAPTER ONE

Early History

When the Bedford line was first promoted, in1844, by a group of local business men led by the Mayor, T. J. Green, it received a mixed reception. After the town of Aylesbury had shown its confidence by encouraging a branch off the new London to Birmingham Railway in 1839, it seemed obvious that the new conveyance could only bring benefit to trade. That being said, some townspeople were still inclined to argue for a securely traditional canal branch, connecting Bedford with the Grand Junction Canal at Newport Pagnell, as being less risky and would proffer the common good, whereas the railway could only provide for an exclusive few. This short-sighted view of what railways were doing was not able to forestall the railway lobby. Their ability to counter this opposition was drawn from the not inconsiderable stature of the support of George Stephenson who made strong criticisms of the impracticalities of the canal scheme. His support of the Bedford line must also be viewed in his admitted interest in supplying coal from his Clay Cross Colliery. That being said, it was certainly a sensible plan and in the promoters' interests. The sixteen or so miles to the main line involved few engineering difficulties, as long as a tunnel, which proved not to be necessary, could be avoided at Brogborough Hill.

After a public meeting on 23rd April 1844, when George Stephenson's considerable influence on the route showed a connection with the London & Birmingham Railway at a point near Bletchley at an intermediary station of Bletchley & Fenny Stratford, a rash of dissension broke out amongst the supporters. Many considered the Wolverton Station, as the principal station in the area, as the obvious place for the junction. Stephenson pointed out that this would make the line two miles longer and, in any case, the London & Birmingham Railway would improve Bletchley once the junction with the Bedford line had been made. Talk of an Oxford branch from the same station was in the air as well. As the passing of time proved, this pursuasion was fully justified as a considerable railway community developed at Bletchley serving a number of radial lines.

A prospectus for the Bedford & London & Birmingham

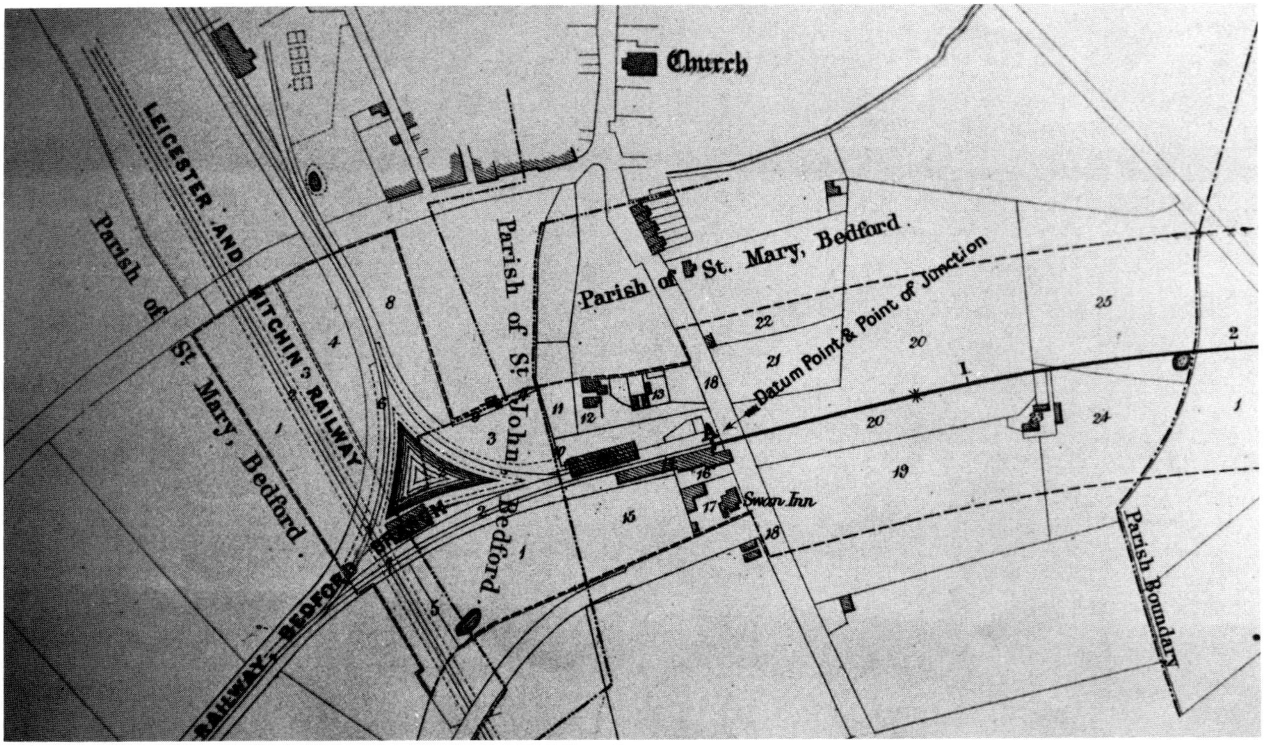

Bedford LNWR Station in 1860 when the engineering survey was carried out for the Cambridge line. This picture gives an indication of the layout of the station from its early days. The main station buildings are the shaded block situated on the southern side of the line, whilst the space on the town side is occupied by an early carriage shed which was, of course, demolished when the new station buildings were built with the opening of the Cambridge line. The branch for the Ouse Navigation can be seen together with the one goods shed and the extra siding near to the cattle pens. This branch crossed the Ampthill Road on the level, until necessity brought the construction of a bridge a few years later. At the centre of the triangle, near the locomotive shed, is the pond that was created for a supply of water. The Leicester and Hitchin line was added to the complex in 1857.

Bedford County Council Archives

Railway was drawn up on 28th May 1844, with the engineers being named as George and Robert Stephenson. In addition, a provisional committee of seven local dignitaries was named as directors, along with seats for two directors representing the interests of the London & Birmingham Railway. Capital was to be £125,000 divided into £50 shares. At the first general meeting, on 29th July 1845, with Thomas John Green in the chair, the report on proceedings stated, 'the immediate commencement and active prosecution of the necessary works so as to ensure the opening of the line by the summer of next year.' When complete, it was to be worked by the London & Birmingham Railway who would pay 4 per cent together with half of any surplus profit and provide locomotives and rolling stock for 5 per cent interest and 2½ per cent depreciation. Also, if authorized by two thirds of the shareholders of the new company, the London & Birmingham Railway may purchase the same on terms to be agreed.

The would-be railway promoters' protracted opening date was no gesture of fevered optimism, for an important and well-staged turf cutting ceremony was arranged at a site a few yards on the Bedford side of what would later become Ridgmont Station. Planned originally for 10th December, it was regrettably postponed until the following Saturday, which meant that the actual lifting of the soil, by the Duke of Bedford who was a subscriber to the Company and across whose land the line would be built, could not be attended by him. His place was taken by the Duchess.

At about 2.00p.m., amongst the profusion of flags and standards guiding the eye in the direction of the proposed line, a carriage and four, with scarlet liveried postillions, arrived with the Duchess and her escort, Lord Alford, who was in attendance to give assistance. Her Grace was welcomed by Mr T. J. Green, Chairman of the new Directors, together with Theed Pearce, the Secretary. A deputation from the London & Birmingham Railway was in company with interested observers from the Eastern Counties Railway, at that time hoping for a link with them at Cambridge from a Bedford extension. Messrs Grissel, Peto & Jackson, contractors for the building of the line, would, no doubt, be thinking of their vigorous enterprise over the next twelve months. The populous was composed of county families and clergy. Her Grace's arrival was announced by a salute of cannon, with cheers from the assembly accompanied by the strident harmonies of a local band. After the Duchess had pressed the spade into the ground, Lord Alford took off his hat and coat and proceeded to fill a specially constructed barrow. This was followed by the cheers of the assembly as he wheeled the full barrow, tipping the first load of Bedford Railway spoil. He then led the way to a splendid marquee and another cannonade preceded the national anthem. Two hundred ladies and gentlemen sat down to a luncheon whilst the beautiful grained oak barrow, and spade, in electrotype silver, were taken away for preservation, suitably inscribed: 'With this barrow, the works of the Bedford & London & Birmingham Railway were commenced by His Grace the Duke of Bedford who turned the first sod on the 13th

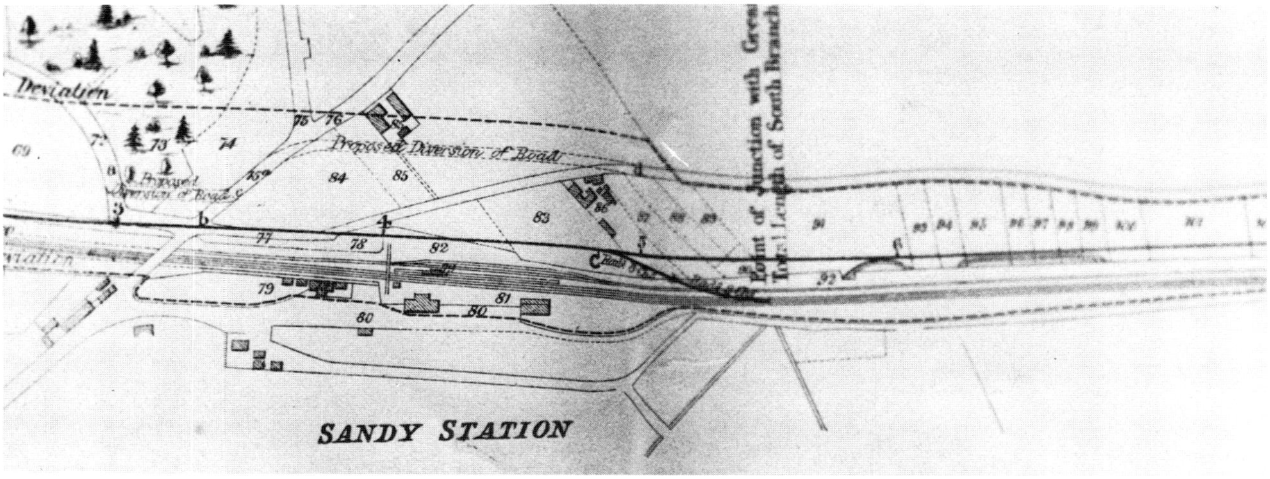

With the compilation of the Cambridge line survey, a glimpse is also afforded of the layout of the other stations involved. This section, dealing with Sandy, not only shows the early Great Northern Station layout but also the loop on the Bedford and Cambridge side, that is, in fact, the lines of the Sandy & Potton Tramway, which extend up to the road bridge on the left. It is interesting to note that the first Great Northern layout had the platforms staggered. The 'up' platform, serving the Sandy & Potton loop, had a footbridge between that and the 'down' side platform. A proposed junction, by the Bedford & Cambridge Railway, who also required, by their alignment, a diversion of the public road, is indicated south of the station.

Bedford County Council Archives

Day of December 1845 upon lands in the parish of Husborne Crawley and County of Bedford.'

Mr Peto, speaking for the contractors, regailed the gathering with the hope that long before the completion of the contract, 31st July 1846, the contractors should have the pleasure of handing over the works, fully completed, and this was reported in the *Railway Record* on the following Wednesday.

During the construction of the Bedford line, the London & Birmingham Railway was to undergo its own major crisis and become amalgamated with the Grand Junction Railway, (Birmingham & Liverpool & Manchester), to form, on 16th July 1846, the London & North Western Railway, who adopted the undertakings of the Bedford line of the former company.

At a shareholders meeting on 27th February 1846, it was stated that there was hope that the line could be completed by 31st July of that year. It was also stated that an application had been made in the present session of Parliament for a Bill to extend the line to Cambridge financed by independent capital. This would have the support of the still extant London & Birmingham and the Eastern Counties railways, that would lease the line for 4 per cent, plus half of any surplus profits. This early scheme for a Bedford to Cambridge railway did not, however, pass standing orders.

Building on the Bedford line was fairly straightforward with the exception of the Brogborough Hill area, for which the Company had, at first, considered a tunnel. This expensive excavation was avoided by a slight deviation to the south. Nevertheless, the alternative cutting caused difficulties with falling earth and five of the workmen were injured.

By September, the line was ready for the Board of Trade inspection which took place in the following October, when Major-General Pasley, accompanied by Directors Bruyers and Bury of the LNWR, traversed the line in the inspection train. The principle details of Major-General Pasley's report on that day were as follows. Starting from Bedford, a mention is made of the half mile long branch to the River Ouse, which trailed from the Bletchley direction, the first section of which would eventually be a triangle. The Ouse Navigation, which opened in 1689, could not survive firstly the competition of the Grand Junction Canal and then the keener competition of the railway, even though the railway brought connection at Bedford. The report continues with a mention of sixteen crossings, these anachronistically survive as a characteristic of the line to the present day and at that time there were, in addition, two on the Ouse branch. Each of the crossings have gates that closed across the road and the railway and each had attendant lodges for the gatekeepers and their families. Twenty footpaths crossed the rails on a level. The rails were of the bullhead type in 15 ft. lengths arranged on transverse sleepers with a mixture of finished timber and half trees, all chaired and spiked, resting on a 2 ft. depth of ballast.

Bletchley, where a large new station is to be built, with a roof span of 510 ft. covering the rails and platforms of the main line and the new line, will eventually have an extension to Oxford. The Company also have in view, extensions and junctions at Bedford, where a temporary station has been erected, although the main station is nearly complete. There is an engine house for four engines. Intermediate stations from Bletchley are as follows: Fenny Stratford (1 mile), where a bridge has been built for the A5 (Watling Street) Road; Woburn (4 miles); Ridgmont (7 miles); Lidlington (8½ miles); and Marston (10 miles); the latter eventually being named Millbrook. All the stations have booking offices and waiting-rooms with lodgings for a station master or clerk. Some of these buildings have been built of lath and plaster with roughcast panels between the wooden framework, and have brick fireplaces and chimneys. Others have been built entirely of brick and a certain amount built with small sandstone blocks and free stone quoins. The platforms at all the stations are more extensive than is usually the case on new lines and should be very convenient for the public. The line is built with two lines of rails throughout and sidings at Bletchley, with a large turntable of 32 ft. diameter, for turning engines and tenders, and a number of smaller turntables for turning carriages individually. Major-General Pasley seemed more than satisfied and could recommend the line for opening on 19th of that month. The day was satisfactorily concluded with a luncheon for the inspecting officer and Directors at the Swan Hotel, Bedford. The line had taken eleven months to build.

An aside to the direct railway business was a careful clause in the Act to protect the rights of the Grand Junction Canal at Fenny Stratford. At that point the railway was required to observe the rightful commerce of the waterway by keeping its bridge in perfect repair, with a soffit arch clearance of not less than 10 ft., with 8 ft. over the towing path. The width was to be not less than 21 ft. of water and 9 ft. clearance for the towing path. During the construction, and whilst any repairs are necessary, there must be left not less than 16 ft. of navigable waterway, and any obstruction to the canal business would be charged to the Railway Company at the rate of £10 per hour, and if longer than 72 hours, at £30 per hour.

Although the year entered is incorrect, it has been retained for its interest. An approximate period for the photograph can be deduced as being between 1872 and 1879, as the engine, one of the standard Trevithick/Allan 6 ft. 2-2-2 Singles, is fitted with a Webb chimney which would suggest a period after Webb's appointment as Chief Mechanical Engineer, in 1871, until the withdrawal of these locomotives by 1879. Note the early slotted post semaphore, utilizing one lamp for each direction, with the spectacle castings arranged lower than the arms. The tiny signal/pointsman's hut can be seen at ground level, and is set slightly back from the post.

Geoff Webb

London and North Western Railway. (SOUTHERN DIVISION.)

BEDFORD and BLETCHLEY TIME and FARE TABLE.

On and after the 1st December, 1846.

(The Time and Fare Tables for the other Sections are issued separately.) **The Clocks are set according to the Longitude of each Station.**

NOTE. The arrival time denotes when the Trains *may be expected*, but Passengers, to ensure being booked, should be at the PRINCIPAL STATIONS **five minutes** earlier, and at the INTERMEDIATE STATIONS **ten minutes** earlier.—The doors of the Booking Offices will be closed punctually at the hours fixed for the Departure of the Trains, after which no person can be admitted.——Carriages intended to receive Passengers who are expected by the Trains at the terminal Stations, should be on the Arrival Side of such Stations, five minutes, at least, before the time specified in the Tables.——Passengers cannot be re-booked at the Road-side Stations by the Train in which they are travelling.

DISTANCES From Bedford. Miles. By Main Line.	By Junction Lines.	FROM BEDFORD, (1) To LONDON. (Via Bletchley.)	TRAINS DAILY, (except on Sundays.) MORNING.			AFTERNOON		On SUNDAYS MORN	AFT.	Passengers' Fares from BEDFORD. First Class.	Second Class.	Third Class.
			h. m.	h. m.	h. m.	h. m.	h. m.	h. m.	h. m.	s. d.	s. d.	s. d.
—	—	Trains leaving BEDFORD	7.30	9.45	11.50	2.10	5.50	8.20	3.45	—	—	—
		Arrive at			P.M.							
—	6	MARSTON	7.45	9.50	12. 5	2.25	6. 5	8.35	4. 0	1 0	0 9	0 6
—	7¾	LIDLINGTON	7.46	—	12. 6	2.26	6. 6	8.36	4. 1	1 6	1 0	0 8
—	9¼	RIDGMOUNT	7.48	—	12. 8	2.28	6. 8	8.38	4. 3	1 6	1 0	0 9
—	12	WOBURN SANDS	8. 5	10.13	12.25	2.45	6.25	8.55	4.20	2 0	1 6	1 0
—	15	FENNY STRATFORD	8.13	—	12.33	2.53	6.38	9. 3	4.28	2 6	2 0	1 3
16½	—	BLETCHLEY (Joins Main Line)	8.20	10.26	12.40	3. 0	6.40	9.10	4.35	2 6	2 0	1 4
22½	—	LEIGHTON	8.35	10.38	1. 7	3.15	-	—	4.55	3 0	2 0	1 5
31½	—	TRING	8.55	—	1.32	3.38	7.18	—	5.18	4 0	3 0	2 0
35	—	BERKHAMPSTEAD	9. 5	—	—	3.48	—	—	—	4 6	3 0	2 2
38½	—	BOXMOOR	9.15	—	—	3.56	—	—	—	4 6	3 6	2 3
42	—	KINGS LANGLEY	9.22		—	—	—	—	—	5 0	3 6	2 5
45½	—	WATFORD	9.30	11.20	2. 2	4.12	7.48	—	5.54	5 6	4 0	2 8
51½	—	HARROW	—	—	—	4.28	—	—	—	6 6	5 0	3 2
63	—	LONDON about	10.10	12. 0	2.45	5. 0	8.30	—	6.45	8 6	6 0	3 11

DISTANCES To Bedford. Miles. By Main Line.	By Junction Lines.	TO BEDFORD, (1) From LONDON. (Via Bletchley.)	TRAINS DAILY, (except on Sundays.) MORNING.			AFTERNOON		On SUNDAYS MOR.	AFT.	Passengers' Fares to BEDFORD. First Class.	Second Class.	Third Class.
			h. m.	h. m.	h. m.	h. m.	h. m.	h. m.	h. m.	s. d.	s. d.	s. d.
63	—	Trains leaving LONDON	7.30	11. 0	—	3.45	5.30	7.30	—	8 6	6 0	3 11
		Arrive at										
[illegible]	—	HARROW	7.52	—	—	—	—	—	—	6 6	5 0	3 2
[illegible]	—	WATFORD	8. 9	11.37	—	4.18	6. 7	8. 9	—	5 6	4 0	2 8
[illegible]	—	KINGS LANGLEY	8.15	—	—	—	—	—	—	5 0	3 6	2 5
[illegible]	—	BOXMOOR	8.29	—	—	—	—	—	—	4 6	3 6	2 3
[illegible]	—	BERKHAMPSTEAD	8.39	—	—	—	—	—	—	4 6	3 0	2 2
[illegible]	—	TRING	8.48	12.14	—	—	6.37	8.48	—	4 0	3 0	2 0
[illegible]	—	LEIGHTON	9. 8	12.34	—	5. 6	6.57	9. 8	—	3 0	2 0	1 5
[illegible]	—	BLETCHLEY (Joins Bedford Line)	9.23	12.45	3.15	5.18	7.10	9.23	4.50	2 6	2 0	1 4
	15	FENNY STRATFORD	9.35	1. 5	3.20	—	7.20	9.35	4.55	2 6	2 0	1 3
	12	WOBURN SANDS	9.45	1.15	3.30	5.33	7.30	9.45	5. 6	2 0	1 6	1 0
	9¼	RIDGMOUNT	9.51	1.21	3.36	—	7.36	9.51	5.11	1 6	1 0	0 9
	7¾	LIDLINGTON	9.53	1.23	3.38	—	[illegible]	9.53	5.13	1 6	1 0	0 8
	6	MARSTON	10. 3	1.33	[illegible]	[illegible]	[illegible]	10. 3	[illegible]	1 0	0 9	0 6
[illegible]		BEDFORD about	10.15	[illegible]	4. 0	[illegible]	8. 0	10.15	5.35	—	—	—

Bedford branch trains through to London shortly after the opening on 1st December 1846.

J. Pritchett Collection

CHAPTER TWO

The Line

Opening day for the Bedford Railway was arranged for October 1846. The enthusiasm of the protagonists became a little clouded, however, when, owing to recent heavy rains, a 'slip' of earth near Fenny Stratford Station forced a postponement until 17th November. After the hiatus, the new railway owners were to manifest their satisfaction with even greater emphasis as celebratory eulogies flowed thick and fast on the great day. At 12 noon, a train of thirty three carriages, with 600 persons on board, travelled from Bedford Station to Bletchley with all the pomp of a victorious Roman legion, accompanied by the Bedford Brass Band, and drawn along by two Bury engines. Travelling quite slowly, taking one and a half hours to complete the journey, was doubtless to afford the passenger spectators the opportunity to admire all the new works. If completed, the half-timbered Gothic style of the main stations would gain special admiration. Curving around the rather sharp 20 chain radius curve into Bletchley Station a discordant note, in this paean of triumph, was struck, for at that point, three of the coaches became derailed. Thankfully, it was encumbent upon the train to proceed very slowly and no injury was incurred, although the muddy progress, on foot, for the occupants of the train, to reach the station through the drizzle of a grey day must have been less than elegant. Once there, they were treated to a demonstration of their engines being turned on a new device called a turntable.

Through a cheering throng, the train returned to Bedford to the pealing of church bells and a champagne reception given by the Duchess of Bedford. As with the opening of many new railways, the evening was to behold what became the customary banquet. This was for 200 guests and was held in the Bedford Assembly Rooms.

In the minute type and closely compact columns of early newspapers, the *Bedford Times* composed five full columns of report of that evening in its issue for 21st November 1846. There was enough information to fill a good many pages of this book. Sufficiently, a brief extract can summarize the proceedings and, hopefully, portray the euphoria of the scene. It is stated that all the town shops were closed for the day and that the people of Bedford were given a day's holiday, which reflects the generous mood of the enterprise. Mention is made of the improved mode of laying rails, 'Whereby the least possible vibration is caused to the carriages in transit.' This could be a reference to the supplanting of wooden sleepers as against the stone blocks used at first on the London & Birmingham Railway.

Unfortunately, the Duchess had to be without the Duke on the second affirmation of the line's success, when, along with the Directors of the Bedford Railway, she was joined by the representatives of the LNWR and the General Manager, Captain Mark Huish, who had developed a reputation for being a malevolent skirmisher in railway conflicts.

The Chairman of the Bedford Railway Company opened proceedings by speaking, at great length, in praise, firstly of the speed and efficiency with which the works had been completed, and expressed credit to Mr Jackson, who alas could not be present and was working upon the Newmarket line from Cambridge. He spoke, with regret, of the failure of the Cambridge line extension that had failed to pass standing orders. However, he offered praise for the Oxford & Bletchley Railway which, at that time, was going through legislature and which he felt would be certain of success. Laying great emphasis on the day when a successful attempt is made upon the obvious gap between Bedford and Cambridge, he spoke of such a line having a 'plethora of routes, springing from each end, that would eventually tie the country from the Wash to the Bristol Channel, from port to port and from the North Sea to the Atlantic.' Further to take advantage of a powerful presence from the Euston boardroom, he regales them in no uncertain manner, enthusing the Company almost to the point of embarrassment. 'I am pleased to say that all our communications with them have been of the most gratifying character and we have received the greatest courtesy and kindness from them. What a wonderful Company this is; how excellent is its arrangement; how great is its traffic; and how immense are its resources; how justly it has been termed the first railway in the world; and richly does it deserve the great confidence reposed in it (hear! hear!). Much of the high character is owing to those gentlemen in whom the management is invested and who are now the subject of this toast.' No doubt the gentlemen concerned could feel the full weight of unrestrained praise.

Later in the proceedings, the Chairman called upon the Directors of the Oxford & Bletchley Railway (not yet formed with the Buckingham & Brackley Junction Railway into the Buckinghamshire Railway) now under construction. Amid loud cheers, Sir Harry Verney rose to reply. He spoke of the grand prospect of through communication on their lines. 'With the metropolitan markets for our own produce, and we shall have brought into our own markets the products of other places which has hitherto been costly. I am connected with agriculture, and in that respect I view railways with peculiar satisfaction, for I believe them to be of the greatest possible benefit to agriculture. Gentlemen, we want an improved system of farming; we want drain tiles for our land and bricks for our houses, (how prophetic the mention of bricks would prove to be in view of the enormous manufacturing undertakings that grew along the Bedford line), . . . and if they brought us nothing but cheap fuel (railways), that alone ought to be sufficient to ensure our hearty support of these great schemes.'

On conclusion of the exhaustive speeches and the shower of congratulations, the assembly withdrew on omnibuses, paid for by the Company, to take guests to their respective homes. After such a long and eventful day, the Directors of the Bedford Railway could dream of the prosperity of their line as a short link that would one day unite the two distant cities of Oxford and Cambridge. An egalitarian gesture of the celebrations was the repast, consisting of roast beef, or game, followed by plum pudding, supplied by the Company to the workmen on the line. The *Railway Record* of 28th November 1864 beamed approval for the men that had often been chastised for unsavoury behaviour in the words – 'sixty three men sat down, not one was intoxicated, though ample opportunity was afforded.'

Stations which were opened on the first day remained the same throughout the lifetime of the line, apart from some changes in name. Ampthill was eventually renamed Millbrook, obviously to avoid confusion with the later Midland line station closer to the village. Ridgmont was altered from Ridgmount and Woburn became Woburn Sands in 1851.

As mentioned, the line was leased from the outset by the LNWR with fares being half of those charged on the stage-coach services also enabling passengers to reach London in half the time of the former equestrian means.

The railway was something of a death blow for the Ouse Navigation who had already severely felt the blast of competition from the building of the Grand Junction Canal. Predictably, the stage-coach was to suffer in a dramatic way, the *Bedford Times* coach ceasing business on the Saturday after the line had opened. London connections for Bedford withered quickly. Some coach proprietors stayed the prospect of ruin by running feeders to rail-heads, but with the opening of the Oxford to Bletchley line in 1851, the Oxford to Cambridge coach was well on the way to extinction. The roads which they had used were maintained by the Turnpike Trusts who were forced to reduce their tolls by half. As a result, road development was to be retarded for another century.

Bradshaw's Shareholders Guide of 1850 gives the conclusive arrangement of the Company; 16½ miles leased by the LNWR at 4 per cent per annum and half of any surplus profit. The whole of the capital consisting of 2,500 shares of £50 each (£125,000). The Company took 1,522 shares leaving only 978 in the hands of the public. The guarantee is payable half-yearly in March and September.

Directors at the Act of Incorporation were Thomas John Green, Mayor of Bedford, Henry Littledale of Kempston, T. A. Green of Pavenham, T. Barnard of Bedford, R. Newland of Kempston, G. Witt of Bedford, I. Elger of Bedford with two London & Birmingham Railway Directors, J. B. Boothby and T. Young both from Middlesex. With the exception of the last two, they were very much a local group.

The first train service dates from 17th November.

Euston (dep)	7.30 a.m.	11.15 a.m.	4.00 p.m.	5.30 p.m.
Bedford (arr)	10.15 a.m.	1.15 p.m.	6.30 p.m.	8.00 p.m.
Bedford (dep)	7.15 a.m.	10.00 a.m.	2.10 p.m.	5.50 p.m.
Euston (arr)	10.20 a.m.	12.30 p.m.	5.00 p.m.	8.15 p.m.

Coal prices took a drastic competitive jolt from 1s 9d (8½p) per cwt to 11d (4½p) per cwt which vindicates earlier criticisms that the railway would not share a common benefit.

Cambridge Railway Station.

CHAPTER THREE

Bedford and Cambridge

The LNWR became interested in the proposed extension, by local business men, to Cambridge from Bedford in October 1858 when Lord Chandos, Chairman of the Company, enquired on the terms of such a line on behalf of the Company.

A proposal to cross the area, indeed to link Oxford and Cambridge, was not new for there had been such a proposal for an Oxford to Cambridge Railway, via Bedford, as early as 1836, which had faded away. It must be pointed out that at that time the railways had the support of the citizens of the towns, but not that of the universities who feared that they would enable students to travel too easily. This they felt would be too great a distraction from their rightful purpose, wasteful soirees in London, with the capital being accessible with too great an ease. However, this defensive stance could hardly be maintained against a transport revolution affecting the entire country. By 1846, a modified outlook countenanced the plans laid out by that famous engineer, Joseph Locke for a connecting line of 73 miles in length. Although this railway did have the support of the universities, it met with strong opposition in the House of Lords and became truncated to merely the Royston & Hitchin section. Nevertheless, his planned route does have a ruminative interest. This route was from Cambridge to Hitchin, Luton and Cheddington, along the Aylesbury branch to that town, between the villages of Long Crendon and Thame and finally into Oxford, with a station 600 yards north of the Martyr's Memorial. Taken at once, it was no modest plan, but the remnant finally built was to play a peripheral role in the eventual development of the Bedford & Cambridge Railway, for it was eventually extended from Royston to Shepreth and Shelford, on a section of line built by the Eastern Counties Railway that had been part of a line sanctioned to reach Bedford, via Biggleswade, promoted by that notoriety, George Hudson, in 1846. This was an attempt by him to spite the plans of the nascent Great Northern Railway whose London to York line included a branch to Bedford from Sandy. This branch, and Hudson's promotion, lapsed in the face of an investment crisis and very high costs for the Great Northern Railway on their main line. Ironically, the Royston & Hitchin section became a Great Northern ally and, as mentioned, the powers to extend to reach Cambridge were exacted from Hudson's Act, after the GNR had been running omnibuses from the station at Shepreth to Cambridge in 1851.

The fruitless ventures of internercine speculation left the Bedford & Cambridge situation frustratingly unfulfilled until the head of a notable Bedford family, William Henry Whitbread, initiated a company called the Bedford, Potton & Cambridge Railway and, as chairman, brought together the following interested parties: James Howard, Bedford; Thomas St. Quintin, Potton; Sidney Stanley, Cambridge; Edward Cropper, Kent; Matthew Lyon, Stafford; William Williams, Bedford; The Hon. C. S. Clements, London; Earl de la Warr, Bourne, Cambridgeshire; William Stuart, M.P., Bedford; George Smith, Potton; William Dennis, Gamlingay and Lieut-Colonel W. Bartholomew Higgins, Turvey, Beds.

A public meeting was held on 3rd March 1859 with Mr W. H. Whitbread in the chair. It was stated, in the course of the proceedings, that the line would be entirely independent of the Eastern Counties Railway and that for the carriage of goods, it would be a competitor. The County of Bedford had subscribed £34,000 to the undertaking including £5,000 from the Duke of Bedford and £5,000 from Mr Whitbread, whilst Cambridgeshire had at present taken shares only to the extent of £3,000. A committee was organized for the purpose of canvassing the town and University of Cambridge. From this transcribed a public meeting at Cambridge, in February of the following year, where Earl de la Warr confirmed his support stating that the line would be of great advantage to the public and university. He was supported by Revd. J. Cartmell, Master of Christs' College, with unanimity from the rest of the assembly.

The Bill for the Bedford, Potton & Cambridge Railway collided, in 1859, with the Eastern Counties Railway trying to oppose and prevent the Great Northern Railway from reaching Cambridge from Royston by forcing the former Company's hand on their lapsed powers from Shepreth to Cambridge. In this conflict the GNR afflicted the ascendant Bedford, Potton & Cambridge Railway Bill claiming that the gap from Bedford would be closed if the section which they required was built by using the Bedford (Midland) to Hitchin, circuitous route. It was, however, enough to force the Bedford, Potton & Cambridge Railway to take stock of the situation. This was followed by an agreement between the small company, supported by the LNWR together with the GNR, that if the Bedford & Cambridge Railway (Potton now removed from the title) got their Act, unopposed by the GNR, the GNR themselves could submit a Bill for a line from Shepreth to a junction with the Bedford & Cambridge Railway near what eventually became Lord's Bridge Station and that the Bedford & Cambridge Railway would not oppose such a Bill. An obvious marriage of convenience. A new Bedford & Cambridge Railway Bill was introduced in 1860 with the Eastern Counties Railway springing to the defence of its claim and making a sanguine case of the LNWR/GNR caprice by stating the following: 'The discreditable conduct of Euston Square as well as the indelicacy of the Great Northern, which, after the advantages it had derived under the Royston & Hitchin agreement, is ready to accept a portion of the plunder intended to be abstracted from the Eastern Counties'. Through their rhetoric and mortification, the Eastern Counties Railway did not carry the day and the Bedford & Cambridge Railway received the Royal Assent on 6th August 1860. In conclusion, the Eastern Counties Railway built the last link from Shepreth to Shelford Junction leased to the GNR who were not forced to take up their option in the Bedford & Cambridge Railway to build the line to Lord's Bridge.

Work on the line began in April 1861 in a very business-like manner without the effusive speeches which precluded the Bedford line. The engineer for the line was Charles Liddell, who also built the Leicester & Hitchin line. He was supported by a contractor of no small reputation, Joseph Firbank. Rights protecting the rightful commerce of the Ouse Navigation were contained within the Act and were similar to those for the canal at Fenny Stratford.

A unique feature of the Act was the purchase of a small railway called the Sandy & Potton Railway which had pre-empted the course of the line by some 3½ miles between the two stations.

Although landowners had been divided in their attitude to railways, Sir William Peel of Sandy, son of the famous statesman Robert Peel, was in little doubt as to their usefulness. Before his career as Captain in the Royal Navy brought his life to an end in 1858, after sustaining wounds in the Indian Mutiny, (he died at Cawnpore in April), he was to instigate this little railway. Alert to the benefits of the Great Northern lines opening at Sandy, in 1850, near the family estates, he took up the interests of the people of Potton for a connecting link, saying that not only would he give permission for it to pass through his lands, but that if extra land was offered to continue the line on reasonable terms, he would build the entire railway at his own expense. The additional land of 1 mile 8 acres was so purchased and in May 1856 construction commenced.

One of the Ramsbottom 0-6-0 'DX' class locomotives of the LNWR, stands on Bletchley Shed. These engines were precursors of medium goods work to the later 18in. goods engines that worked on all local branch lines.

L&GRP/ Courtesy David & Charles

An official Board of Trade inspection by Captain Wynne took place on 5th November 1857. He stated that from Sandy GNR to the village of Potton was a permanent way of 3 miles 2 furlongs of 'contractor's rail', 59lb per lineal yard with sleepers one yard apart and all joints fished. The line was found to be satisfactory for passenger traffic.

Before then, on a brilliant and warm sunny day, 25th June 1857, the line opened for goods traffic with a new engine having been purchased from George England & Co., Ironworks, Hatcham for £800, making its first official journey on the line and proudly bearing the name of Captain Peel's frigate, *Shannon*. The railway had cost

Below The terminus of the Sandy & Potton Tramway, the entrance to which is by the Biggleswade Road on the right (broken line). A reasonable guess at the various buildings would be, from left to right; main station building with a small staff office, and the building for the locomotives, as illustrated in this book. The building alongside the rails is probably a goods landing, whilst the shaded area, away from the rails, may well be the coal staithes mentioned by the journalist on the opening day. As the locomotive shed, now surviving, does not have a structure abutting the rear, it can only be assumed that this was the building that housed the steam pump for bringing water up from a well for the engines.
Bedford County Council Archives

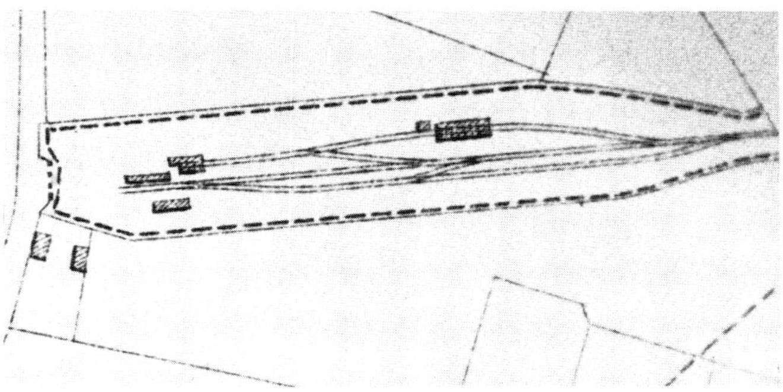

£15,000 to build but its value in transporting fruit and vegetable merchandise out and bringing manure and fertilizer into Captain Peel's and other estates would soon recover this outlay. Captain Peel had extended his own estate by a 1,000 acres in 1853 turning its income of £70 per annum to £500 per annum and was now adding the benefits of this railway.

The line was opened on that fine summer's day by Lady Peel, as Captain Peel was on naval service. The scene was described thus by the reporter of the *Illustrated London News*. 'The country through which the branch passes is of a light, yet rich and prolific character principally employed in the raising of garden produce, its vegetables being famous in Covent Garden quotations. The little and truly English town of Potton was hung with banners, and woods around had contributed whole trees which were made to meet at their tops as if they had grown in the rustic streets which were also spread with triumphal arches of evergreens. Bands of music conducted the guests in procession to the market place where an excellent luncheon was served. Some good songs contributed to the enjoyment of the day, and the presence of a vast concourse of elegantly dressed ladies within the dining booth added its customary grace to the assembly. The *Bedford Mercury* made more prosaic observations, 'There is no booking office or waiting-room at Potton where a coal staith was so far as clean as a drawing-room. There was a warehouse for goods and secondly an engine shed, where we found a little stationary engine of ½ horsepower (to operate a pump to bring up water from a well). The band arrived at about 11.00a.m. and at 12 noon members of the committee went to meet the train from Sandy. On the return, the band was under the self appointed leadership of a drunken tomfool.'

The line began to carry passengers in November 1857 after the Board of Trade's inspection. Its total rolling stock of two earth wagons, one trolley and a brake van would hardly suffice and so carriage stock was hired from the Great Northern Railway at Sandy. Signalling was primitive, even by the standards of the period, consisting of waving a red flag to make the train stop.

Once the Bedford & Cambridge Railway had received the Royal Assent and construction was under way, the line was destined to close. This took place in 1861. Much of the route was relaid with the new railway, except to the terminus at Potton which was diverted from the course that now led to the new station nearby. The line was bought by the Bedford & Cambridge Railway for £20,000 including *Shannon* which was resold to Joseph Firbank for use in the building of the line. Another engine, No. 2, named *Little England* was bought by the LNWR for £350.

The little independent railway had a very short life but in that time employed a typical group of railway staff to operate it. There was a superintendent for the first year who became a manager for the last two years; one station master, a clerk, one engine driver with an assistant engine

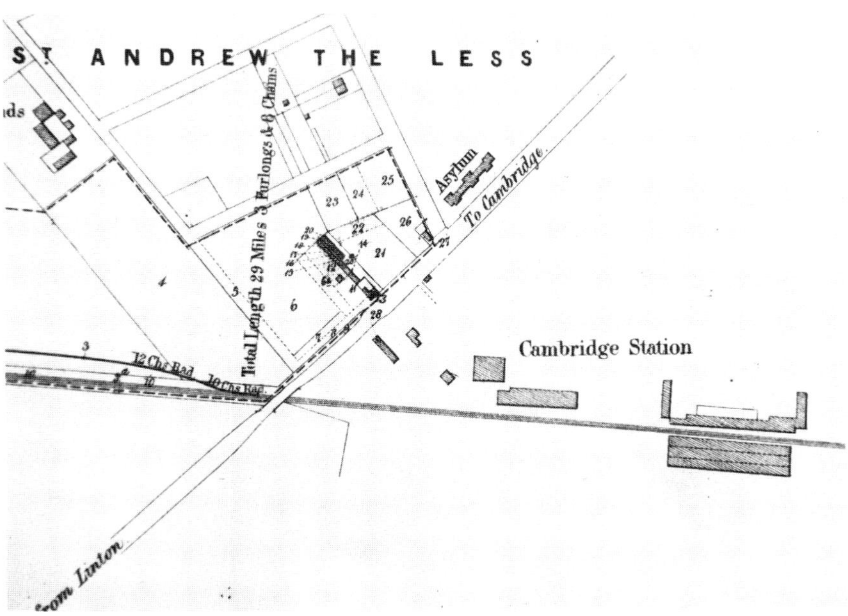

The proposed junction with the Great Eastern Railway at Cambridge before the Hills Road bridge. The former Eastern Counties Station is still only a modest structure and although having been enlarged since opening, the original arcaded front can be seen extending from the shaded area. The traditional long single platform, at Cambridge, was not always the case, as before the rebuilding by the Great Eastern, an 'up' platform was required. This was removed with the extension of more lines and the building of the long platform to take all arrivals and departures.
Bedford County Council Archives

A footplate view of the engine shed at Bletchley. *L&GRP/ Courtesy David & Charles*

driver/fireman, one guard/brakesman, one porter and two labourers that became platelayers in the third year. Total receipts for the year ending 31st December 1860 were £540 against an expenditure of £386 leaving net profits of £154.

All the stations along the Bedford & Cambridge line were built as sited by Charles Liddell, with the exception of Gamlingay, where he complained of not being able to site the station where he would have liked, closer to the village, as the trustees of the highway refused to let him make a diversion of the road at that point.

The Cambridge station was to be sited within an area abounded by Linton Road and Brooklands Road and not, at that time, jointly in the Eastern Counties Railway station.

By 1st July 1862, independence of the Eastern Counties Railway came to an end and a convenient amalgamation of railways in the area brought the Great Eastern Railway into existence from that date. With the rebuilding of Cambridge Station in hand, it was expediant to approach the Bedford & Cambridge Railway for the cost of some of the enterprise, rather than the smaller company going to the expense of building its own station a few hundred yards away. Reason prevailed and a bay was allotted at the south end of the station for LNWR Oxford and Bedford trains. This came to be shared with the GNR's rigorous path through from Hitchin by 1864.

On Friday, 4th July 1862, only three days after the formation of the Great Eastern Railway, a train of twenty six new and very spacious carriages left Bedford at 9.04a.m. containing Directors, shareholders and their friends, picking up other invited parties along the line, to arrive at Cambridge at 1.30p.m. The link between Oxford and Cambridge had at last become a reality. The line was officially opened to the public three days later, but for handling the all important goods, it was to wait a further three weeks until 1st August as all the structures and equipment were not yet ready for use.

The Bedford & Cambridge Railway Company was not destined for a long period of independence after the critical first two years of the line's opening. This was due to them experiencing some difficulty in raising the required capital of £240,000, with the LNWR contributing £70,000 as prospective lessees, and appointing three of its Directors to the board of fifteen. The LNWR also insisted that these three should sit on the Joint Committee for supervising the construction of the line with two other Directors, one of which was W. H. Whitbread who was in the Chair. They also agreed to devote part of their receipts from through traffic to a fund to be used to guarantee up to 4 per cent per annum on the cost, (to a limit of £300,000), of constructing the line. Also included in the Act was the LNWR's agreement to run not less than four trains each way from Bletchley to Cambridge and two each way between Oxford and Cambridge on each weekday.

Problems began to develop after the opening of the line when the Company was forced to raise £80,000 in mortgages against a revised estimate of the line's cost, £370,175, which brought the Bedford & Cambridge Railway to confer with the LNWR with a view to procuring the extra capital.

The LNWR agreed to pay the interest on the £80,000 and guarantee 3½ per cent per annum for five years on the share capital of £240,000 and 4 per cent thereafter, but would have nothing to do with the excess. The Bedford & Cambridge Railway were grieved as they felt that it had been the LNWR's influence on the Joint Committee that had caused the revised estimates by insisting on more substantial constructions than the Company could afford at the outset, supplanting iron for timber at river bridges and ensuring that the stations and ancillary buildings were completed to a finished standard. Acrimony between the two companies brought the Bedford & Cambridge Railway to promote a Bill repealing the clauses that gave the LNWR control of the Company's capital which became law on 23rd June 1864. In effect, this forced the LNWR to absorb the smaller company and its liabilities for 4 per cent on a capital of £240,000 and to relieve the Company of debentures and other liabilities. Shares of the Bedford & Cambridge Railway were converted into LNWR stock and by an Act of July 1865 became part of that Company. The final cost of the line was £370,000.

CHAPTER FOUR

The Line

Stations which opened on the first day did not include Willington on the 20 mile post from Bletchley, although the village applied unsuccessfuly for a station shortly after the line was opened. It would be another thirty years, in 1903, before they would see that requirement fulfilled. Three bridges over the River Ouse from Bedford to Willington were part of the added burden to construction costs. These were built of wrought iron girders and supported by piers of cast-iron columns and timber piling with brick abutments. The fact that these, and the bridge over the River Ivel at the 22½ mile post were built for a single line only must have inhibited any prospect of doubling the track. Indeed, during extensive rebuilding of the Ouse bridges and the strengthening of the Ivel bridge in 1916, doubtless due to heavy wartime trains, it was still not financially expedient to rebuild them for double track. The section of the line between Bedford and Willington had a complicated history of additional sidings and removal of defunct sidings. The first known siding was opened on 15th November 1912 and was for Bedford Council and called Summerhouse Hill Sidings, situated on the 18 mile post. Its original intention was to facilitate a sewage works, but, in contrast, it was eventually used for collecting sugar beet. A number of minor alterations to these sidings took place in February 1922.

In October of the same year, Sterling Foundry opened their siding on the 16 mile post which is, in fact, on the eastern side of the London Road bridge at Bedford Station, facing the original site of Bedford No. 2 signal box.

A new loop and signal box called Goldington were opened during World War I and were added to the block sections. This was closed in 1938.

On 2nd February 1932, the LMS opened Newnham Sidings for the Bedford Corporation with a bridge over the 'new cut' into the council store yard. Controlled by a ground frame with electric token, this was situated on the Willington side of the No. 4 Ouse bridge at 17 mile post.

With the outbreak of World War II, the Bedford No. 2 box was moved, along with the double/single line junction to bridge No. 3 on the 17 mile post, the River Ouse bridge being nearest Bedford. Goldington box was made a block post again until after the war when it was removed, with the loop, on 5th June 1951.

In 1948, the Central Electricity Generating Board selected a site for a new power-station near the Summerhouse Hill Sidings on the 'down' side. This station was opened by a gentleman familiar to the Bedford & Cambridge Railway, Major Simon Whitbread, Lord Lieutenant of Bedfordshire, on Friday, 16th August 1958. Part of the reason for choosing the site was the proximity of the railway. For the new power-station the old Bedford Corporation Siding was removed on 16th September 1951 and a new siding into the power-station put in during the following month. This was controlled by a ground frame released by Bedford No. 2 box.

The electric telegraph was opened throughout between Bletchley and Cambridge in July 1863. Train control until 1877 was on the time system, as outmoded as the early LNWR signalling with slotted post semaphores that proved so fatal in the Abbots Ripton accident on the Great Northern Railway in 1876 when they became clogged with snow. With the increasing speed of timetables and density of traffic, it became necessary for signalling to be more thoroughly controlled with new equipment and it was also necessary for the design and introduction of better semaphores. The LNWR had their earliest experiments with the Tyer No. 1 system of tablet between Bedford and Blunham in 1878 and installed a twenty lever signal box at the latter station. Absolute block was brought in between Sandy and Cambridge on 9th November 1880, and the electric train staff between Sandy and Bedford in 1888, for the first time on the LNWR.

Bedford and Cambridge Railway.

ON FRIDAY, JULY 4,

A Train for the Directors and Shareholders of the Line, will run as under:—

MORNING.

Leave	Bedford	9. 0	a.m.	Leave	Cambridge	11. 0	a.m.
Arrive at	Blunham	9.13	,,	Arrive at	Lord's Bridge	11.14	,,
,,	Sandy	9.22	,,	,,	North Road	11.31	,,
,,	Potton	9.34	,,	,,	Gamlingay	11.45	,,
,,	Gamlingay	9.42	,,	,,	Potton	11.52	,,
,,	North Road	9.58	,,	,,	Sandy	12. 3	noon
,,	Lord's Bridge	10.14	,,	,,	Blunham	12. 9	,,
,,	Cambridge	10.30	,,	,,	Bedford	12.30	,,

AFTERNOON.

Leave	Bedford	3.30	p.m.	Leave	Cambridge	5.30	p.m.
Arrive at	Blunham	3.43	,,	Arrive at	Lord's Bridge	5 44	,,
,,	Sandy	3.52	,,	,,	North Road	6. 1	,,
,,	Potton	4. 4	,,	,,	Gamlingay	6.15	,,
,,	Gamlingay	4.12	,,	,,	Potton	6.22	,,
,,	North Road	4.28	,,	,,	Sandy	6.33	,,
,,	Lord's Bridge	4.44	,,	,,	Blunham	6.39	,,
,,	Cambridge	5. 0	,,	,,	Bedford	7. 0	,,

Euston Station, *1st July*, 1862.

Double track was installed in two parts, from Sandy to Gamlingay on 20th October 1870 and from Gamlingay to Cambridge on 10th July of the following year.

Just before the installation of the wrought iron lattice bridge over the GN main line at Sandy, the line had its first public road crossing at Girtford. Unlike the Bedford branch, built fifteen years earlier, public road crossings proved the exception rather than the rule. Road access to Girtford was necessary quite early as the line had what must have been its first business siding there. What was termed a 'vegetable station' was opened on 6th July 1863, a commercial prospect that was largely the raison d'etre of the lines existence. As required, the necessary habitat for the gatekeeper of the crossing, a small house, was built alongside. Other early sidings were put in at Potton in February 1868 and at Gamlingay in September 1869, both for brick-making factories. Another 'vegetable' siding was put in at Willington on 15th September 1896. Girtford also became the site of what must have been one of the shortest lived 'Halt' platforms on Britain's railways. It was opened on 1st January 1938 and closed on 17th November 1940.

After Sandy and Potton, the three remaining intermediate stations are more openly spaced. These are situated in rural Cambridgeshire, under wide skies in fields of vegetables, flowers and orchards of the market gardening interest. Most of such produce, intended for LNWR metals, was handled by the stations with the exception of one location where a siding was put in near the villages of Toft and Kingston and named such after its opening on 12th July 1911. The key for this siding was obtained from Lord's Bridge signal box.

To enter Cambridge, the LNWR line joined the Great Eastern line 320 yards south of the station, a few yards beyond the site of the later installed Hills Road signal box. Cambridge Station was opened by the Eastern Counties Railway on 30th July 1845, but needed to be rebuilt for the requirements of expanding traffic. This was accomplished on 16th November 1863 when the newly formed Great Eastern Railway proudly announced, in the press, the opening of the new station with its characteristic single platform design. 'All of the arriving and departing trains are now reached from one platform 1,254ft. in length; these trains are from London, Hitchin and Bedford from the south end; and those for Norwich, Peterborough, St. Ives and Bury from the north end. Passengers will no longer be compelled to ascend and descend staircases to pass from the booking office to the carriages. For the present, the new refreshment room will be used for the booking office until the space occupied by the tunnel and present entrance is converted into an office.'

Bletchley Station staff assemble in front of 'Problem' class 2-2-2 locomotive, *Waverley*, in 1904. Until the scrapping of these engines in the latter part of the decade, the LNWR proclaimed no repainting of them after October 1903. They had become regular coursers of the Oxford to Cambridge route. Except for pilot work, they lost their main line duties with the introduction of heavier trains in the 1890s. Nevertheless, they retired in sprightly fashion with the six wheel coach rakes on the 'Oxbridge' line, although *Peel* had the misfortune to be the train engine in the Bedford accident. It is warming to see that two of the faithful trace horses that hauled wagons around the station area are not left out of such an assembly. The high-ballasted track would allow these devoted servants the ease to plod along to perform their daily duties.

Sid Sellers Collection

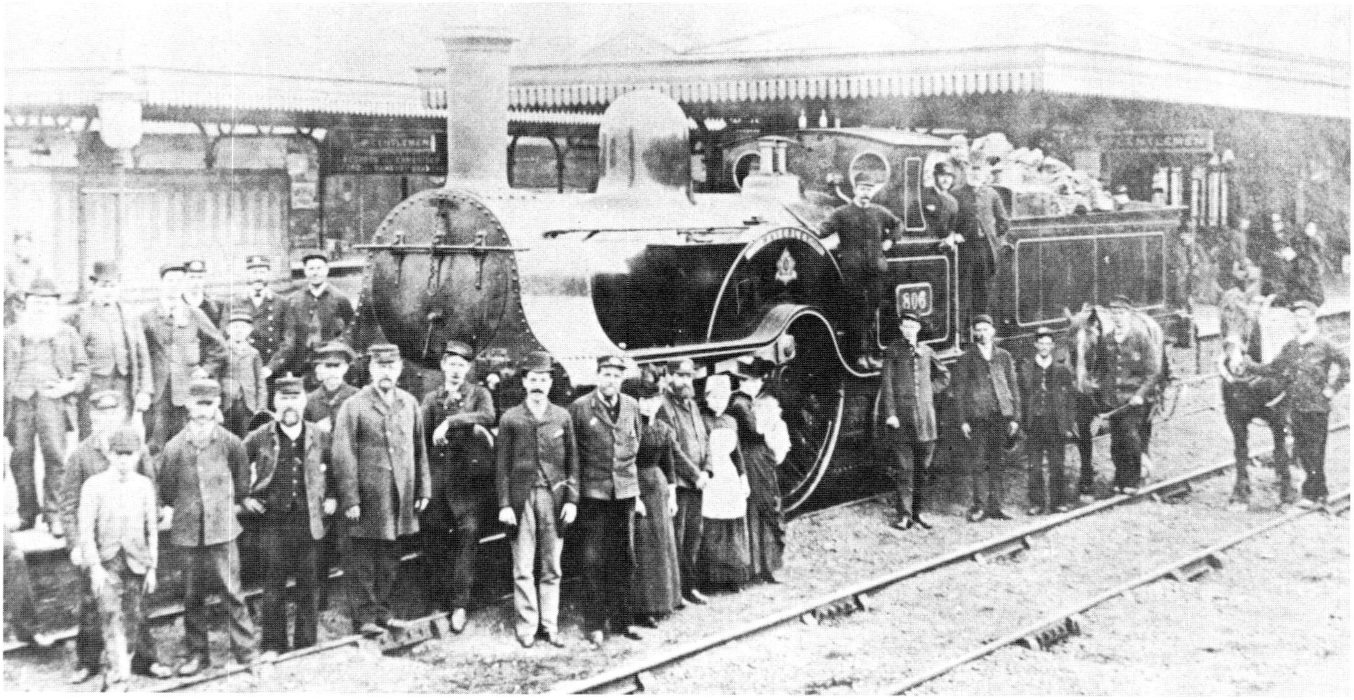

CHAPTER FIVE

Bletchley

Until the Bedford line was built, the menial little wooden station at Bletchley was but an intermediary stop close to the much larger neighbour of Wolverton. During construction of the London & Birmingham Railway in 1838, a journey between Rugby and Denbigh Hall, north of Bletchley, had to be covered by horse transport. It was during the period of the coronation of Queen Victoria that the void was hastily shuttled by stage-coaches, gigs, wagons, carts and every variety of equestrian vehicle in the area. With this discordant fault in the line completed by 20th September 1838, the temporary station at Denbigh Hall was not reluctantly closed down and the new station of Bletchley & Fenny Stratford came into being between the two villages. This joint name survived until the construction of the Bedford Railway who gave the latter village a station of its own, although both communities grew steadily towards the main line railway.

How Bletchley would have developed, had George Stephenson allowed himself to be influenced by the persuasion that wanted the Bedford line to go to Wolverton, must now remain a matter of conjecture. For, unlike Wolverton, Bletchley on its cross of lines, became an operational centre. Alongside the area of the station there developed a railway community of descendants of those early patriarchs of the footplate; moustached and bearded men of the Scottish expresses that hurled forth at 80 or 90 miles an hour along the West Coast Main Line. Bletchley men knew the great age of steam well, together with the dismal weariness of many long hours spent away from home and the resultant struggle to return home faced with the adversaries of bad weather and a locomotive long over-due for overhaul.

Signalling was no less a concentrated vigil, and eventually there were six boxes in operation; Bletchley No. 1, with its 96 levers controlling the southern section and the Oxford branch; No. 2, north of the station with 68 levers controlling the section up to No. 3 box (50 levers) which controlled the main line with the fast to slow line junction and the loop line from Denbigh Hall into the marshalling yard and trains departing from that yard. No. 4 box, consisting of 25 levers, was opened on 2nd December 1934 to control the new sidings between Bletchley and Fenny Stratford built on the northern side of the Cambridge line. The Bletchley end of these sidings was controlled by No. 5 box, consisting of 80 levers. This box replaced a ground frame in 1912 and received levers from No. 2 box for the branch. Curiously, there never was a No. 6 box and No. 7 box was, in fact, a pointsman's box at the north end of the main shunting yard. There was also a ground frame called No. 9 box. Signalmen, together with engineering staff, permanent way men and station staff operating in continuous shifts, can give some idea of the intensity of railway operations and how this community grew within the railway in the Bletchley area. A prospect of this develop-

Bletchley in the 1900s. A tree-lined scene with a few genteel carriages, emanates a reflective mellow composure against modern times. The charming scrolled casting on the lamp brackets is in harmony with the neat line of railings.

Author's Collection

ment was witnessed, as early as 1852, under the sagacious pen of one Reverend Boughton of Bletchley Rectory. He sat in his gig both day and night to take a personal census with which he hoped to petition the Company to build a bridge to replace the crossing on the Bletchley to Fenny Stratford road, alongside the station. His detailed account of the scene at the station, with trains to Oxford included, is a mixture of acerbic asides to the Company and sympathy for the staff. 'If you want to get to the platform that the 'up' trains start from, you have, on emerging from the booking office, to walk over a narrow platform (1), then over two lines of railroad (Oxford), then up two steps on to another platform (2 & 3), then down two steps and across four lines of the main railway, then up two steps on to another platform (4 & 5). There are two more lines beyond the Bedford and beyond that, the outside wall of the station. All of this is in a distance of 50 yards and totally unprotected. There are eleven porters, six on duty by day, with one head porter. They come on duty at 8 o'clock in the morning and remain until 11 or 12 at night. At the gates where the public road crosses, one man is stationed and on Saturday last, between 7a.m. and 7p.m. he opened these gates 89 times; the gates being 26½ft. long across a gap of 72ft.; he also had to attend to the points, nine in number in a distance of 533ft. from one another and also to take care of the signals. I am sure that he did not sit still for 5 minutes the whole of the Saturday for all of his twelve hour duty.' The obvious danger of people crossing the running lines was not removed until a subway was opened six years later when some extensions to the station buildings were added. The road crossing was not removed until the building of a bridge in 1881 when the entire station was also rebuilt with a hotel and the offices that lasted until the 1960s. A footbridge replaced the earlier subway in this construction. During this rebuilding, an all-over roof was constructed across the platforms which were extended to 600ft. in length, with the exception of platform No. 1, which had served a declining role as Oxford trains tended to arrive and depart at platform No. 2.

By the turn of the century, the heavier and more comfortable trains, with fast schedules, meeting connections across the 'Oxbridge' line and the developing London commuter trains, gave Bletchley a major main line junction atmosphere. Expresses swept through the station at anything from 50 to 70 miles per hour which, although not spectacular by modern standards, must have looked so when compared with some of the 'Highflyer' single wheelers still operating on pilot work. The general effect was also dramatically amplified by the low-lying roof and staccato rhythm of jointed rail. At night, the high signals, aglow with their lamps after a vertiginous climb by the lampman, reflected their cluster of lights along the rails, and probably the most striking effect of a summer twilight would be the postal special that came through the station around 9.25p.m. A distinctive train with lights not only along the roof but also along the footboards. Bletchley was, in fact, a dropping and pick-up point for the first travelling post office.

Outstanding at Bletchley amongst the traffic on the Cambridge branch were the numerous horse-boxes, many of which conveyed the fine bloodstock to Newmarket Races

The station approach from alongside the Jacobean style hotel on the right. Behind the post office buildings, in the distance, can be seen a little of the locomotive shed roof with its high draughting flues.

BR/OPC Collection

Turning to face the access roadway, a fine view of this arrangement of curved gables, built in brick with stone dressings and lattice diaper brick-work, is provided. Although its rambling formality was to be swept aside by the gale of modernity that came with the early 1960s, its distinctive profile is now perhaps missed in the unrelieving corporate style of thirty years later. Both views were photographed in the early 1950s.

BR/OPC Collection

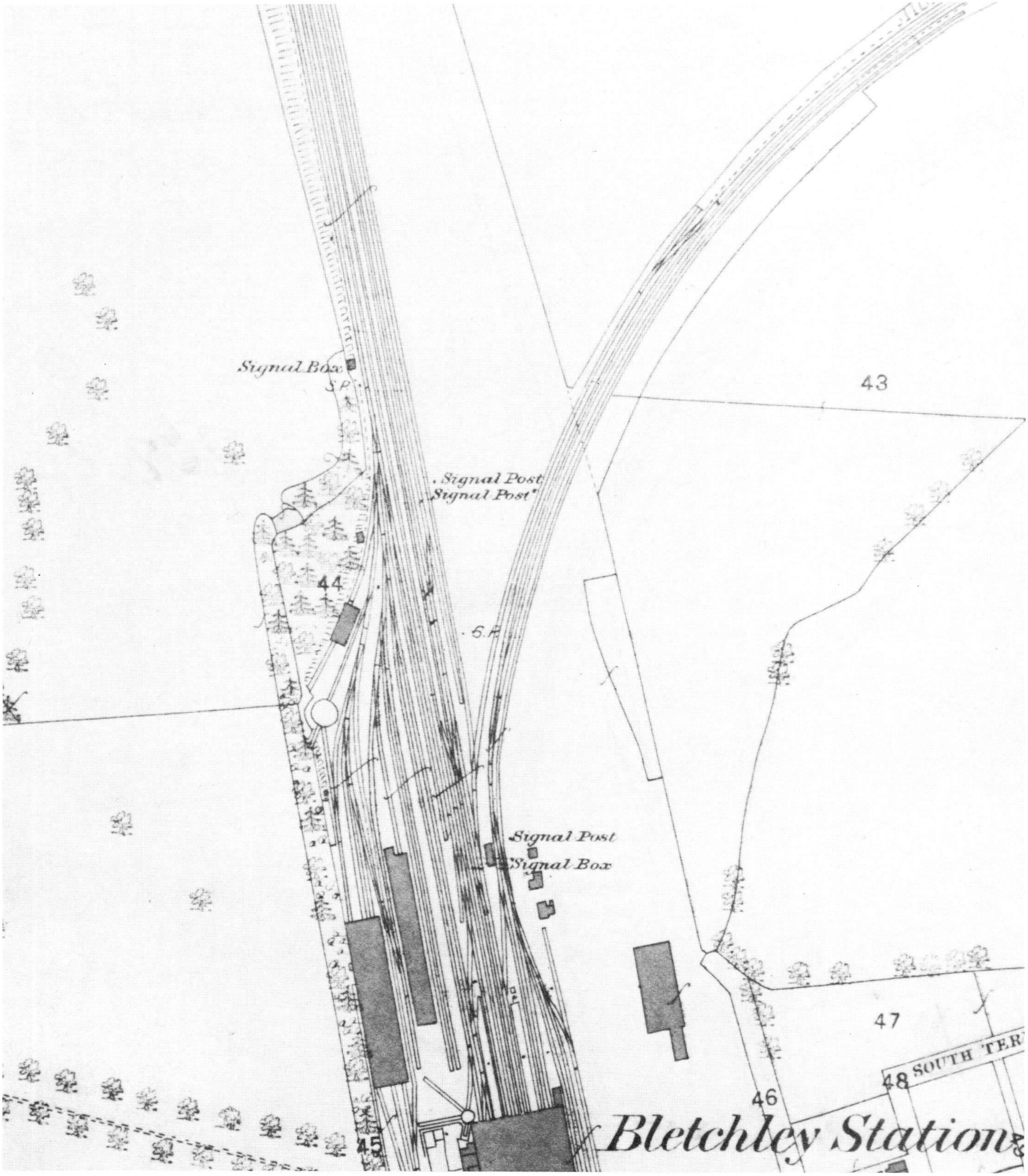

Bletchley north, in 1880, with the Bedford and Cambridge branch curving to the right. Locomotive facilities on the left are shielded, by trees, from Sir Herbert Leon's Bletchley Park Estates.

Courtesy of the Ordnance Survey

or to special hunts in the vicinity. All these horse-boxes were finely liveried with the owners' initials or coat of arms on the side. Less regal were the Company horse-boxes with the dependable 'Shires' entrained within. These horse-boxes were sometimes hauled by no less dependable 'Shires', four of which were stabled in the station area for shunting vehicles.

Other traffic on a more prosaic daily level included the Scottish mail, after passing through the rugged border country and the Westmorland fells from its night start of 8.42 from Carlisle arriving in the temporal hours at 2.42a.m. and stopping for five minutes. Five minutes was all the time there was between that train and the perishable parcels from Holyhead that pursued it down the main line at the same speed. From midnight onwards, there would be a steady procession of fast and slow goods trains going north and south. Meat and fish, together with various other footstuffs was carried on trains which ran between the long ceaseless progression of returning empties.

During the day there were 29 main line stopping trains 'down' and 32 'up' with a 'slip' coach detached from the 4.05p.m. Euston to Birmingham train. In the other direction trains leaving Birmingham at 7.30a.m. and 10.05a.m. also 'slipped' a coach at Bletchley. This arrangement provided convenient communication for trains on the Cambridge branch arriving at Cambridge at 10.41a.m. and 1.20p.m. A morning express from Aberdeen also 'slipped' a coach which was attached at Crewe, arriving in Bletchley at 6.20a.m. 'Slip' coach working was evidently suspended during World War I and was not reinstated. Trains from Oxford crossed over the running line to reach platform 4 (7) for Cambridge. Until the late 1930s, Bletchley platforms were confusingly numbered 1, 2, 3, 4 and 5, but later each separate platform face was allocated a number.

In 1913, control offices were set up on Bletchley No. 5 (8) platform. These consisted of a telegraph office, rolling stock and traffic inspectors' offices, telegraph linesmen's offices, a carriage and wagon examiners' room, a mess room, a lamp room and lavatory stores.

The station remained largely unchanged after 1881 until the facelift, in 1952 costing £20,000 which proved to be no more than a minor prelude to the drastic changes brought about by the electrification of the main line in the 1960s.

Bletchley locomotive steam shed, situated at the northern end of platform 1, developed in accord from small beginnings. Its allocation increased from a twelve engine fleet, eight in service with four spare, to a total of seventy five engines during World War II. Little is known of the original three road structure, built of wood and galvanized iron, except that it must have provided only limited accommodation. It required extension in the 1860s but appears to have been blown down in 1876. The LNWR standard brick shed with hipped roof replaced it and this in turn was totally rebuilt with a glazed roof in 1953, only to be removed completely in 1965.

After lasting until 1917, a 50ft. turntable was replaced by a more suitable 60ft. turntable in that year when the old one was removed to Banbury. Another turntable of 1846, that used to avoid the Bedford line engines crossing the main line to the sheds, was removed from the freight yard in 1909. The water tank house, that had once been the habitat of the shed foreman, supported a 60,000 gallon tank on its roof.

Under the control of Bletchley were seven sub-sheds: Oxford, Cambridge, Banbury, Leighton Buzzard, Bedford, Newport Pagnell and Aylesbury. Under the control of the shed foreman were 240 men of different grades; ten links of enginemen. Amongst the locomotives used at Bletchley were the four cylinder compound coal engines of which there were three. There were also thirteen 18in. goods engines, six 5ft. 6in. and six 4ft. 6in. tank engines, with four 'Precursor' 4-4-2 tanks and four shunting engines. Several 6ft. and one 6ft. 6in. 'Jumbo' and a four cylinder compound 'Jubilee' class called *Agincourt* served as a relief. There were four other express passenger engines and two railmotors with a spare engine unit. The staff at Bletchley had an ingenious method of removing wheels without a crane. They used a hydraulic wheel drop, installed in 1906, capable of dealing with wheels up to 7ft. 6in. in diameter. There were two hydraulic valves for operating the lift, one at 700lb per sq. in., and another at 2,000lb per sq. in. and they were both used for lifting, but the second was only required for the last few inches of lift, to act on the springs enabling the axle-boxes to be released from the horns. In the case of a driving wheel, connecting rods and probably valve motion would have to be disconnected. Descending some 10ft. with the wheel, the 9ft. base came into contact with some cross bars which released rails mounted on girders inwards at rail level under the locomotive. This allowed the locomotive, minus the particular wheels, to be towed away. Wheels could be lowered underneath an engine in five minutes and the entire operation of disconnecting the wheels took an hour. There was also a set of hydraulic sheer legs on shed for lifting tenders or reloading wagons. A 10 ton breakdown crane was also stationed at the Bletchley shed.

BEDFORD, WOBURN, and BLETCHLEY.—London and North Western.

Miles.	Fares 1 cl. s. d.	Fares 2 cl. s. d.	Fares 3 cl. s. d.	Up.	Week Days mrn	Week Days mrn	Week Days aft	Week Days aft	Sun mrn
				Bedford ...dep	8 20	10 25	3 0	5 55	7 25
6	1 0	0 9	0 6	Ampthill (Mrstn)	8 32	10 36	3 11	6 8	7 37
7¼	1 6	1 0	0 7½	Lidlington	8 39	...	3 17	6 15	7 44
9¾	1 6	1 0	0 9	Ridgmount	8 45	...	3 23	6 22	7 50
12	2 0	1 6	1 0	Woburn	8 52	10 50	3 30	6 30	7 57
15	2 6	2 0	1 3	Fenny Stratford .	9 0	...	3 37	6 39	8 5
16¼	2 6	2 0	1 4	**Bletchley** J. ar	9 5	11 0	3 42	6 45	8 10
52¼	7 6	5 9	4 1	42 RUGBY ...arr	10 59	12 38	5 32	9 12	11 [illegible]
63	8 6	6 6	4 0	45 LONDON ...,,	10 30	12 45	6 30	8 30	10 20

Down.	Week Days mrn	Week Days mrn	Week Days aft	Week Days aft	Sun mrn
42 LONDON dep	7 30	10 30	3 30	5 45	7 30
42 RUGBY ... ,,	8 19	9 37	2 55	5 15	...
Bletchley J.dp	9 35	12 5	4 58	7 45	9 30
Fenny Stratfor d.	9 39	12 9	...	7 49	9 34
Woburn...........	9 47	12 17	5 11	7 58	9 45
Ridgmount	9 55	12 25	...	8 6	9 54
Lidlington.........	10 1	12 31	...	8 12	10 1
Ampthill(Mrstn)	10 7	12 37	5 26	8 17	10 7
Bedford ...arr	10 20	12 50	5 40	8 30	10 25

Trains between Bletchley and Bedford in 1853, including the fares. Note the abbreviated Woburn, the Ridgmount spelling and Ampthill which became Millbrook.

Peter Webber Collection

Left By the early 1950s, it must be admitted that Bletchley's platforms were looking a little careworn and found some pleasant relief in this afternoon sunshine. Nevertheless, some desirable gems of the past shine through the haze. This view is of the 'up' and 'down' slow lines between platforms 5 and 6. The wide pitched roof, with its long row of sunlit tie rods, has lost its fine glazed end screens since LNWR days. The deep valances and flat wide canopy echo the original company style unmistakably. The porter's footstone at about original platform height can be seen. Platform 7 is clearly asserted in this view towards platform 8, the Cambridge line platform. A round-topped archway leads to the finely balustraded footbridge above, which provided an agreeable open causeway between trains, unlike its disturbingly shuttered replacement of today.

BR/OPC Collection

Right One of the Bletchley men, Bert Goodman, leans back from the cab for indication that he can take 'Precursor' class locomotive, *Bucephalus*, away with the 1.20p.m. to Rugby. From Rugby he would then bring the 3.40p.m., known as 'The Mails', to Euston. The engine was, in fact, withdrawn in June 1936. The area in front of the engine provides a tantalizing glimpse of the Bletchley of yesteryear. The water column is, of course, a thing of the past, and behind it a fraction of Bletchley No. 2 box can be seen. Bletchley No. 5 box is visible, with the front of the smokebox of a 'Super D' peeping round it. Behind the hut, one of the 'imported' Lancashire & Yorkshire saddle tanks shunts the Bletchley yard. The hut itself provided an interesting and a less obvious use. This was, in fact, the working stable hut for the trace horses (note the hitching rail). Between duties in the station the horse would remain safely enclosed until the day's work was done, when it would return to the main stable.

L. Hanson

Topped with coal and replenishing its water supply, 'Precedent' class No. 866, *Courier*, prepares to leave Bletchley shed for duty in 1923. These locomotives were once champions of the Euston to Carlisle route until gradual displacement brought them on to secondary lines. Bletchley's allocation worked many of the passenger trains between Oxford and Cambridge and it is quite possible that *Courier* is destined for one of the termini on this particular day.

L&GRP/Courtesy David & Charles

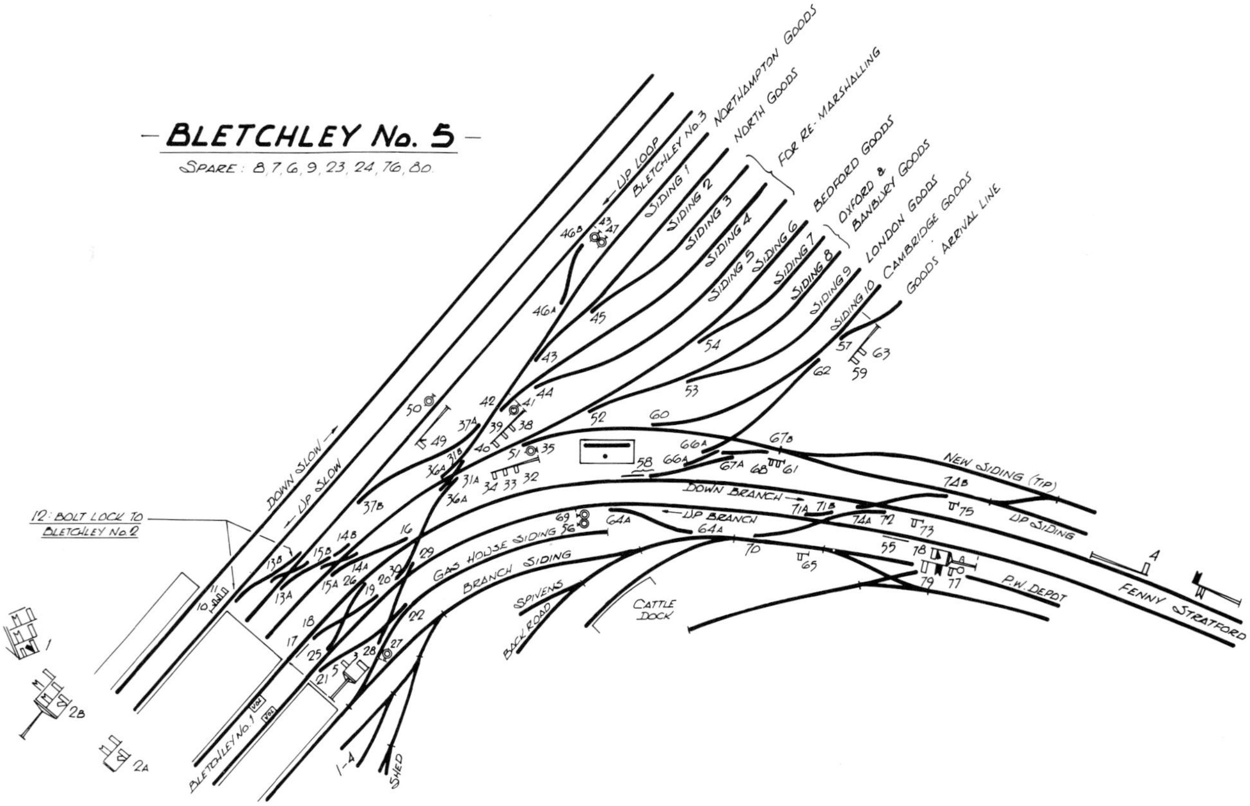

Above Bletchley shed's new glazed roof is shown to very good effect in this photograph taken in the late 1950s. The new roof was built during the period 1950–53. Piston valves in the bench vice are having new stainless steel rings fitted. Bletchley 'Ds' were exemplary by reputation; strong hard-working engines affectionately regarded by the men that drove them.

BR/OPC Collection

Left Declining years of Bletchley shed in the late 1950s, with Midland Railway Class '4 Freight' standing alongside an LMS '8 Freight'. By this time, only the 'Super D' maintained an appearance of the last vestiges of the LNWR dynasty. The top of the water tank house is missing. A new installation has been built by this time.
John Spencer

Above Tea by gaslight in the old Bletchley Station refreshment room. During the rebuilding in the early 1960s, an entirely new refreshment room was opened.
BR/OPC Collection

Bedford and Cambridge. May.

Down. LONDON TO CAMBRIDGE.

Single Line. Bedford to Cambridge.

Distance from Cambridge.	Stations		1 Goods.	2	3 Passenger	4 Goods.	5 Passenger	6	7 Passenger
			A.M.		A.M.	A.M.	A.M.		A.M.
92¼	LONDON	dep.	...	...	...	...	6 30	...	11 0
...	Blisworth		...	...	...	...	...	...	...
...	OXFORD		...	...	...	...	8 0	...	9 15
...	BLETCHLEY (*for Bedford*)		4 0	...	...	7 0	9 28	...	12 15
½	Fenny Stratford	arr.	...	...	...	7 5	9 33	...	...
41½	Woburn Sands	arr.	4 15	...	...	7 18	9 40	...	12 24
		dep.	...	...	...	7 28	...	...	...
39	Ridgmont		...	...	...	7 34	9 47	...	12 32
37	Lidlington		...	...	...	...	9 53	...	12 38
35½	Ampthill	arr.	4 35	...	...	7 50	9 59	...	12 44
		dep.	4 45	...	...	...	...	...	...
29¾	Bedford		5 0	...	...	8 10	10 14	...	1 0
...	BEDFORD for Cambridge	dep.	5 20	...	8 5	8 30	10 19	...	1 5
23¾	Blunham	arr.	5 40	...	8 18	8 48	10 34	...	1 20
21¼	Sandy (Junc. with Gt. Northern)	arr.	5 52	...	8 28	**8 57**	**10 42**	...	**1 29**
		dep.	6 2	...	...	**9 13**	...	...	...
17¾	Potton	arr.	6 13	...	8 42	9 25	10 52	...	1 39
		dep.	6 20	...	...	9 33	...	...	...
15¼	Gamlingay		6 28	...	**8 49**	9 40	11 0	...	1 46
10¾	Old North Road	arr.	6 43	...	8 59	**10 5**	11 12	...	**1 58**
		dep.	6 58	...	...	**10 15**	...	...	...
5½	Lord's Bridge		7 12	...	9 11	10 30	11 25	...	2 12
...	CAMBRIDGE		7 35	...	9 23	11 0	11 39	...	2 25

No. **4** leaves Sandy 9.13 a.m., after 8.10 a.m. Passenger Train from Cambridge; Old North Road 10.15 a.m., after departure of 9.45 a.m. Passenger Train from Cambridge.

No. **8** leaves Sandy 4.8 p.m., after 3.10 p.m. Passenger Train from Cambridge, and Gamlingay, 4.40 p.m. after arrival of 3.40 Goods Train from Cambridge.

Down. LONDON TO CAMBRIDGE.

Stations.	8 Coal.	9	10 Passenger	11	12 Passenger	13	14 Passenger	15	16 Passenger	Sundays 1 Passenger	Sundays 2	Sundays 3
	P.M.		P.M.		P.M.		P.M.		P.M.	A.M.		
LON.	...	...	...	...	4 0	...	...	...	7 0	10 0	...	...
Blis.	...	...	...	...	4 20	...	...	...	...	...	...	...
OXF.	...	...	1 15	...	4 15	...	5 20	...	7 30	10 0	...	...
BLE.	1 30	...	2 38	...	5 55	...	6 35	...	9 5	11 50	...	...
F. S.	1 35	...	...	...	...	...	6 39	...	9 9	11 54	...	...
W. S.	1 48	...	2 50	...	6 5	...	6 47	...	9 17	12 2	...	...
,,	1 58	...	...	...	...	...	...	...	...	...	...	...
Ridg.	2 4	...	...	...	...	...	6 55	...	9 25	12 9	...	...
Lid.	...	...	...	...	...	...	7 1	...	9 31	12 15	...	...
Ampt.	2 20	...	3 6	...	6 18	...	7 7	...	9 37	12 21	...	...
,,	...	...	...	...	...	...	...	...	...	...	...	...
Bed.	2 40	...	3 18	...	6 30	...	7 20	...	9 50	12 36	...	...
BED.	3 0	...	3 23	...	6 33	...	...	...	...	12 40	...	...
Blun.	3 19	...	3 38	...	6 47	...	...	...	...	12 55	...	...
Sandy	**3 35**	...	3 46	...	**6 55**	...	...	...	...	1 3	...	...
,,	**4 8**	...	...	...	...	...	...	...	...	...	...	...
Pott.	4 19	...	**3 56**	...	7 6	...	...	...	...	1 13	...	...
,,	...	...	...	...	...	...	...	...	...	...	...	...
Gam.	**4 39**	...	4 4	...	7 14	...	...	...	...	1 21	...	...
O.N.R.	4 59	...	**4 16**	...	7 25	...	...	...	...	1 33	...	...
,,	5 7	...	...	...	...	...	...	...	...	...	...	...
L. B.	5 22	...	...	...	**7 37**	...	...	...	...	1 46	...	...
CAM.	5 42	...	4 38	...	7 50	...	...	...	...	2 0	...	...

Up. CAMBRIDGE TO LONDON.

Single Line. Cambridge to Bedford.

Distance from London.	Stations		1 Passenger	2	3 Passenger	4	5 Passenger	6	7 Goods.
			A.M.		A.M.		A.M.		A.M.
...	CAMBRIDGE	dep.	...	...	8 10	...	9 45	...	11 50
...	Lord's Bridge	arr.	...	...	8 24	...	9 59	...	12 5
...	Old North Road	arr.	...	...	8 37	...	...	...	12 25
...		dep.	...	...	...	...	...	...	12 35
...	Gamlingay		...	...	**8 49**	...	10 23	...	12 50
...	Potton	arr.	...	...	8 58	...	10 31	...	1 0
...		dep.	...	...	...	...	...	...	1 15
...	Sandy (Junc. with Gt. Northern)	arr.	...	...	**9 11**	...	**10 42**	...	**1 25**
...		dep.	...	...	...	...	...	...	**1 40**
...	Blunham		...	...	9 21	...	10 48	...	2 0
...	BEDFORD		...	...	9 36	...	11 2	...	2 25
...	Bedford for Bletchley	dep.	7 15	...	9 40	...	11 5	...	2 55
...	Ampthill	arr.	7 26	...	9 51	...	11 16	...	3 10
...		dep.	...	...	...	...	...	...	3 20
...	Lidlington		7 32	...	9 57	...	...	...	...
...	Ridgmont		7 38	...	10 3	...	11 25	...	3 30
...	Woburn Sands	arr.	7 45	...	10 10	...	11 32	...	3 40
...		dep.	...	...	...	...	...	...	3 50
...	Fenny Stratford		7 53	...	10 18	...	...	...	3 59
...	Bletchley		7 58	...	10 25	...	11 44	...	4 5
...	OXFORD		9 40	...	11 50	...	1 25	...	...
...	Blisworth		...	...	...	...	...	...	...
...	LONDON		10 0	...	12 15	...	1 30	...	...

7 leaves Sandy 1.40 p.m. after 1.5 p.m. Passenger Train from Bedford.

Up. CAMBRIDGE TO LONDON.

Stations.	8 Passenger	9	10 Passenger	11 Goods.	12	13 Passenger	14 Goods.	15	16	Sundays 1 Passenger	Sundays 2	Sundays 3
	P.M.		P.M.	P.M.		P.M.	P.M.			A.M.		
CAM.	1 35		3 10	3 40	...	6 5	7 15	...	...	9 0	...	...
L. B.	...	...	3 24	3 55	...	6 18	**7 32**	...	...	9 14	...	...
O.N.R.	**1 59**	...	3 37	**4 10**	...	6 30	8 0	...	...	9 27	...	...
,,	...	...	...	**4 18**	...	...	8 10	...	...	...	...	...
Gam.	...	...	3 49	**4 34**	...	6 40	8 22	...	...	9 37	...	...
Pott.	2 15	...	**3 57**	4 51	...	6 49	8 35	...	...	9 47	...	...
,,	...	...	...	5 0	...	...	8 45	...	...	...	...	...
Sandy	2 25	...	**4 7**	5 12	...	**6 57**	8 57	...	...	9 57	...	...
,,	...	...	...	...	...	...	...	...	...	...	...	...
Blun.	...	...	4 15	5 36	...	7 5	9 12	...	...	10 5	...	...
BED.	2 45	...	4 30	5 56	...	7 19	9 32	...	...	10 25	...	...
Bed	2 50	...	4 35	6 20	...	7 23	9 45	...	...	10 35	...	...
Ampt.	3 0	...	4 45	6 35	...	7 33	...	...	...	10 46	...	...
,,	...	...	...	6 45	...	...	...	...	...	...	...	...
Lid.	...	...	4 51	...	...	7 39	...	...	...	10 52	...	...
Ridg.	...	...	4 56	6 55	...	7 45	...	...	...	10 58	...	...
W. S.	3 12	...	5 4	7 5	...	7 51	...	...	...	11 5	...	...
,,	...	...	...	...	...	...	...	...	...	...	...	...
F. S.	...	...	5 10	7 20	...	7 58	...	...	...	11 13	...	...
Bletc.	3 22	...	5 15	7 30	...	8 5	10 40	...	...	11 20	...	...
OXF.	4 50	...	6 55	...	...	9 30	...	...	...	12 55	...	...
Blis.	4 0	...	...	...	...	...	...	...	...	...	...	...
LON.	5 55	...	7 5	...	...	10 40	...	...	...	2 15	...	...

No. **11** leaves Old North Road 4.18 p.m. after 3 23 p.m. Passenger Train from Bedford, and Gamlingay 4.40 after 3.0 p.m Coal Train from Bedford.

No. **14** leaves Lords Bridge 7.38, after arrival of 6.33 p.m. Passenger Train from Bedford.

Train Staff Stations.

Bedford, Sandy, Potton, Gamlingay, Old North Road, Lord's Bridge, Cambridge.

Goods Trains, Up and Down, will call at Girtford's Siding, between Blunham and Sandy, by Signal, to leave and take up Waggons.

The working timetable for May 1864, when the line from Bedford to Cambridge was single all the way

An excellent view from Watling Street road bridge at Fenny Stratford, looking down on the LNWR station. The space occupied by the wagons on the 'down' siding was, in later years, the site of a new platform. Of great interest is the area to the left and behind the wagons, the siding for Rowland Brothers. Comparison with the diagram for this siding would aid scrutiny. A shadow of the narrow gauge crane tramway can just be seen between the wagons and the trees, whilst in the far distance, is the angular shape of the crane itself.

Lens of Sutton

CHAPTER SIX

Fenny Stratford

Just beyond the first mile post from Bletchley Station is the attractive station of Fenny Stratford with station buildings in the half-timbered Gothic style, with fretted barge boards and white geometrical pattens making it stand out sharply in its surroundings. This attractive style was insisted upon by the Duke of Bedford for stations situated within the Woburn Estates. Consequently, there is a pleasing similarity between all the buildings along the line.

Where the line was to cross the famous Watling Street, (A5), the road was carried over the railway and had, therefore, to be raised some 6 ft. 8 in. to allow sufficient clearance.

Originally, the station had staggered platforms with the wedge-shaped 'down' platform being situated near the Simpson Road crossing. This platform was rebuilt, in 1948, to face the 'up' platform as is the conventional arrangement.

In the early days, Fenny Stratford was the only real community served by the railway at this end of the line, with a population of 635 residing in about twenty five separate buildings situated alongside the Grand Junction Canal. The entire canal was opened to traffic in 1805 which gave Fenny Stratford something of a head start. Coal, bricks, slate and pottery from the Midlands were moving through wharfs on the canal long before the London & Birmingham Railway was surveyed.

Protection of canal interests was included in the Act for the Bedford Railway, mentioned previously. With the opening of the line, the canal was to be of service to the railway in a direct way, for an agreement was made between the Grand Junction Canal and the Bedford Railway on 9th April 1847, to supply no more than 500 gallons of water per day for engines at a cost of £5 per annum.

Had the demands stated in the petition by the villagers for a bridge to be built at the other end of the station at the Simpson Road crossing, in June 1882, been agreed, the incident that followed would not have occurred. Forty three years later, on 7th December, at 8.43 p.m., a motor omnibus crashed through the closed crossing gates, even though they had bright red lamps mounted upon them, and collided with the 6.30 p.m. Cambridge to Bletchley train. Six occupants of the vehicle, including the driver, were killed instantly and four others were seriously injured. Two others had cuts and bruises and only one suffered no injury. The train, which was undamaged, was hauled by No. 1170 *General*, a 2-4-0 locomotive, with four bogie coaches and a brake van, weighing 93 tons behind the tender.

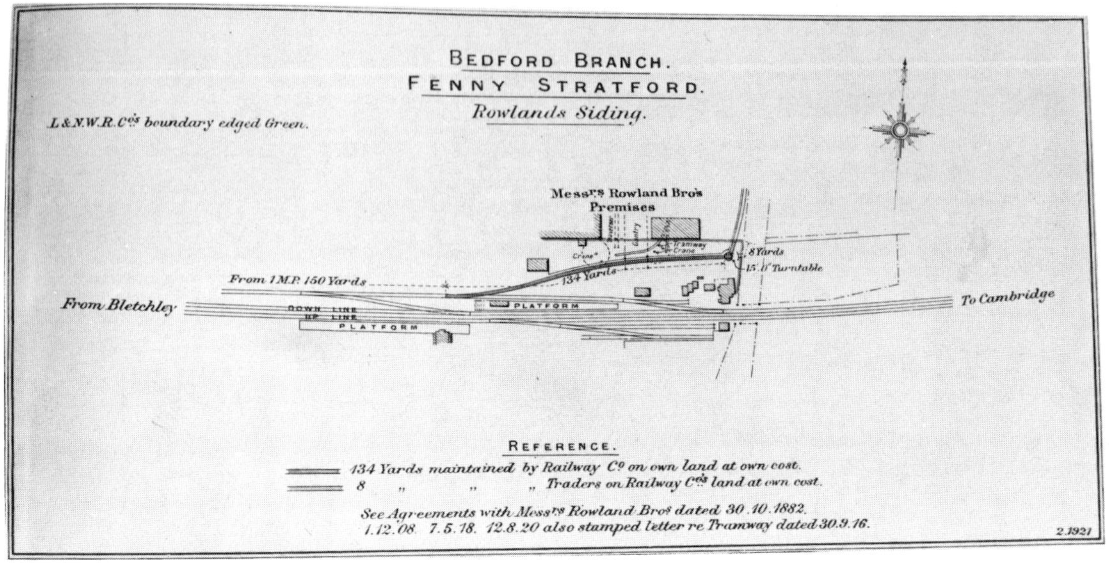

This diagram of Fenny Stratford, in 1921, gives an indication of the original disposition of the 'down' platform; the wedge shape staggered nearer the crossing. The interesting detail of the siding to Rowlands Brothers Timber Merchants, with tramway crane, can also be seen.

J. Pritchett Collection

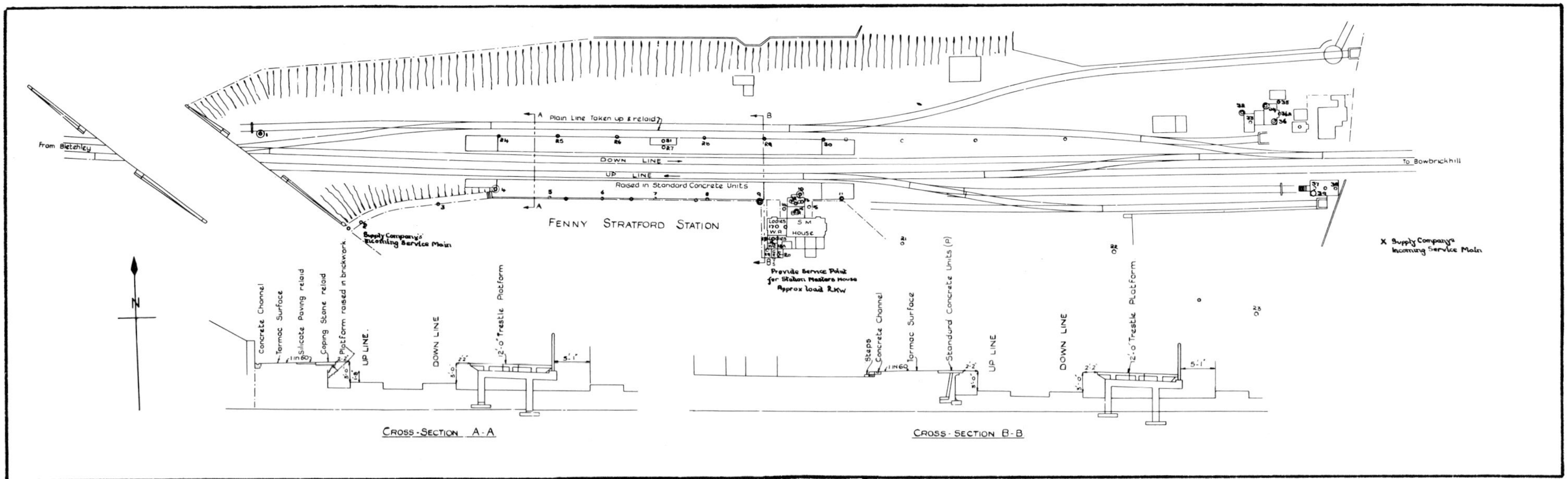

Installation of the new 'down' line platform and electric lighting points at Fenny Stratford in 1948. Rowland Brothers Siding is still in use with its small wagon turnplate giving access to a long extension to the siding at right angles along the Simpson Road. Few goods facilities were installed at Fenny Stratford due to the close proximity of the large goods yard at Bletchley. Lamp hut and permanent way huts are situated alongside the crossing keeper's house, facing the signal box on the Simpson Road side. The skew road overbridge of the A5 (Watling Street) is reached from the platform by a narrow footpath.

Exuberant half-timbering at Fenny Stratford, with high pitched gables, fine fretted barge boards and ornamental tiling. This distinctive style makes the building almost spring into view from its woodland surroundings. Although the 'sausage' emblem of British Railways is evident, little has altered from the original structure apart from the prefabricated concrete block construction of the platform, rebuilt in 1948.

BR/OPC Collection

The view towards Bedford after the 'down' platform had been rebuilt to a facing platform in 1948. The photograph was taken in the early 1960s.

John Spencer

Simpson Road crossing, at the Bedford end of the station, with a type 4 signal box of the LNWR period from 1884 to 1903. The crossing keeper's house modestly follows the building style, being built in roughcast with diaper brickwork on the chimney. The matching 'peep-hole' window can be seen facing the oncoming 'down' trains in both the house wall and the permanent way hut wall, next to the door. A siding in front of the steps of the signal box has been removed in this view taken in the early 1960s.

J. R. Rounthwaite

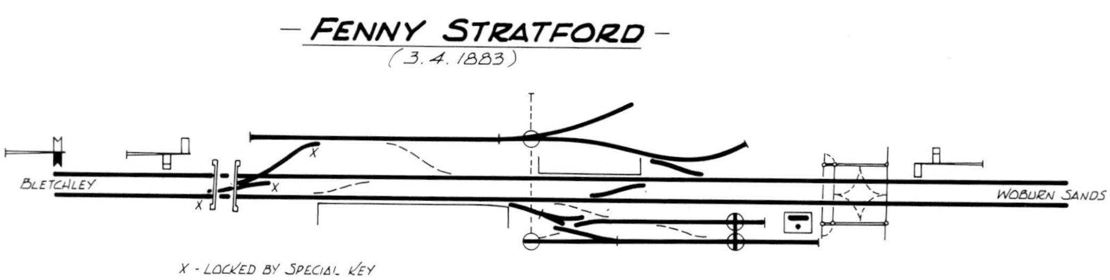

An early diagram of the signalling at Fenny Stratford when semaphore arms for both 'up' and 'down' lines were sited on a single post. The date for this diagram is 3rd April 1883, three years after the installation of 'block' signalling from Bletchley to Cambridge. The 'down' and crossover road, at the Bletchley end of the station, were controlled by a ground frame released by Annett's key from the signal box. Also remaining are four of the 12ft. turnplates that were so familiar on the line in early days.

M. Christensen

A view looking towards Bletchley in the early 1950s, when the platforms were still at rail level.

National Monuments Records

CHAPTER SEVEN

Bow Brickhill Halt

In December 1905, in common with the line between Oxford and Bicester, the LNWR decided to apply their experimental steam railmotor service on the line from Bedford to Bletchley. On 1st December, the new service began using seven halts situated between Bletchley and Bedford. In addition to Bow Brickhill, at the 2¼ mile post, there was Aspley Guise (5¼ mile post), Husborne Crawley (6½ mile post), Wootton Pillinge (11¼ mile post), Wootton Broadmead (12¼ mile post), Kempston Hardwick (13 mile post) and Kempston & Elstow (14¾ mile post). Company records show a Brickyard Halt on the 11½ mile post near Wootton Pillinge, but this never appeared on a public timetable. Bow Brickhill proved to be an exception by having platforms staggered on each side of the crossing which would have enabled the gates to be closed after the motor had entered the platform point. This was not repeated again on the other halts which all conform to the usual arrangement of facing platforms, (if platform was the right word). The halts were of the simplest construction, consisting of an old sleeper base at rail level with a nameboard and oil lamps. This very modest installation, built at an average cost of £43, could be effected as the new vehicle was alighted and mounted by means of folding steps that held the vacuum brake on when opened at the halts. The vacuum could not be restored until the conductor, who took the fares en route, folded them back against the vehicle. Operating at a modest pace, the new lightweight machine worked quite well, except when it broke down which, unfortunately, happened quite often. There were two units in use with one spare engine kept at Bletchley. In 1911, the service was earning 10¼d (4p) per mile against operating expenses of 6¾d (2½p) per mile and was, quite obviously, popular. There were, however, some operating difficulties for the Company. Having a light drawbar

The only structures beside the lodge for the crossing keeper were the waiting-room, plain and neat with fine glazing bars, and the necessary signal cabin, enclosing its four lever frame for operating signals to protect only the crossing. Both structures stand at the original level of the halts, which, when boarding the steam railmotor, was facilitated by the folding steps on the vehicle itself.

K. Bristow

efficiency, the steam railmotor could hardly pull an extra van when required, or, for that matter, an extra coach, which was a crucial limitation in the loading factor. The conditions for the enginemen were the worst imaginable with unbearable heat being generated in a confined space, so that the men were often forced to run with the doors open, which was a rather unsafe practice. As local services evolved they were to prove merely a prototype to the much more successful push-pull workings that followed.

The halts proved much more durable, some of them surviving to this day. They were all suspended in 1917, due to the rostering of heavy wartime traffic, but were reinstated on 5th May 1919, although it is not clear as to how long under steam railmotor operation. It was not long after the war, that the push-pull trains began to operate the service which they did efficiently until diesel trains replaced them in 1959. A number of the halts did not survive beyond 1926 and many were modified with concrete paving and edging replacing the wooden sleepers. As they had been originally intended for a single loading point on the train, they had short platforms of about 50 ft. in length. Therefore, with the introduction of diesel trains, they required rebuilding with conventional height platforms of timber of about 300 ft. in length. Stewartby was converted to a station in 1932 and was controlled by one man.

The motor service shown in *Bradshaw's*, for July 1905, included a Bletchley to Sandy working.

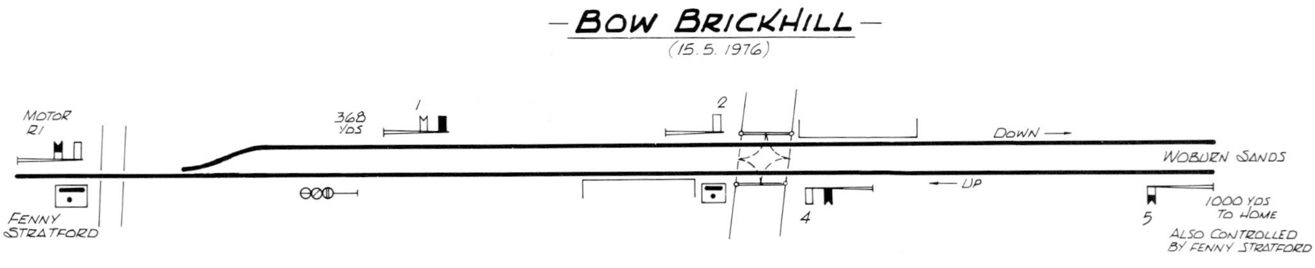

A Bow Brickhill diagram, altered only slightly, with the single line section put in between Bletchley and Fenny Stratford. The halt was never a 'block' post. Signalling is for protection of the crossing.

M. Christensen

This unique view of a steam railmotor, bound for Bedford, photographed at Woburn Sands, was taken in 1908 from a position standing alongside the crossing gates.

Harry Pikesley

Details of the coach fitting interior were included with a drawing in *Oxford to Cambridge Railway (Volume One)*. It is an interesting historical development that diesel multiple units perform the same operation along the Bedford line to this day, with 'paytrain' tickets being issued by the guard on the train.

A motor unit for the steam railmotor, appears curious when denuded from its coach body. This design, by George Whale, is self evidently of light construction, and seems hardly likely to draw upon much reserve drawbar capacity.

BR/OPC Collection

A glance in the Bedford direction, on 30th July 1965.

R. Powell

Bow Brickhill crossing, halt and signal box. This was the only halt to have the staggered platforms that were raised in timber in 1959 with the introduction of diesel trains. This late afternoon view is looking towards Bletchley.

Author's Collection

Disregarding their oncoming train, which appears to be hauled by a 'Precedent' class locomotive, this group, pictured in the early 1900s, pose before camera and the momentary record of photograph. Appropriately, Woburn Sands must represent the apogee of the half-timbered style, as it was on the insistence of the Duke of Bedford that this style was adopted, the family residence of Woburn Abbey being situated nearby. Before rebuilding, the platforms were edged in stone blocks and, quite often, they were the old stone sleepers lifted from early lines after being replaced by wooden ones. Little has changed from this scene to the present day, except that the district around the station has become much more built up and urbanized.

Author's Collection

CHAPTER EIGHT

Woburn Sands

Woburn, meaning a stream, was the name given to the Cistercian Abbey, founded in 1145, six miles from the village of Bletchley. Upon dissolution, in 1540, it went to the King who passed it on to one, John Russell, or Baron Russell of Chenies, a forebear of the Dukes of Bedford. The older village of Woburn was largely untouched by the arrival of the railway, in 1846, at a place called Hogsty End, which could hardly be allowed to carry such a prosaic representation of the locality into the new commerce of railway communication. So it was that the station carried the more urbane name, Woburn Sands; the word Sands being added for the layer of greensand upon which it stood. The building is in the attractive half-timbered style to be found elsewhere on the line.

With the opening of the railway, a little community began to develop at Woburn Sands and a small brickyard, alongside the station, was owned by Eastwoods who later moved to Kempston to expand their business in the Fletton method of brick-making. Also in July 1871, the Woburn Sands & Aspley Guise Gas Company sidings were built on the 'down' side of the line and, of course, the coal offices that would despatch from their new sidings. From 1848, Woburn Sands had a goods depot which was equipped with two 12 ft. and four 11 ft. turntables. The yard was handling the highest tonnage of coal between Bletchley and Bedford, 3,393 tons, throughout that year.

Woburn Sands crossing, with a type 4 signal box and a handbell affixed. This bell was used by the signalman to warn of the imminent closure of the gates. The closure was effected from the box, by turning a large 'nautical' wheel which transferred the movement to the rodding and the gatepost by the mesh or a gearwheel on the gatepost base (see below). The wheel and mechanism were brought from Oxford Road signal-box, near Oxford, when that crossing was removed in 1935 (see *Oxford to Cambridge Railway, (Volume One)*. With the development of the motor car, Woburn became possibly one of the busiest crossings on the line. Today, the crossing has been replaced by automatic crossing barriers.

BR/OPC Collection

A view along the Dunstable to Newport Pagnell road, at Woburn Sands, around the turn of the century. The rurality of the neighbourhood is clear. The original crossing gates are closed over a road as yet unsurfaced. Through the bars of the gate, grassy mounds can be seen growing. The name on the private owner wagon on the right is frustratingly cropped from view, but there is some identification interest in the small lettering of 'E V' & 'G N R'. Of further interest in this particular scene, is the side road entrance on the right, in front of the wagons. Before the railway was built, this also crossed the path of the line's survey. With the building of the line, this was truncated to the use of a single crossing point.

Harry Pikesley

A very early print of Woburn Sands, probably taken during the latter part of the nineteenth century. The high ballast is typical of the period. The view of open country around the station gives a good example of how it all probably looked at the time of the opening of the line in 1846. Evidently, the photographer's interest has gained everyone's attention and immobility, as such photographs were often taken on very long exposures.

Author's Collection

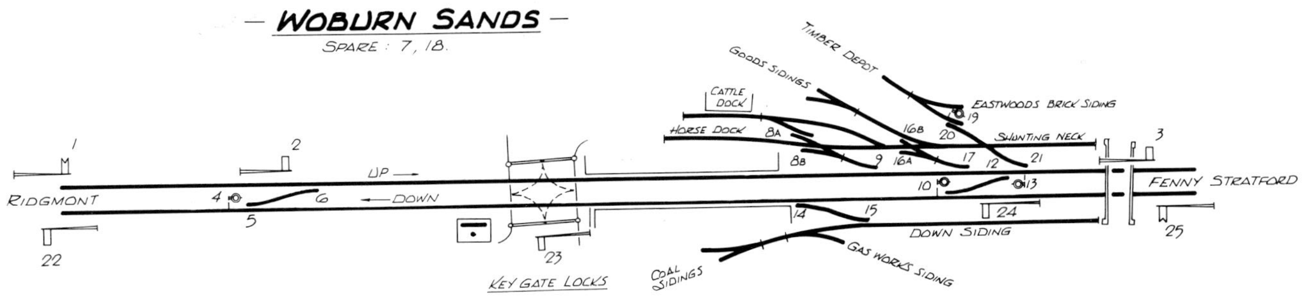

A Woburn Sands signalling diagram of the early twentieth century. Note the timber depot, a great deal of timber being supplied from the Woburn Estates.

M. Christensen

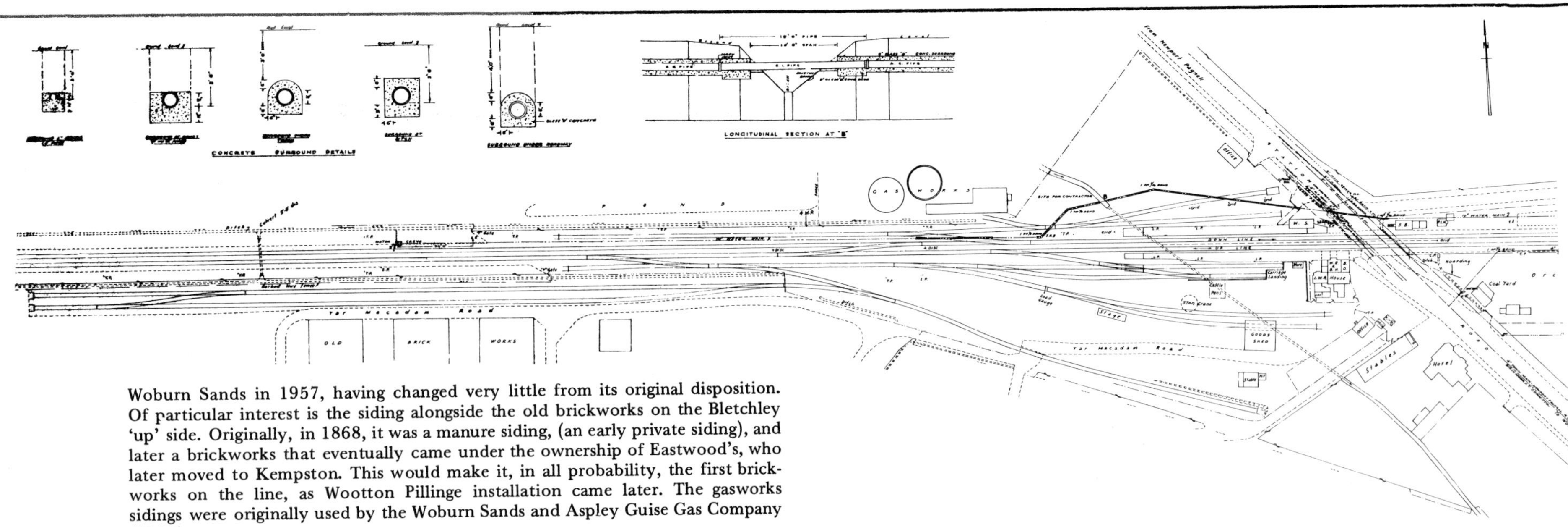

Woburn Sands in 1957, having changed very little from its original disposition. Of particular interest is the siding alongside the old brickworks on the Bletchley 'up' side. Originally, in 1868, it was a manure siding, (an early private siding), and later a brickworks that eventually came under the ownership of Eastwood's, who later moved to Kempston. This would make it, in all probability, the first brickworks on the line, as Wootton Pillinge installation came later. The gasworks sidings were originally used by the Woburn Sands and Aspley Guise Gas Company (1870).

BR/OPC Collection

A British Railways standard Class 4, 4-6-0 locomotive, makes a cautious approach, to the old footpath just west of the Woburn crossing, with its train of unfitted goods empties, in the mid-1960s.

John Spencer

WOBURN SANDS.

Footpath leading out of Lower End Road.—This footpath crossing is situated 200 yards east of Woburn Sands station. Guards of up freight trains which come to a stand at the station must, if necessary, divide the train, the rear portion being left between the footpath crossing and the level crossing gates, and the front portion drawn ahead clear of the level crossing gates.

A reference to the footpath at Woburn Sands.

C. Gibbins Collection

A charming representation of the station in the early days painted on the public house sign situated alongside the station.

Author's Collection

I am particularly indebted to B. V. Garland, for his time and effort in calculating and drawing up this profile from figures published by the LNWR in 1910.

B. V. Garland

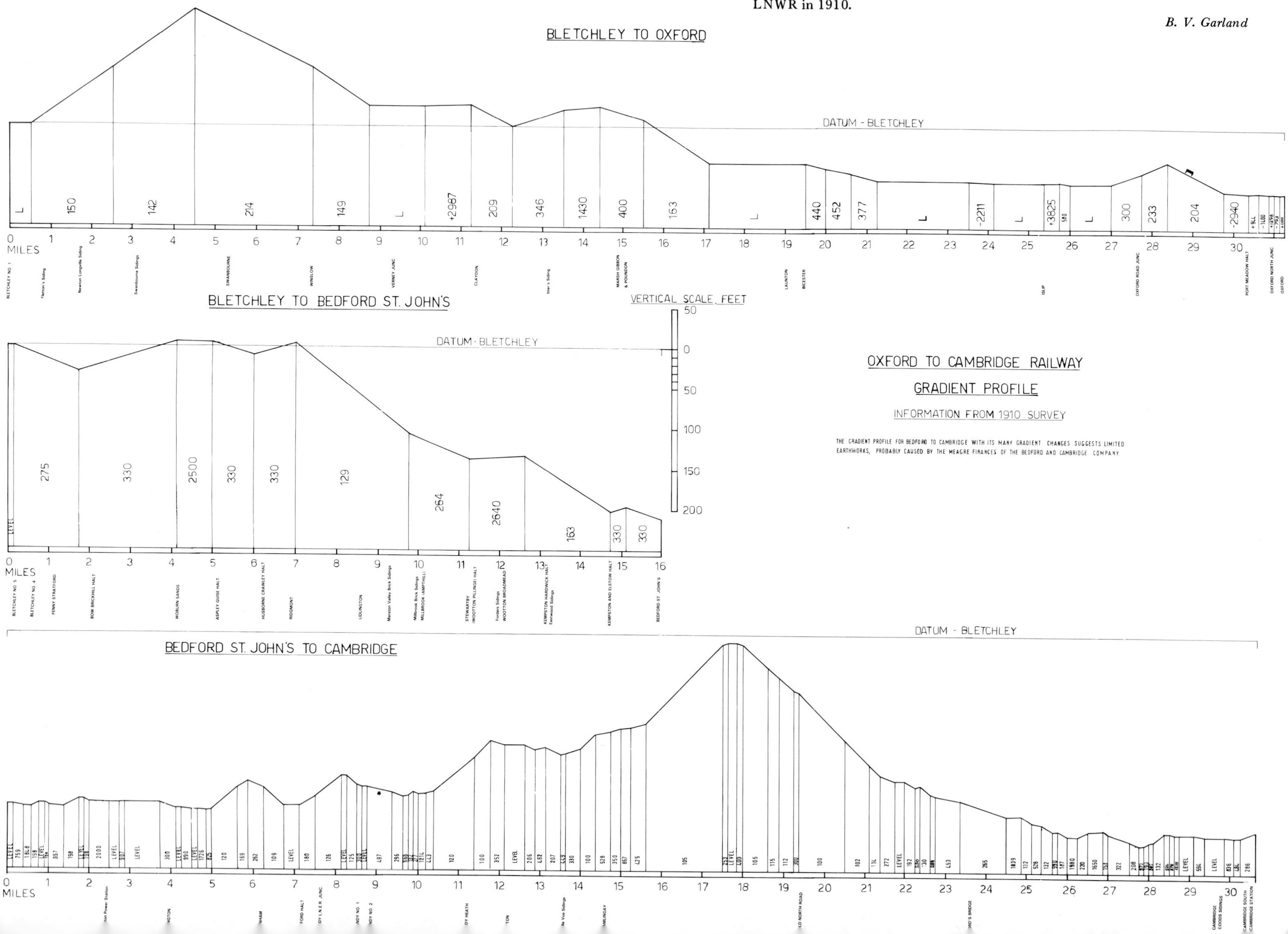

Aspley Guise Halt, in 1953, looking in the Bletchley direction, and showing the brick shelter, built by the LMS, who also supplanted the wooden sleepers of the original platform with concrete paving. Gates were held across the road at this halt, which required no signals. The crossing keeper in the adjacent lodge could be summoned by the road traveller who could effect this by pulling a bell at the gate side. Nowadays, a member of the railway staff attends the gates from a hut which contains train indication instruments.

National Monuments Records

CHAPTER NINE

Aspley Guise

The crossing acquired its small two platform halt in the installations of 1905. It was an unusual crossing insomuch as the gates were left across the road and the keeper had to be summoned to open them, for road traffic, by means of a bell. The halt was closed during World War I and reopened on 5th May 1919.

The lodge at Aspley Guise. The, by now, familiar style is evident once more.

Author's Collection

A Bletchley-bound BR Class 4 standard locomotive, brings its loose-coupled train of mineral empties through Apsley Guise Halt in the early 1960s. The original nameboard has been replaced by a BR enamel sign in maroon, but the old LNWR oil lamps maintain their use along the platform. The speedy reconstruction of the platforms was accomplished, ingeniously, with drainage pipes, filled with concrete, holding the cross member supports in the ridges.

John Spencer

A rambling '4 Freight' locomotive, No. 44447, on the Bletchley to Bedford pick-up goods, passes through Aspley Guise. Another Bletchley engine of the same class was regarded with great esteem. This was No. 43841 which always steamed freely and answered every call with great effort. It is the familiar unresolved enigma of engines of the same class, but not the same kind.

John Spencer

As mentioned in the text, push-pull working proved most successful on the Bletchley to Bedford line, with a fairly intensive passenger usage over a number of short distance stops. Following the tentative beginnings with the steam rail-motor, the successive push-pull trains got into their stride with the 'motor tanks' of the LNWR, followed by the ex-Midland 1F 0-4-4 tanks of the LMS. British Rail carried the push-pull workings up to pre-diesel introduction, as seen here at Aspley Guise. The view is looking in the Bletchley bound direction.

J. R. Rounthwaite

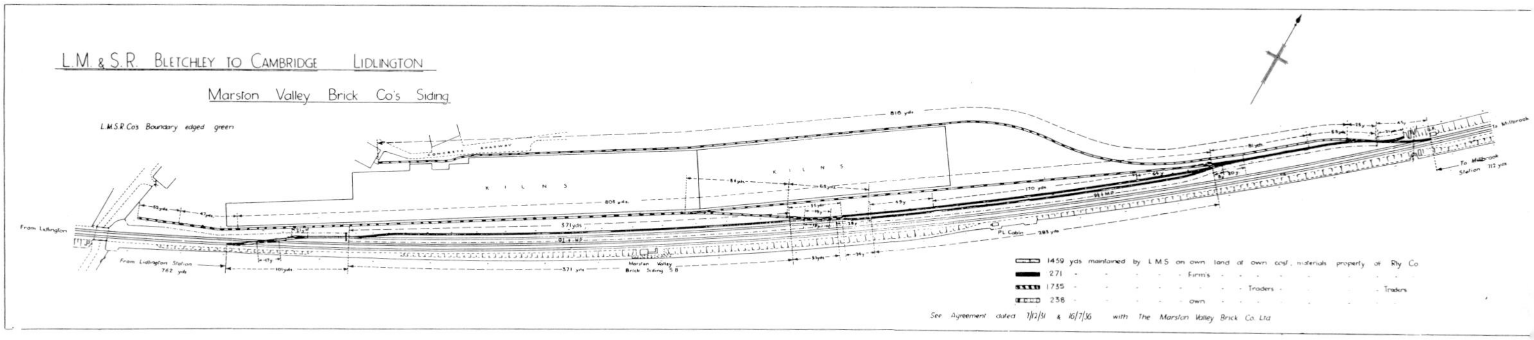
L.M. & S.R. Bletchley to Cambridge Lidlington
Marston Valley Brick Co's Siding
L.M.S.R. Co's Boundary edged green
K I L N S
K I L N S
From Lidlington
From Lidlington Station 762 yds
805 yds.
816 yds
371 yds
101 yds
371 yds
170 yds
Marston Valley Brick Siding 5 8
PL Cabin 285 yds
To Millbrook
To Millbrook Station 712 yds
1459 yds maintained by L.M.S on own land at own cost, materials property of Rly Co
271 - Firm's
1735 - Traders - Traders
238 - own
See Agreement dated 7/12/31 & 16/7/36 with The Marston Valley Brick Co. Ltd

PLEASE RING FOR CROSSING KEEPER
OUT OF ORDER

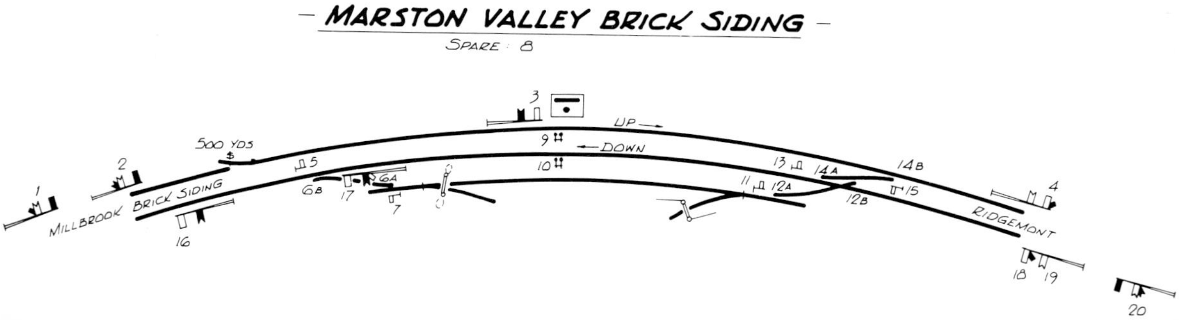
– MARSTON VALLEY BRICK SIDING –
SPARE: 8
UP
DOWN
500 YDS
MILLBROOK BRICK SIDING
RIDGEMONT
1
2
3
4
5
6A
6B
7
9
10
11
12A
12B
13
14A
14B
15
16
17
18
19
20

Ridgmont in 1979. The exposed frame was moved from a hut on the other side of the road crossing in 1934, the instruments being installed in the bay windowed room facing the platform. Next to the bay window, under the gables, is the old LNWR station number, 155. This oddly retained its position long after it had ceased to apply. The station platform was rebuilt similar to the others mentioned at Fenny Stratford and Woburn Sands.

Author's Collection

CHAPTER TEN

Ridgmont

At Ridgmont, the station buildings followed the familiar half-timbered style of three other stations on the line, although each structure had variations on the style. Ridgmont is still a signalling block post with the frame, once at ground level, alongside a small hut containing the instruments on the other side of the road but on the same side of the crossing. However, with the introduction of staff economies on 30th January 1934, the instruments were brought into the booking office and the lever frame placed just outside the door. This enabled the signalman to operate his instruments, to open and close the gates and also to attend to the booking of tickets.

Until World War I, the surroundings of 1846 changed very little at this rural crossing point. During that period, on 25th July 1918, the Ministry of Munitions opened a siding at the 5¾ mile post, on the Aspley side. This was manned by German prisoners of war who cut and loaded wood on to the railway wagons in the siding.

The most drastic change to the scene came with the sudden expansion of the London Brick Company with a new factory, dwarfing the station, in 1930. New sidings were installed alongside the works with ground frames released by Annett's key held by the signalman. This entire installation was situated on the Bedford side of the crossing, at the 7 mile post.

Between Ridgmont and Aspley Guise, on the 6½ mile post, was the small crossing and halt of Husborne Crawley. It was converted to a 'block' post with a signal box upon the installation of sidings for the RAF fuel supply on 15th September 1939. However, the sidings, but not the halt and crossing, survived the building of the nearby M1 motorway when an important road link was bridged across the line in 1959. The halt had not, from its inception, been one of the more successful, being closed not only during World War I but again in 1941. It was never truly recalled to passenger service and was removed, completely, in 1949.

A station group of 9th August 1917, with station master, Mr Abbey, on the left. With him are Porter Charlie Fleet and Signalman Albert Woodlett. It is noticeable in this view, that the frame has not yet been brought over to this side of the road for staff economies. In the background is the Bedford Arms public house, a companionable hostelry near the station, dating from the days when there were no other buildings nearby. The station number is visible over the bay windowed room, as mentioned previously.

R. Carpenter

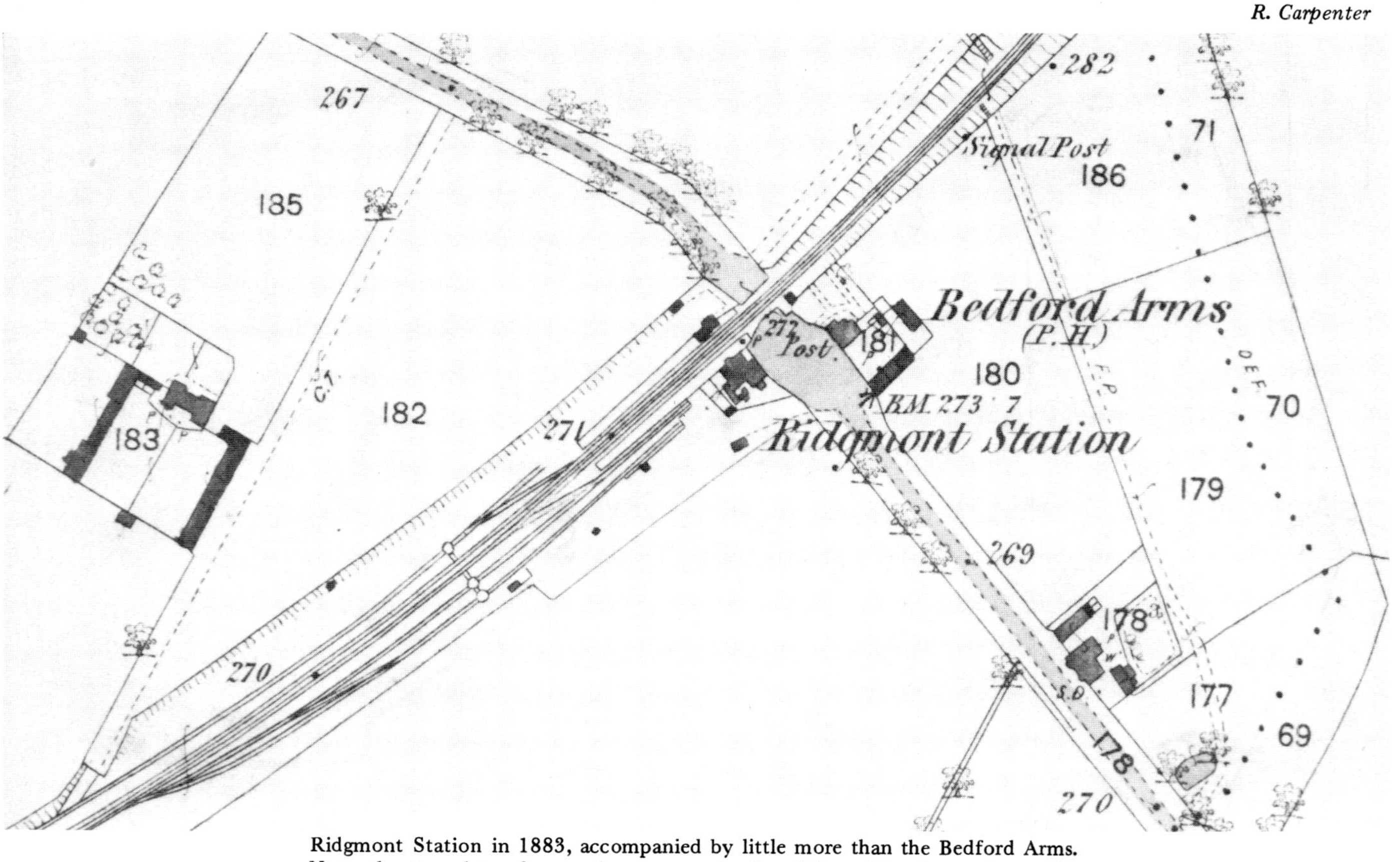

Ridgmont Station in 1883, accompanied by little more than the Bedford Arms. Note the turnplates for moving wagons in the sidings. The footpath on the other side of the signal post is on the site of the turf cutting ceremony of 1845.

Courtesy of the Ordnance Survey

A view looking towards Bedford over the crossing, with the Ridgmont brickworks of the Marston Valley Company nearby.

Author's Collection

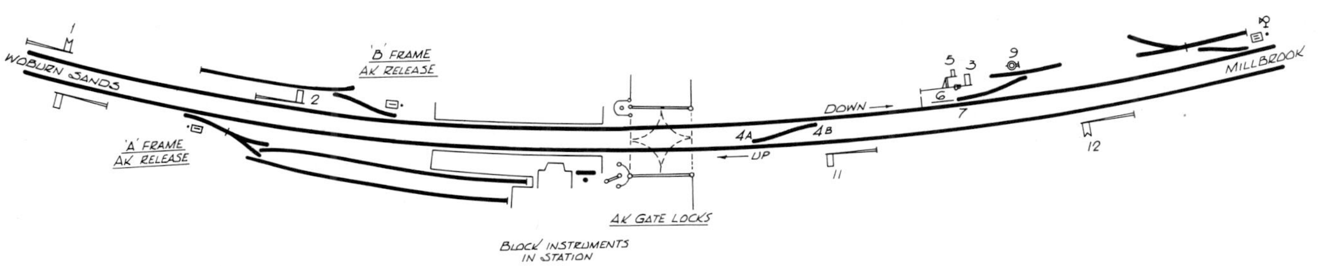

A Ridgmont diagram with sidings released by Annett's key. Marston Valley sidings were released from Ridgmont as Lidlington was not a 'block' post. The diagram is circa 1960.

M. Christensen

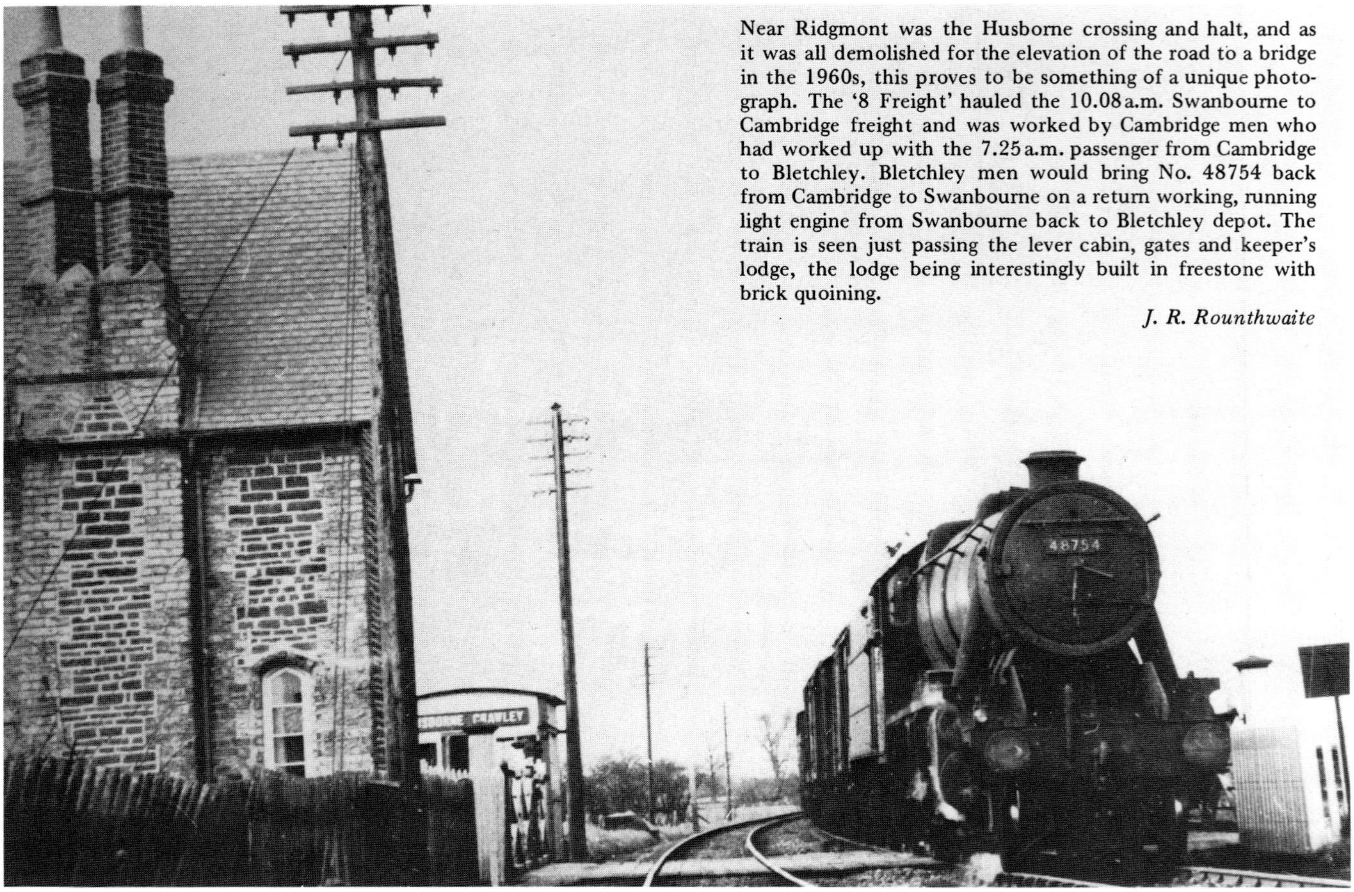

Near Ridgmont was the Husborne crossing and halt, and as it was all demolished for the elevation of the road to a bridge in the 1960s, this proves to be something of a unique photograph. The '8 Freight' hauled the 10.08 a.m. Swanbourne to Cambridge freight and was worked by Cambridge men who had worked up with the 7.25 a.m. passenger from Cambridge to Bletchley. Bletchley men would bring No. 48754 back from Cambridge to Swanbourne on a return working, running light engine from Swanbourne back to Bletchley depot. The train is seen just passing the lever cabin, gates and keeper's lodge, the lodge being interestingly built in freestone with brick quoining.

J. R. Rounthwaite

Another view, taken on 21st May 1964, shows standard 4-6-0 locomotive, No. 73014 with the Bedford 9.43 a.m. stopping train to Bletchley (normally a diesel multiple unit working) having just left Ridgmont. This gives a distant view of the alterations to the site on the previous photograph. The new concrete bridge is evident and an indication of the position of the '8 Freight' in the previous view would be just a little further than the two car unit, Nos. M56225 and M50942, near the fifth coach of the steam-hauled train. Points were installed at the same spot for the wartime petrol storage depot sidings, which are just visible at the edge of the photograph. In the opposite corner are the tall chimneys of Ridgmont brickworks.

Ian Hall

Little more than a halt, as there are no sidings or goods facilities. Nevertheless, a fine stout presentation of yellow and red brickwork with the same distinctive roofing covered with ornamental ridge tiles. A small room and chimney over the entrance porch are interesting features. The station master, in these latter years of the nineteenth century, stands proudly before his charge with his porter. Seated behind, it is possible that his family have also come out to pose for what was an uncommon occurrence at that time; the taking of a photograph. Much is unchanged today, although the building is no longer a dwelling and the station platforms have been rebuilt to a standard height. This particular view is looking towards Bedford.

Crown Copyright (NRM)

CHAPTER ELEVEN

Lidlington

Signalling at Lidlington was in the block post system until 1900. After that time the levers beside the crossing hut controlled the signals to protect the station and crossing.

Lidlington differs among the stations on the line by being built in the style of the crossing lodges rather than that of the half-timbered black and white buildings. It was built in yellow gault brickwork with red brick dressings and the very distinctive ornamental roof tiles that were such an attractive feature on the steeply pitched roof. The four centre archway of the porch is beneath a small bedroom with a tiny dormer window looking out on to the station.

Lidlington is unusual, even amongst small stations, in that it is without any sidings or goods facilities, simply having two facing platforms. *Herpath's Journal,* of 1848, mentions an 111ft. siding at Lidlington but this must have been involved in the construction of the line as it does not appear on any map or listing in the Clearing House Index. A space behind the 'up' platform suggests a probable location of this contractor's siding. One can reasonably assume, from the expansion of Millbrook Station nearby, that all of the goods traffic requirements could be supplied from there.

Bill Evans and his companion in front of his keeper's hut, and in the same position as the porter in the previous photograph, with the lever frame for signals to protect the crossing on his right. Nearing retirement, Bill served for thirty years on the branch, much of the time at Lidlington. During his off duty hours he would serve the village in that traditional occupation of coal fire days, chimney sweep. Truly a character of the line.

Author's Collection

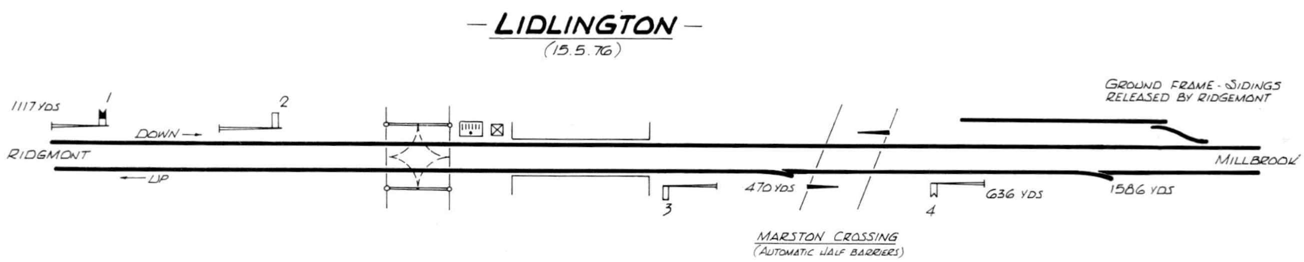

Lidlington on 15th May 1976, when the Marston crossing had become a half-barrier automatic crossing. Marston Valley Brick (LBC) Siding was released by Ridgmont instruments. Note the two catch points installed after the breakaway accident in 1929.

M. Christensen

Lidlington, as seen from the train, looking towards Bletchley.

Author's Collection

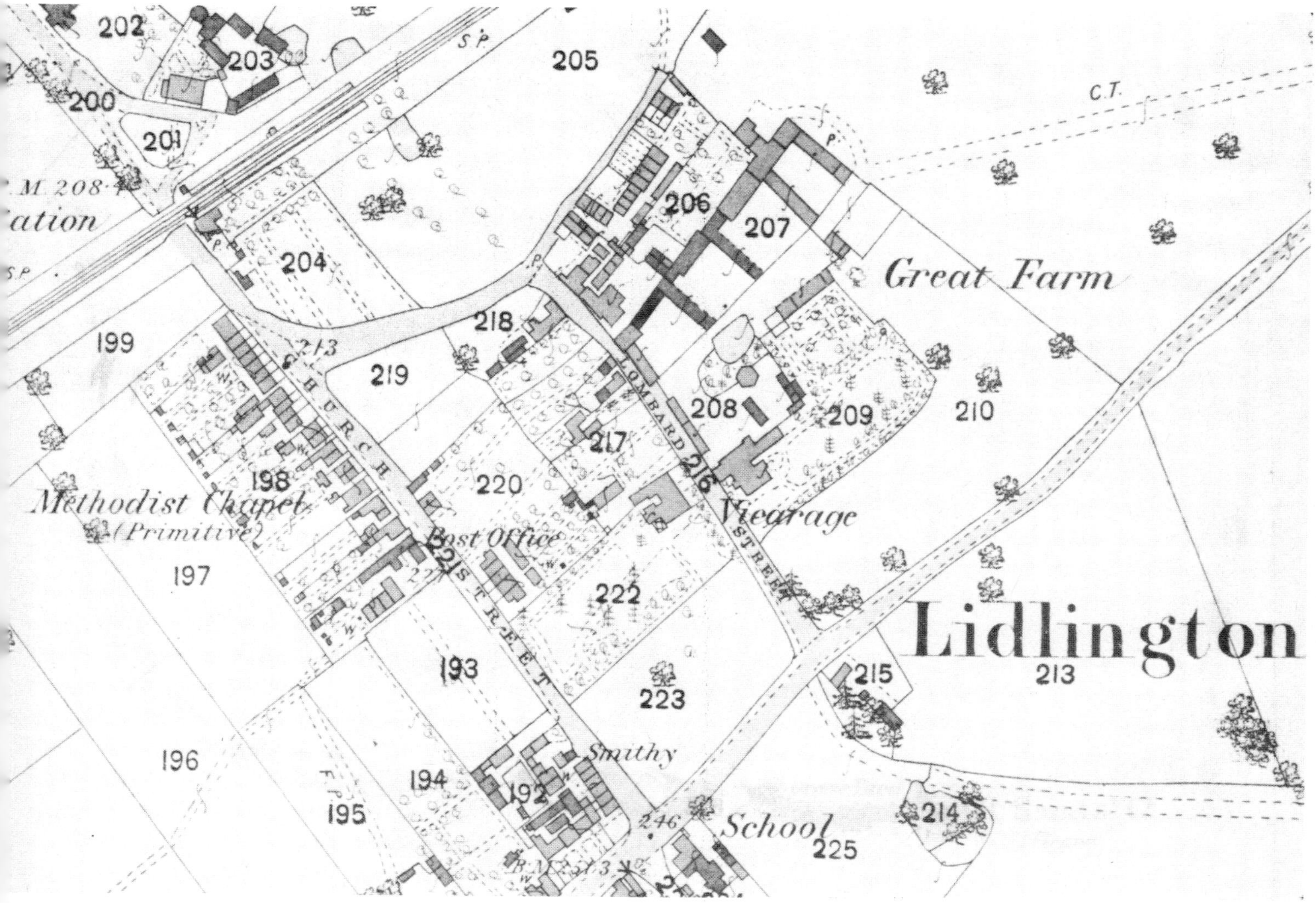

Lidlington in 1883. The station has changed very little from this to the present day.

Courtesy of the Ordnance Survey

Less than a mile beyond the station, the line passes over the Marston crossing on the Marston Moretaine to Lidlington road, its crossing lodge and keeper's hut once situated, like Ridgmont, in complete isolation. Similar to Ridgmont, it was destined to be in the shadow of a large brickworks of the Marston Valley Brick Company. Built in 1930, this plant eventually became part of the London Brick Company. A group of seven sidings for the works was controlled from a new signal box installed in 1933, having one additional ground frame that was electrically released from the box.

A novelty of the crossing at Marston was that the signs for the crossing were once displayed in Italian, as well as in English, for the benefit of a large emigrant work-force at the brickworks.

This did not remain the only distinction on the line, as on 2nd July 1961, it was the second only crossing on British Rail to be fitted with the half barrier automatic controlled gates.

A Cravens two car unit forms the 4.00p.m. (SO) Bedford St. John's to Bletchley train and is seen passing over Marston crossing. In 1961, Marston was the second crossing on British Rail to be converted to half barrier automatic control. The crossing house is now privately owned.
Author's Collection

Millbrook is the fourth and final station along the line to exemplify the half-timbered style. It is also the only station to retain the traditional platforms which allows a contemporary view of the standard platform style of the LNWR, with Staffordshire blue paviours and stone edging. Thereby, the wooden steps brought into use with the new designs of coaching stock working on the line in 1906 are still retained. Also of the LNWR era is the wooden signal post, uncharacteristically upper quadrant. The brick built signal cabin is beyond the gates on the other side of the line, giving an indication of the original arrangement at Ridgmont.

Author's Collection

CHAPTER TWELVE

Millbrook

This station was originally named Marston, when opened in 1846 but the name was changed to Ampthill in 1850, which is what it may well have remained had not the Midland Railway built their new line closer to that village in 1868. The obvious confusion was removed by the LNWR, with Ampthill Station being called Millbrook in March 1877 after a period of being called Millbrook for Ampthill. A large catering establishment on the other side of the road, called the Morteyne Arms, bears witness to the stations developing trade and activity. This activity included numerous sidings, intensive coal traffic, (3,278 tons in 1848), cattle and goods with stables in the goods yard and a wagon repairers. Millbrook increased its activity still further with the development of the brick industry. A new siding was installed near the station on 7th May 1928 and the station master was put in charge of five clerks who concentrated much of their work on the brick traffic that came to a peak in the 1930s.

It is with regard to this kind of traffic that the Morteyne Arms came to witness the inquiry into the kind of accident that is something of a nightmare for enginemen, and signalmen, working heavy trains on steeply graded sections of the line. This accident took place on 21st October 1929 as the hard working 0-8-0 G1 class locomotive, No. 9059, was approaching the Ridgmont Station 'up' distant signal with the 6.45p.m. from Forder's Siding with more than 800 tons behind the tender. The rear 35 vehicles broke loose leaving only 16 with the engine. Lead by a twenty ton four wheel brake van, the vehicles ran loose for 3½ miles before they collided violently with the 2.30p.m. goods from Cambridge to Bletchley killing the fireman of the goods train and injuring the driver and the guard. The guard of the brick train was injured whilst jumping clear. The total length of the goods train was 380 yards and was entirely vacuum-braked being hauled by 4-6-0 No. 5468 of the 'Experiment' class and composed of 35 wagons and a 20 ton brake van;

Millbrook in the 1950s, still with the characteristic blue paviors on the low platform, and the LNWR signal at the crossing. In the distance is the works of the Millbrook Brick Company.

Lens of Sutton

The lever frame for the points and signals, originally on a brick base, with the LNWR-style separate lettering screwed on to the nameboard. A little of the Morteyne Arms can be seen in the background.

Author's Collection

Millbrook Station crossing in the mid-1950s. Note the signal frame raised on the brick base, which would facilitate greater visibility for the signalman for shunting operations taking place in the yard on the other side of the crossing. In latter years, the frame was resited at ground level as Millbrook is now no more than an unstaffed halt.

H. C. Casserley

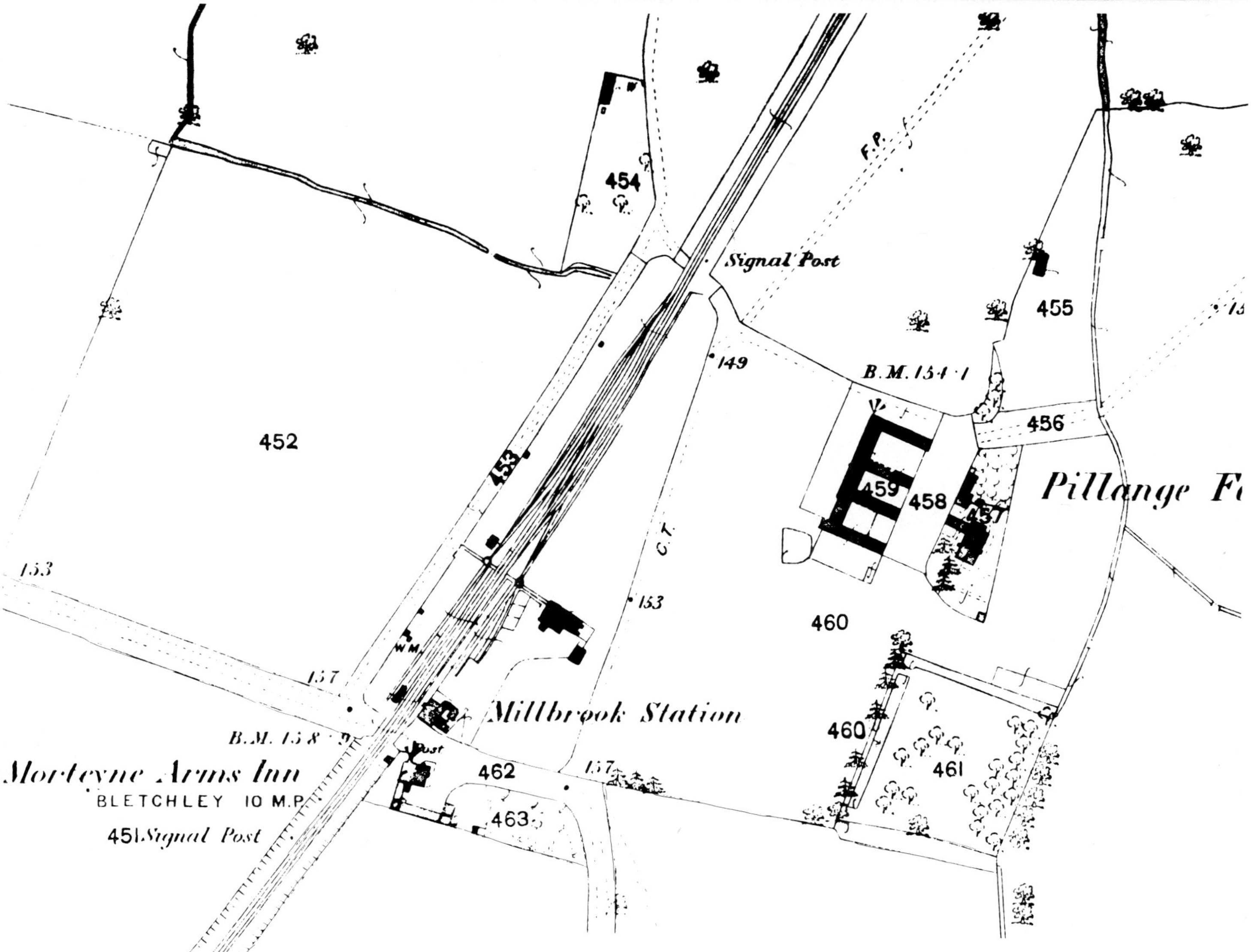

Millbrook Station in 1883. Note the goods shed at right angles to the siding. The other building close by is the small stables.

Courtesy of the Ordnance Survey

a gross weight of 550 to 600 tons. As a result of the impact, the goods train engine overturned on its right side fouling the 6ft. and 'up' line between two heaps of wagon debris, consisting of the brake van and wagons from the brick train together with three wagons from its own train. Twenty three intact wagons from the brick train were now at a standstill.

by sorrow, had there been a full passenger train involved, the results may have produced a horrifying tableau in the history of the line. It is interesting, therefore, to relate the sequence of the resulting enquiry and its contribution thenceforth to the evolvement of the high degree of safety on our railways.

The breakaway had come near the summit of the 1 in 129 climb from Millbrook at the 7 mile post, virtually at Ridgmont Station. A driver's description of the events were as follows.

The authorized load for this train was 55 wagons including the brake van. The engine did not, at any time, slip and the weather conditions were good. It was just that the train was becoming too much for the engine at that time and the train was brought to a stand near the 'up' Ridgmont distant signal. The driver decided to let the train roll back about two wagon lengths to get a fresh start to finish the climb. Assuming, correctly, that the guard would apply his brakes, he restarted the train and then saw the lights of the brake running back down the grade. The engine lurched as it restarted and he felt sure that this was when the breakaway occurred. He immediately went to Ridgmont Station and told the signalman what had happened, leaving sixteen wagons that still remained with his engine in a siding. As a light engine, he then went on to Bletchley to summon the breakdown train. The driver stated that he had been working the brick trains for years and that this was the first

Now derelict, but an interesting piece of antiquity that was once so common in the early days of railways. Now very few remain. This turnplate gave access to the goods shed and the cattle dock from a siding trailing in from the Bedford direction.

J. R. Rounthwaite

time that his engine had stalled, although always working the same type, a heavy goods class of engine.

At the other end of the train, two guards were to have a harrowing experience. J. H. Coley was in charge of the train whilst F. J. Burridge was returning to Bletchley at the end of his shift of duty as shunter at Forder's Sidings. When the engine came to a stall, Coley put on the brake and it was never taken off again. As the engine reversed into the slack in all of the couplings and before it could tighten them with its restart, the breakaway occurred, which was unusual as it is the sudden strain on the gradient that finds the weakest link. Unaccountably finding the train running back, Guard Burridge took the brake stick and jumped off with the intention of putting on ten or twenty of the wagons brakes as they went by. The train was, by then, travelling at thirty miles per hour, and he was unable to effect any restraint. Coley could do nothing but stand in his van at the head of a speeding train that must soon meet with disaster. This he beheld in the lights of the distant goods train from which he was only twenty wagon lengths when he jumped off.

The driver of the goods train said that he was running ten minutes late, but slowing down as the 'up' Millbrook distant was against him. He first saw the three red lights of the brake van when he was 300 yards beyond Wootton Pillinge crossing (later Stewartby). Owing to the curve he did not, at first, realize that the vehicle was moving or even on the same line. A number of seconds later he realized the dreadful situation and put his engine in reverse by opening the regulator. He estimated his reverse speed to be about 25 miles an hour at the time of the collision.

Relief Signalman A. E. Hull was on duty in the Ridgmont Station box, and he received 'train entering section' for the brick train at 6.59p.m. The train and its sixteen wagons appeared at the station at 7.38p.m., thereupon Hull immediately gave an emergency telephone call to Millbrook which was not instantly answered by Signalman Gurney. Gurney then gave 'vehicles running away on the line' on the block bell. As a 'down' passenger train from Bletchley and the 'up' goods train were both in section, he had been out to close the crossing gates across the road. This took him rather longer than usual as there was a great deal of road traffic. This resulted in seconds which were vitally lost, for as he returned to the box and received the emergency telephone call from Ridgmont, he moved quickly to the frame to set the cross-over points that would put the runaway on the 'down' line and out of the path of the oncoming goods train, but unfortunately he was too late to effect this manoeuvre and could only watch helplessly as the runaway went speeding by. It should be mentioned that the 'down' passenger train was now held in the distance as it had not yet been accepted by Forder's box.

Lidlington, in between and no longer a block post, was manned by F. W. Thorn, signalman/porter, who had tried to warn Gurney before Hull at Ridgmont, but could not get any reply; probably as Gurney was still out attending to the traffic and the gates. This must have been of great personal anguish for him to watch a possibly avoidable disaster speed by and be unable to summon the box to effect that chance.

After the crash, an examination of the train by the Bletchley carriage and wagon foreman found the last link of

A closer view of the siding entrance to Marston Valley Brickworks, between Lidlington and Millbrook in 1981. In the distance, looking back towards Bletchley, is a fragmentary glimpse of the only significant difficulty for the builders of the line, Brogborough Hill. The cause of the notorious 1 in 129 climb was not spectacular by comparison with many lines but was a formidable obstacle for a very heavy brick train.
Author's Collection

the front portion coupling to be broken in two places, each of the fractures containing a weakening flaw that could not be detected by normal examination. This type of coupling was now obsolete, and consisted of three wrought iron links, each 2 ft. in length.

Mildly contradicting the driver's confidence in his engine, Gurney mentioned that engines becoming overpowered by their load happened, on average, about once every three months. When it did, the usual procedure was to divide the train leaving part in a siding. His experience was based on 29 years service in the Millbrook box. Some allowance on timings had been made for these heavier trains from 1st August 1929, since which, eight 50 wagons trains had been hauled by the same class of locomotive being allowed fifty minutes for the section between Forder's Sidings and Bletchley. This includes twenty five minutes for the section between Millbrook and Ridgmont, the 1 in 129 incline, whereas normal goods trains were allowed fifteen minutes for the climb.

In the Ministry of Transport report, it was mentioned that the Company should consider installing 'catch points' in advance of Lidlington and Millbrook. It also stated that the driver showed some lack of judgement in not dividing his train.

Consequently, Lt.-Col. E. P. Anderson was able to report, on 6th December 1930, that 'between Lidlington and Millbrook stations, two sets of connections have been made near the 9¼ mile post, one to serve the siding on the west side of the line, belonging to the Marston Valley Brick Co., and at the south end, a trailing connection has been laid on the 'up' line, with a trailing single slip (cross-over road) in the 'down' line. At the north end, a trailing connection has been made in the 'down' line for the siding. All are worked from a new signal box called 'Marston Valley Brick Siding' with 19 working levers and one spare. Correct locking and track circuits have been provided. And with regard to the misfortune of October 1929, connections are on a 1 in 129 rising gradient to Bletchley where catch points have been installed and approved.'

An indication of the ascendent development of brick-making at that time was the opening of yet another brickworks, called Marston Moretaine, near Millbrook, opened on 13th September 1933. Although not close enough to the line for a siding, the bricks were brought the distance of one mile to Millbrook Station by road and then loaded into rail wagons.

General Instructions for working Down Inclines—continued.

From the direction of	Proceeding towards	Point at which train must come to a stand for wagon brakes to be applied.	Point at which train must come to a stand for wagon brakes to be released.
Bedford	Cambridge	Between Gamlingay and Old North Road, at 34 mile post	At 37¾ mile post.
Bletchley	Bedford...	Near Ridgmont Station, at 7 mile post	At 10 mile post (Millbrook Station).
Banbury or Oxford ...	Bletchley	4½ mile post, between Swanbourne and Bletchley	Midway between ¾ and ½ mile posts.
Dunstable...	Stanbridgeford... ...	Dunstable, down distant signal...	Forder's Siding signal box.

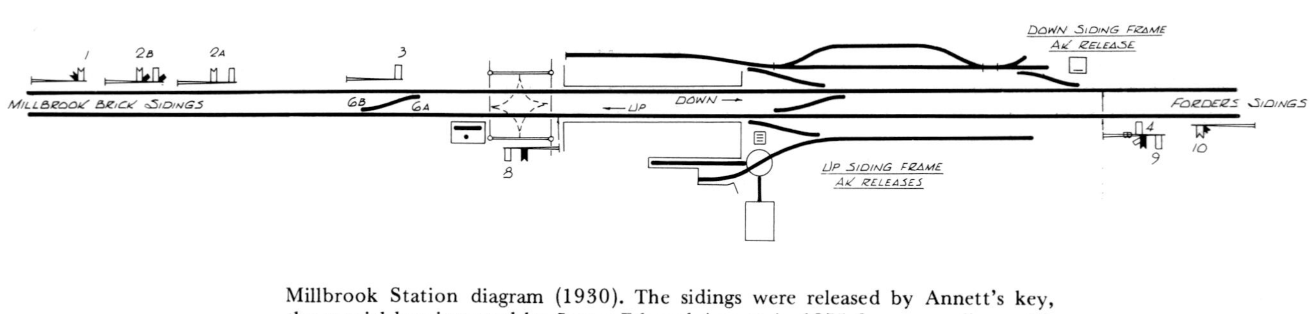

Millbrook Station diagram (1930). The sidings were released by Annett's key, the special key invented by James Edward Annett in 1875 for use on lines with little used sidings. Although 'little used' it could hardly apply to Millbrook at the height of brick production. A more detailed description of the use of the key is contained in *Oxford to Cambridge Railway (Volume One)*, on page 94. An extra brick siding was added at Millbrook with a small box on 7th May 1928.

M. Christensen

Single Line between BEDFORD and SANDY.—Electric Train Staff. | Train Staff Stations—BEDFORD, BLUNHAM, and SANDY.

Distance from Cambridge	UP.		1	2	3	4	5	6	7	8	9	10	11	12	13	14	15	16	17	18	19	20	21	22	23	24	25	26	27
				Pass		MOTOR		Pass	Pass		Pass	MOTOR	Goods	Goods		Goods	Pass	Goods	Goods	Pass	MOTOR	Goods		Light Engine		Pass		Eng. and Break	
													S	S O				IH S	S O	T S 0		TH O						S O	
				a.m.		a.m.		a.m.	a.m.		a.m.	a.m.	a.m.	a.m.		a.m.	a.m.	p.m.	p.m.	p.m.	p.m.	p.m.		p.m.		p.m.		p.m.	
...	Cambridge ...	dep.	...	...	...	...	...	7 45		...	9 42	...	...	...	...	10 20	11 23	...	...	...	...	...	...	...	...	1 50	...	...	...
5⅛	Lord's Bridge ...	arr.	...	...	...	...	...	7 55	...	...	9 51	...	...	...	...	10 30	...	...	...	...	...	...	...	C	...	1 59	...	...	...
		dep.	...	...	...	...	...	7 56	...	...	9 52	...	...	...	...	10 45	X	...	...	...	...	...	...		...	2 0	...	...	...
10⅝	Old North Road	arr.	...	...	...	...	...	8 5	...	...	10 0	...	...	...	...	11 5	11 42	...	...	...	...	...	...	...	...	2 9	...	...	...
		dep.	...	...	...	...	...	8 6	...	...	10 1	...	...	...	...	11 55	11 43	...	...	...	...	...	...	...	...	2 10	...	...	...
15¼	Gamlingay ...	arr.	...	...	...	...	...	8 14	...	...	10 9	...	...	...	...	12 5	11 51	...	...	...	...	...	...	...	...	2 18	...	...	...
		dep.	...	...	...	...	...	8 15	9 38	...	10 10	...	10 20	10 20	...	1 0	11 53	...	...	...	...	...	...	...	...	2 19	...	...	...
16½	Dennis' Siding ...	,,	...	...	...	...	...	...	...	...	...	...	X	X	...	...	...	...	...	...	...	...	...	...	...	...	...	...	...
17⅝	Potton	arr.	...	...	...	...	...	8 20	9 42	...	10 15	...	10 30	10 30	...	1 10	11 57	Arrives Forder's Siding 12.45 p.m.	Arrives Fenny Stratford 1.40 p.m.	...	...	...	...	...	...	2 23	...	...	...
		dep.	...	...	...	...	...	8 21	9 45	...	10 16	...	10 35	10 35	...	1 15	11 58			...	...	...	...	...	...	2 24	...	...	...
21⅜	Sandy	arr.	...	...	...	...	...	8 26	9 50	...	10 21	...	10 55	10 55	...	1 25	12 4			...	...	...	...	...	...	2 29	...	...	...
		dep.	...	...	...	...	...	8 31	9 51	...	10 22	...	11 40	11 40	...	1 35	12 6	...		12 45	...	...	...	...	...	2 32	...	...	...
22¾	Girtford Siding ...	,,	...	...	...	...	...	...	...	...	...	...	...	...	...	1 50	...	...		...	...	...	...	...	...	...	...	...	...
23¾	Blunham	arr.	...	...	...	...	...	8 35	9 55	...	10 26	...	11 50	11 50	...	1 55	12 10	...		12 49	...	...	...	...	...	2 36	...	...	...
		dep.	...	...	...	...	...	8 36	9 57	...	10 27	...	1 2	1 2	...	2 15	12 11	...	...	12 51	...	...	...	...	...	2 37	...	...	...
26	Willington	,,	...	...	...	...	...	8 41	10 2	...	..	...	1 22	1 22	...	...	X	...	...	12 56	...	...	...	...	...	2 42	...	...	...
30	Bedford	arr.	...	...	...	...	...	8 47	10 9	...	10 36	...	1 34	1 34	...	2 30	12 21	...	...	1 2	...	...	...	...	...	2 48	...	...	...
		dep.	...	7 20	...	...	...	8 52	10 15	...	10 39	10 55	...	1 45	...	...	12 25	12 35	12 35	...	1 15	1 37	...	2 20	...	2 58	...	3 10	...
31	Kempston & Elstow	,,	...	...	...	...	...	...	...	...	...	10 59	...	...	...	...	...	...	...	...	1 19	...	...	...	...	...	...	...	...
33	Kempston Hardwick	,,	...	...	...	...	...	...	...	...	...	11 3	...	...	...	...	...	...	...	...	1 22	...	...	...	...	...	...	...	...
33¾	Wootton Broadmead	,,	...	...	...	...	...	...	...	...	...	11 7	...	...	...	...	...	...	...	...	1 26	...	...	...	...	...	...	...	...
34	Forder's Siding ..	,,	...	...	...	...	...	...	...	...	...	...	...	2 10	...	...	...	1 0	...	...	...	...	...	2 30	...	...	...	3 20	...
34⅝	Wootton Pillinge ...	,,	..	..	...	...	...	...	...	...	...	11 11	...	...	...	...	...	...	...	...	1 30	...	...	...	...	...	...	...	...
34⅝	Wootton Pillinge Siding	arr.	...	...	...	...	...	...	...	..	...	...	...	Arrives Willington 1.12, Forder's Siding 1.55	...	...	...	...	...	...	...	...	...	...	...	...	...	...	...
		dep.	...	...	...	...	...	...	...	...	...	..	...		...	...	...	...	...	...	...	...	...	...	...	...	...	...	...
35⅞	Millbrook for Ampthill	arr.	...	7 30	...	...	...	9 2	10 24	...	...	...	...		...	.	12 35	...	...	...	...	...	...	...	...	3 2	...	...	...
		dep.	...	7 32	...	...	...	9 4	10 26	...	...	11 15	...		...	...	12 36	...	X	...	1 34	X	...	...	...	3 4	...	...	...
37¼	Lidlington ..	arr.	...	7 35	...	...	...	9 7	10 29	...	..	...	...		...	Arrives Girtford 1 40 p.m.	...	...	...	...	...	...	...	...	...	3 7	...	...	...
		dep.	...	7 36	...	...	...	9 8	10 30	...	...	11 19	...		...		...	...	...	...	1 39	...	...	...	...	3 8	...	...	...
39¼	Ridgmont ...	arr.	...	7 39	...	...	...	9 11	10 33	...	...	...	...		...		...	...	1 0	...	...	2 2	...	...	...	3 11	...	...	...
		dep.	...	7 40	...	...	...	9 12	10 35	...	...	11 24	...		...		...	...	1 20	...	1 44	2 10	...	...	...	3 13	...	...	...
39¾	Husborne Crawley ...	,,	...	...	...	...	..	...	...	...	...	11 27	...		...		...	...	...	..	1 47	...	...	...	...	...	...	...	...
40⅞	Aspley Guise	,,	...	...	...	...	...	...	...	...	...	11 31	...		...		...	...	...	...	1 51	...	...	...	...	...	...	...	...
41⅞	Woburn Sands...	arr.	...	7 45	...	...	...	9 17	10 40	...	...	..	...	2 30	...		12 46	1 25	...	...	...	2 20	...	...	...	3 19	...	...	...
		dep.	...	7 47	...	9 0	...	9 19	10 42	...	...	11 34	...	3 5	...		12 49	2 10	...	...	1 54	2 30	...	...	...	3 21	...	...	...
43⅞	Bow Brickhill...	,,	...	...	...	9 5	...	...	...	..	...	11 39	...	...	...	...	...	..	...	...	1 59	...	...	...	...	...	...	...	...
44⅛	Fenny Stratford	,,	...	7 53	..	9 8	...	9 25	10 48	...	..	11 42	...	...	...	...	...	...	[illegible]	...	[illegible]	[illegible]	...			[illegible]			...
46	Bletchley ...	arr.	...	7 56	...	9 11	...	9 28	10 50	...	11 0	11 45	...	3 20	...	...	12 56	[illegible]	[illegible]	...	[illegible]	[illegible]							

BEDFORD AND CAMBRIDGE BRANCH.

Single Line between BEDFORD and SANDY.—Electric Train Staff. | Train Staff Stations—BEDFORD, BLUNHAM, and SANDY.

Distance from Bletchley	DOWN.		1	2	3	4	5	6	7	8	9	10	11	12	13	14	15	16	17	18	19	20	21	22	23	24	25	26	27
			Goods and Mail.	Goods and Emps	Goods			Goods	Goods	Pass	Pass		MOTOR	Pass	MOTOR	MOTOR	Pass	Goods and Emps	Pass		Pass	MOTOR	Goods and Emps	Light Engine	Goods	Goods	Pass	Emp. [illegible]	
					MO			M							S O	S	S O	S O	T S 0				S		S O	S		S	
			a.m.	a.m.	a.m.			a.m.	a.m.	a.m.	a.m.		a.m.	a.m.	a.m.	a.m.	a.m.	a.m.	a.m.		a.m.	p.m.	p.m.	p.m.	p.m.	p.m.	p.m.	p.m.	
...	Bletchley	dep.	8 35	4 15	5 0	...	...	5 45	6 50	7 20	8 20	...	8 30	9 20	9 45	9 55	10 15	10 25	...	...	11 55	12 15	12 30	...	1 10	1 10	2 10	2 15	...
1⅛	Fenny Stratford ...	,,	...	...	...	...	...	...	X	7 23	8 23	...	8 33	...	9 48	9 58	10 18	...	...	...	...	12 18	...	...	...	...	2 13	...	...
2⅛	Bow Brickhill ...	,,	...	...	...	...	...	...	...	...	...	...	8 37	...	9 52	10 2	...	...	...	...	...	12 22	...	...	...	...	...	...	...
4⅛	Woburn Sands...	arr.	...	...	...	...	...	...	7 5	7 28	8 29	...	8 42	9 26	...	...	10 23	10 35	...	...	12 1	...	...	C	...	..	2 18	C	...
		dep.	...	...	...	...	...	...	7 35	7 29	8 30	...	...	9 27	9 57	10 7	10 25	12 35	...	...	12 3	12 27	...	...	...	...	2 20	...	...
5⅛	Aspley Guise	,,	...	...	...	...	...	...	...	...	...	...	...	...	10 0	10 10	...	...	...	...	...	12 30	...	...	...	...	...	...	...
6¼	Husborne Crawley...	,,	...	...	...	...	...	...	...	...	...	...	...	...	10 4	10 14	...	...	...	...	...	12 34	...	...	...	...	...	...	...
6¾	Ridgmont	arr.	...	...	...	...	...	...	...	7 34	8 34	...	...	...	...	...	10 30	...	...	...	...	...	...	...	...	...	2 25	...	..
		dep.	...	...	...	...	...	...	X	7 35	8 35	...	...	...	10 7	10 17	10 31	...	...	...	...	12 37	...	...	...	...	2 26	...	...
8¾	Lidlington	arr.	...	...	...	...	...	...	...	7 38	8 38	...	...	...	...	...	10 34	...	...	...	...	...	...	...	...	...	2 29	...	...
		dep.	...	...	...	...	...	..	...	7 39	8 39	...	...	X	10 12	10 22	10 35	...	...	...	...	12 42	...	...	...	...	2 30	...	...
10⅛	Millbrook for Ampthill	arr.	8 54	...	...	...	...	...	8 5	7 42	8 42	...	...	...	...	...	10 38	12 50	...	...	12 12	...	1 5	...	1 50	1 50	2 33	...	...
		dep.	8 56	...	...	...	...	...	8 55	7 44	8 43	...	...	...	10 16	10 26	10 40	1 15	...	...	12 13	12 46	1 25	...	2 10	2 10	2 35	...	...
11⅝	Wootton Pillinge Siding	arr.	...	Willington arr. 7.12.	...	...	...	...	...	...	...	...	...	...	...	...	...	1 20	...	...	...	...	1 30	...	...	...	...	...	...
		dep.	...		...	...	...	...	...	...	...	...	...	...	...	...	...	1 50	...	...	...	...	1 55	...	...	...	...	...	...
11⅝	Wootton Pillinge ...	,,	...		...	...	...	...	...	...	...	...	...	...	10 20	10 30	...	...	...	...	...	12 50	...	...	...	...	...	...	...
12	Forder's Siding ...	,,	...		...	...	...	...	...	...	...	...	...	...	...	...	...	1 55	...	...	...	...	2 0	2 5	...	...	...	...	...
12¼	Wootton Broadmead	,,	...		...	...	...	...	...	...	...	...	...	...	10 24	10 34	...	...	...	...	...	12 54	...	...	...	...	...	...	...
13⅛	Kempston Hardwick	,,	...		...	...	...	...	...	...	...	..	...	...	10 28	10 38	...	...	...	...	...	12 58	...	...	...	...	...	...	...
14⅞	Kempston & Elstow	,,	...	...	...	...	...	...	...	...	...	...	...	...	10 32	10 42	...	...	...	...	...	1 2	...	...	...	...	...	...	...
16	Bedford	arr.	4 8	4 50	5 35	...	...	6 20	9 10	7 54	8 52	...	...	9 45	10 35	10 45	10 50	...	...	...	12 21	1 5	...	2 15	2 25	2 25	2 45	2 55	...
		dep.	4 18	7 0	6 10	...	...	6 40	...	7 58	8 55	...	...	9 47	...	...	...	...	11 45	...	12 24	...	...	...	...	3 20	2 50	3 5	...
20	Willington	,,	...	7 17	...	...	...	...	...	8 5	X	...	...	...	...	...	...	...	11 52	...	12 31	...	...	...	...	X	2 57	...	...
22¼	Blunham	arr.	...	7 22	...	...	...	..	...	8 9	9 7	...	...	9 56	...	...	...	...	11 56	...	12 35	...	...	...	...	3 40	3 1	3 20	...
		dep.	4†30	7 40	6 25	...	...	6 55	...	8 10	9 8	...	...	9 57	...	...	...	...	11 58	...	12 36	...	...	...	...	4 10	3 2	3 25	...
23¼	Girtford Siding ...	,,	...	...	...	...	...	...	...	...	...	...	...	...	...	...	...	...	...	...	...	...	...	...	...	X	...	..	...
24⅛	Sandy	arr.	4 38	7 48	...	...	...	...	...	8 14	9 12	...	...	10 1	...	...	...	...	12 3	...	12 40	...	...	...	...	4 25	3 6	3 35	...
		dep.	4 50	8 25	6 32	...	...	7 2	...	8 16	9 15	...	...	10 2	...	...	...	...		...	12 41	...	...	...	...	5 45	3 11	3 40	...
28⅛	Potton	arr.	...	8 35	6 42	...	...	...	...	8 22	9 21	...	...	10 8	...	...	...	...	...	...	12 47	...	...	...	...	5 55	3 17	3 50	...
		dep.	...	9 30	6 50	...	...	...	...	8 23	9 22	...	...	10. 9	...	...	...	...	...	...	12 48	...	...	...	...	...	3 18	4 15	...
30¼	Gamlingay ...	arr.	...	9 40	X	...	...	...	...	8 28	9 26	...	...	10 13	...	...	...	...	...	...	12 52	...	...	...	...	...	3 22	4 25	...
		dep.	...		...	...	...	...	...	8 30		...	...	10 14	...	...	...	...	...	...	12 53	...	...	...	...	...	3 23		...
35⅜	Old North Road	arr.	...	..	...	...	...	...	...	8 38	...	...	...	10 22	...	...	...	...	...	...	1 1	...	...	...	...	...	3 31	...	...
		dep.	...	...	...	...	...	...	...	8 39	...	...	...	10 23	...	...	...	...	...	...	1 2	...	...	...	...	...	3 32	...	...
40⅝	Lord's Bridge ...	arr	...	...	...	...	...	...	...	8 49	..	...	...	10 32	...	...	...	..	...	...	1 11	...	...	...	...	...	3 41	...	...
		dep.	...	...	...	...	...	...	...	8 50	...	...	...	10 33	...	...	...	...	...	..	1 12	...	...	...	...	...	3 42	...	...
46	Cambridge ...	arr.	5 25	...	7 30	...	...	7 50	...	9 0	...	...	...	10 41	...	...	...	...	...	...	1 20	...	...	...	...	...	3 50	...	...

BEDFORD AND CAMBRIDGE BRANCH.

The working timetable for the busy year of 1909. Note the short distance trip for the railmotor, under diagram No. 11, to Woburn Sands and the return working under diagram No. 4.

Peter Webber Collection

Stewartby Plant had a narrow gauge railway system (2 ft. 11 in.) operating on overhead electrification. It is believed to have been installed in the early 1930s and lasted until 1960. The diminutive box-like 0-4-0 locomotives were built by English Electric of Preston and totalled some seventeen in number. It is also understood that a certain unspecified number was assembled at the plant from parts supplied by English Electric. The entire system and locomotives had disappeared by 1965. After that time, handling of the bricks was carried out with 'Hyster' fork lift trucks for the use of which the entrances to the kilns had to be enlarged. In this illustration, No. 16 has brought its load of 'green' bricks from the pressing sheds to be transferred into the kiln. A pair of trucks is held on the rails fixed to the railway vehicle and pushing them off seems to be a very impromptu arrangement. Nevertheless, in view of the considerable tonnages handled in the 1930s, the little railway must have been very intensively used.

London Brick Company

Although Millbrook is now on the closing edge of the brick-making industry, Stewartby Station is virtually within the intensely active plant, very much in mass production. It was once called Wootton Pillinge Halt and became Stewartby Station in the early 1930s and was, therefore, rebuilt before the other halts on the line.

Author's Collection

CHAPTER THIRTEEN

Stewartby

From a hamlet of two farms developed the village of Wootton Pillinge, which acquired a halt of that name in 1905; a name that would probably have rested in obscurity had not the site been chosen for the development of one of the world's largest brick-making undertakings.

B. J. H. Forder originally came from Hampshire where he had a lime-burning business. His interest in brick-making began in Bracknell and Westoning where he introduced a high degree of mechanization to the process. He set up the first brickworks along the line, using the Fletton process, at Wootton Pillinge in 1897, which was to prove to be the embryo of the enormous development of later years.

The Fletton process was developed at the place of the same name, near Peterborough, where, in 1881, it was discovered from the unique properties of Oxford Clay. This is a grey-green clay beneath the top callow which was known as 'Knotts' having a constant moisture content, allowing the clay to be crushed into granular form and pressed into brick shapes. These bricks could be fired immediately and had the valuable property of being combustible to a large degree, firing themselves. The advantage in saving in the cost of fuel could not be overstated.

In order to achieve the best possible use from this advantage, it still required much research and development to produce the type of kiln that would satisfactorily fire the bricks in large numbers. This resulted in the construction of the Hoffmann Kiln with its continuous fire circulating a number of draughted, but separate, chambers; a revolving fire that never went out. Through holes in the top, extra small amounts of fine coal could be fed in to keep the 1,000 degree temperature from falling. Such large kilns, with their high 250 ft. chimneys, would obviously require large amounts of capital investment. Once this was available, together with a direct rail access, the industry

The keeper's hut, in 1979, in front of the now unoccupied LNWR crossing keeper's house. The house follows the LNWR standard design for company employees. Note the tiny ticket window beside the door in the hut.

Author's Collection

Stewartby frame, a replacement for the one time Wootton Pillinge signal box, was installed in the early 1930s and, therefore, follows the LMS style. Semaphore repeater indicators are situated in boxes above the levers.

Author's Collection

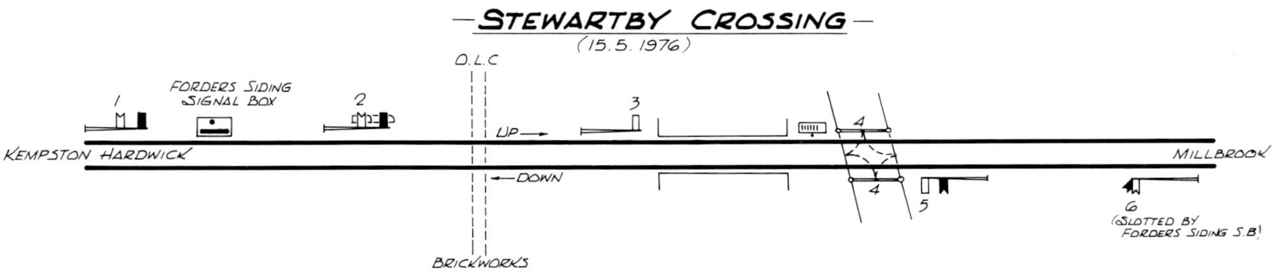

A Stewartby diagram of 15th May 1976. This was not a 'block' post, signals being used to protect the crossing.

M. Christensen

would be liberated from expensive piecemeal manufacture that had hamstrung it since Tudor times. The Bedford line could not have been better constructed to assist the industry for conveying its product to the high demand of the London market.

Forder was assisted in the development of Wootton Pillinge Brick Co. by two Fletton men, George and Arthur Keeble and the Liberal Parliamentary candidate for Peterborough, Halley Stewart, who became first chairman of the Limited Company in 1900. He brought with him other members of the family; Guthrie Stewart, who became chief accountant and Perry Malcolm Stewart became the managing director. Halley Stewart built up the company for long term growth and stability, so that by 1910 it was selling 48 million bricks per year.

After the set-back of ceased production during World War I, the merger of the Company, still called Forder's, began in 1923 with what was then the London Brick Company which was founded at Fletton in 1829.

The new company of London Brick Company and Forder's Limited had reached a staggering 118 million bricks in the year 1926 when they began work on a 'Garden Village' for their employees at Wootton Pillinge. This became the spacious urban style village called Stewartby, (1935), built of 'rustics' and possessing a tranquil quality in its easy lines and sense of mellow affluence. Clearly it extols the virtue of brick in the restraint of domesticity. Stewartby was now the location of the largest brickworks in the world, employing 2,000 people and producing 500 million bricks per year. It became a separate civil parish in 1936, the year when Sir Halley Stewart died, shortly after his ninety ninth birthday.

Growth of the brickworks between the wars was probably one of the most remarkable things ever to affect any short stretch of line of only 16 miles. Eastwood's, who had once worked a small installation alongside Woburn Sands Station, opened a plant at Kempston Hardwick in 1927. In 1929 the Marston Valley Brick Company formed their first works being built alongside the Marston crossing. A second works was opened by them at Ridgmont in 1935 together with an industrial village at Brogborough to house the company's employees. Marston Valley Brick Company itself became second only to the London Brick Company in this country.

With the development of Stewartby, from Wootton Pillinge, the old brickworks sidings close to, and alongside, the halt did not hold enough wagons for the increased production and became an extension to the much larger group of sidings developing at Wootton Broadmead. The Wootton Pillinge signal box was closed leaving the sidings to be operated by a ground frame on 27th April 1931. Wootton Broadmead sidings were then controlled by a new box called Forder's Sidings.

One of the electric locomotives of the London Brick Company's narrow gauge system, hauling 'green' bricks from the pressings to the kiln.
London Brick Company

Many brickworks suffered lost production with the outbreak of World War II with shortage of labour and black-out restrictions. Kilns were used for storing food at Lidlington and Ridgmont whilst tanks were constructed at Stewartby.

With the return of peactime once more, the industry was to undergo reorganization and merger, with the London Brick Company, eventually owning all the local clay brickworks, taking over Kempston Hardwick Works in 1962 and the Marston Valley by 1968. After a peak year in 1973 of 738 million at Stewartby, 406 million at Ridgmont and 167 million at Kempston Hardwick, the works at Marston crossing ceased production and was eventually demolished in 1981.

'Fletliner Trains' is the name given to the brick trains in modern times. They operate via Bletchley and Bedford on to the ex-Midland line usually hauled by two Class 25 diesel locomotives. The modern 'Fletliner' wagon is capable of carrying 32,000 bricks which compared to its pneumatic rival is three lorry loads. The normal loading is two trains each day of 12,000 tons, with regular destinations being Liverpool, Manchester and London. Each train represents a 45 lorry load capacity.

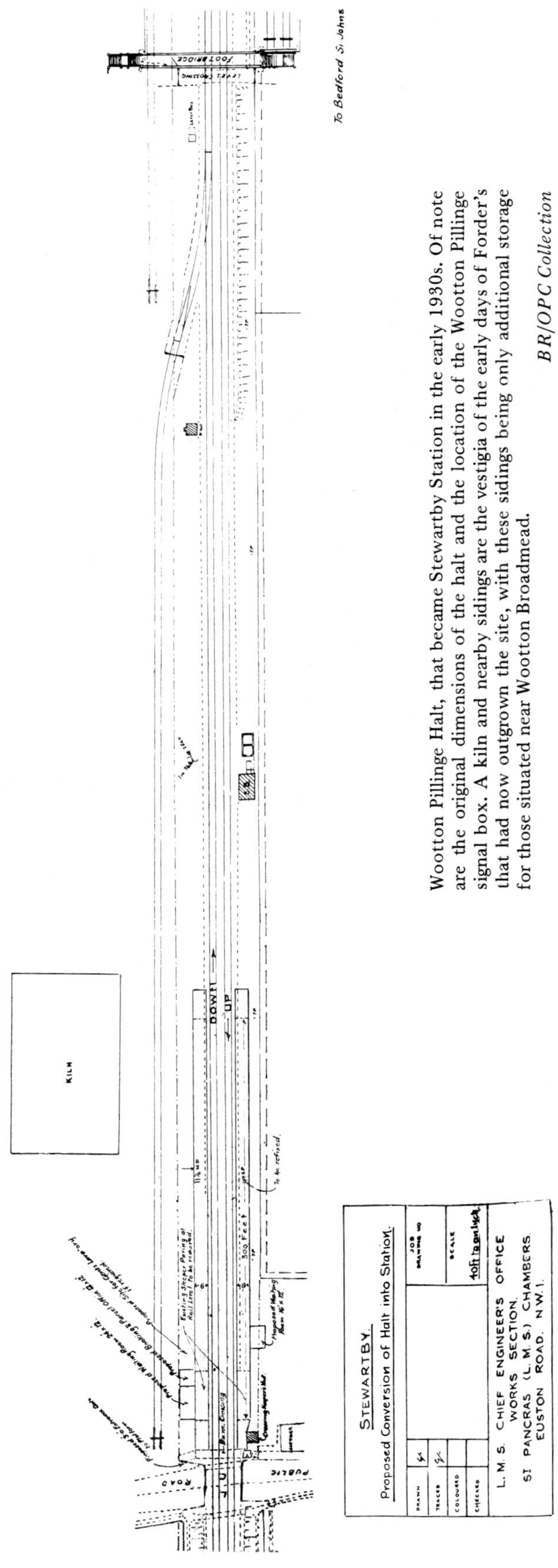

Wootton Pillinge Halt, that became Stewartby Station in the early 1930s. Of note are the original dimensions of the halt and the location of the Wootton Pillinge signal box. A kiln and nearby sidings are the vestigia of the early days of Forder's that had now outgrown the site, with these sidings being only additional storage for those situated near Wootton Broadmead.
BR/OPC Collection

The entrance to Forder's Sidings looking into the heart of the plant, with the Bedford branch passing right through the centre. Forder's Sidings really developed from the late 1920s, necessitating the installation of the Midland pattern signal box by the LMS.

Author's Collection

During the recession of the early 1980s, there have been far fewer brick trains and the prospect is that the entire LBC undertaking along the branch will be altered beyond recognition over the subsequent years. with a large new works replacing all the capacity of the former plants.

Trading under the name 'Easidispose', LBC signed a twenty year contract in 1974 for landfill of their clay pits with rubbish from London, involving one or two container trains per day of 1,000 tons from the Hendon Depot to the handling facilities at Stewartby, these trains being hauled by either Class 47 or Class 56 diesel locomotives. Eventually, the full pits will be covered with soil and the land returned to rural farmland. It is staggering to think that what is included in the photographs in this book of apparent industrial complexity, could one day be the site of languid cows with only the distant hum of the tractor and combine harvester.

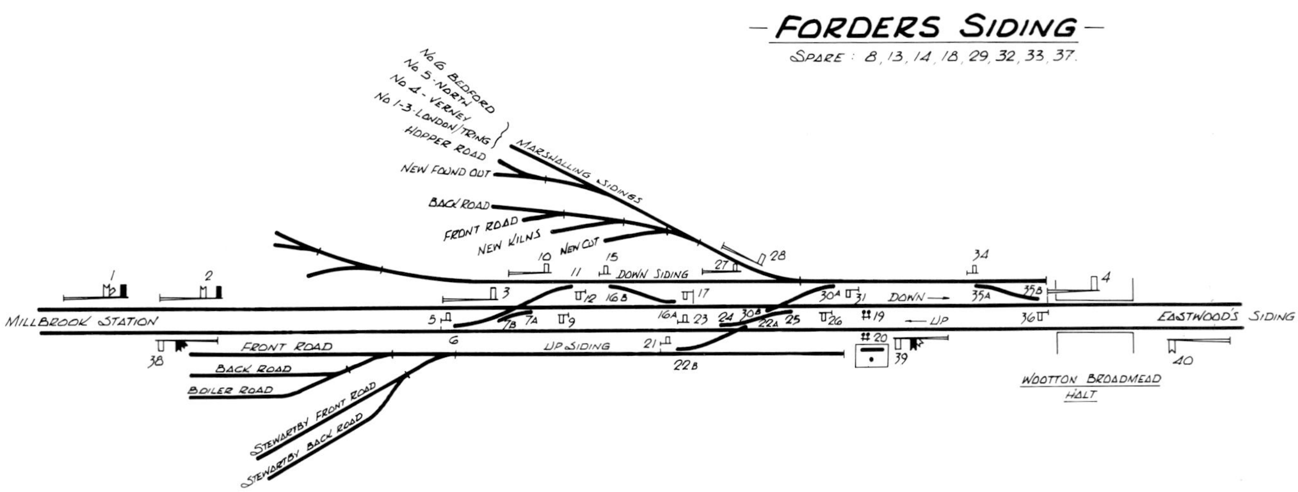

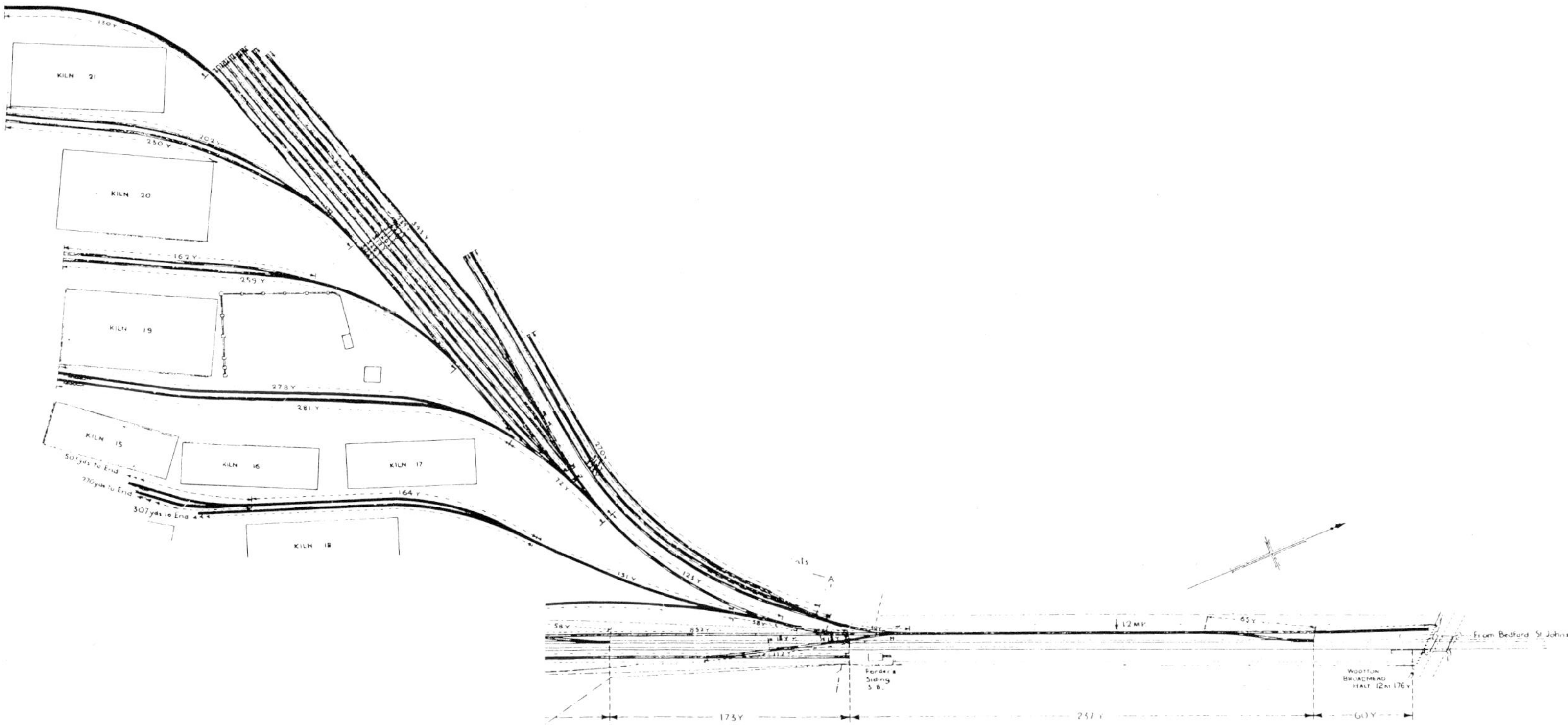

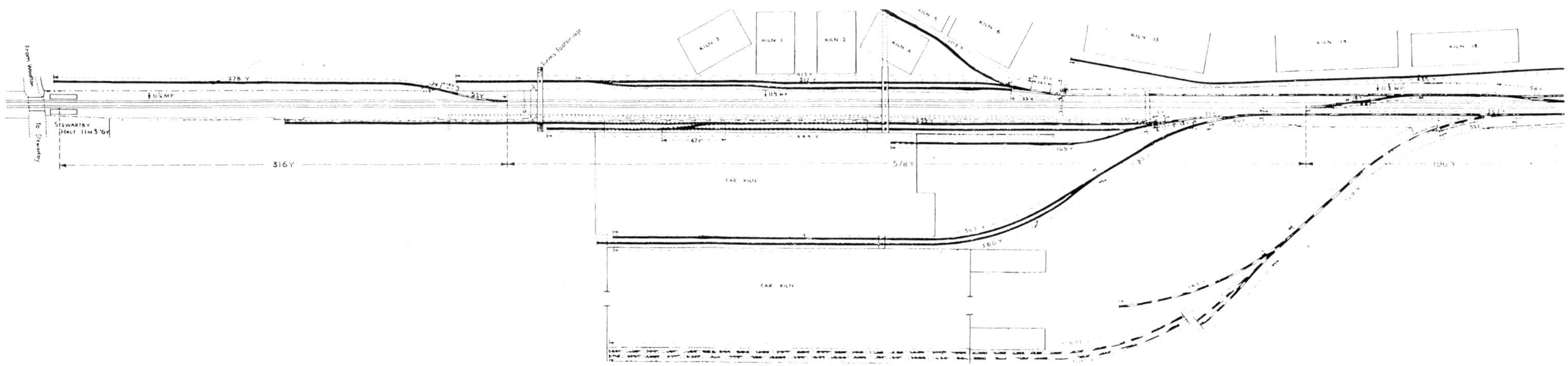

Forder's Sidings and the heart of the brick-making railway interchange. To consider the plant capacity here of 3,500,000 bricks per week, continuing for many years, especially during the 1920s and 1930s when nearly all were moved by rail, gives an indication of the staggering tonnages that must have passed over these metals.

M. Christensen

An excellent study of the Bletchley to Bedford push-pull unit in the Ridgmont area. Ex-Midland 0-4-4 tank, No. 1260 moves briskly past the wood yard as an ex-LNWR 'Super D' passes on its way to Bletchley, ceaselessly occupied with goods work. Note the characteristically tall LNWR semaphore signal.

I.C.A.

A neatly kept halt, on the 13 mile post, called Kempston Hardwick and in the background is Eastwood's Kempston Brickworks. Raising the platform has created an odd alignment against the house window that must have seen many feet. The view, taken in July 1970, but for the raised platforms and television aerial, could just as easily have been taken many years previous as so little has altered.

John Spencer

CHAPTER FOURTEEN

Wootton Broadmead Kempston Hardwick and Kempston Elstow

Three halts between Stewartby and Bedford were all built alongside crossings with the introduction of the steam rail-motor in 1905. All three were suspended from operation during World War I.

Wootton Broadmead Halt, with keeper's hut and signal frame, was situated at the north end of Forder's Sidings, and on the 12 mile post and rather less conveniently situated to local communities than the halts south and north of it, Wootton Pillinge (Stewartby) and Kempston Hardwick. It was suspended from service in 1941 and lingered without use until final closure in 1949.

Kempston Hardwick fared rather better, being convenient for the nearby Eastwood's Brickworks, although not quite as convenient for the village of Wootton. Its platforms have survived in use to the present day, but the crossing keeper's lodge was demolished during the 1960s. A diverting interest nearby was the sidings for the brickyard, which were situated on the Bedford side of the crossing, on the 'up' side of the line, which opened on 16th July 1928. These have now been removed together with their attendant signal box.

Kempston & Elstow Halt experienced exactly the same opening, suspension periods and closure dates as Wootton Broadmead. It was built close to an old road bridge, that crossed over a tributary of the River Ouse, called Cow Bridge. Although the halt has long since been removed, the lodge house still remains as a private dwelling. The most striking feature of this crossing is that it became dominated by the Midland Railway line of 1868 which was carried on a bridge above the house roof-top.

Eastwood's own diesel engine was kept in its own small shed, between shifts of its occupation of shunting bricks to the siding.

John Spencer

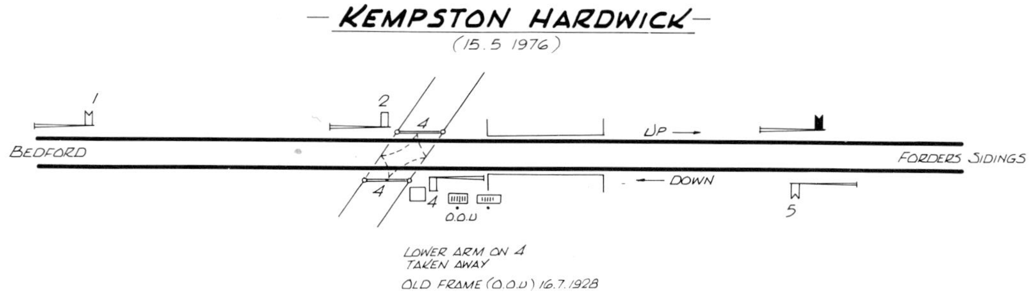

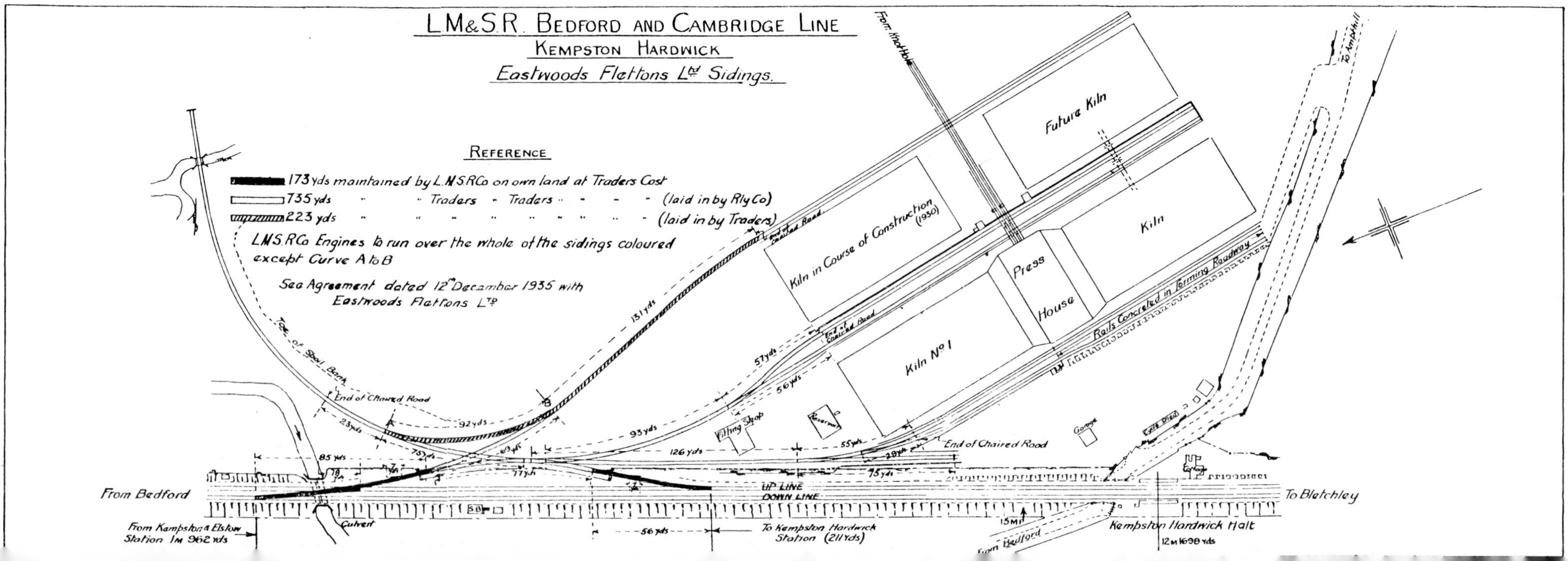

The railway crossing house cottages in Elstow. A top view, is shown, of the house at Cow Bridge, where a keeper was employed from 1846 until 1868, when a diversion of the road by the Midland Railway caused the removal of the crossing. The house was used by a porter, from 30th October 1905 until May 1941, being the staff to the nearby Kempston & Elstow Halt. After the halt was closed, the house was purchased privately.

J. R. Rounthwaite

Another small crossing, closer to Bedford, had this crossing house which was also affected by the diversion of the road. A charming little half-timbered house, now sadly demolished.

J. R. Rounthwaite

LICHFIELD T.V. TO LONDON (EUSTON) AND BRANCHES—continued.

ADDITIONAL RUNNING LINES.	STATIONS AND SIGNAL BOXES, ETC.	Distance from place next above. Miles.	Yards.	UP LINE.	Lie-by Sidings and holding capacity. No. of Wagons. Up Side.	Down Side.	RUNAWAY CATCH POINTS. WHERE SITUATE.	LINE.	Approximate Gradient. 1 in	ENGINE WHISTLES. UP. Main, Fast or Passenger Line.	UP. Slow or Goods Line.	DOWN. Main, Fast or Passenger Line.	DOWN. Slow or Goods Line.	TO	MILES PER HOUR. UP.	DOWN.
	NEWPORT PAGNELL STATION TO WOLVERTON No. 2.															
Staff	**Newport Pagnell**—Station	—	—													
	Between Newport Pagnell and Wolverton														45	45
Staff	**Great Linford**—§Station	1	257													
Staff	**Bradwell**—§Station	1	1130													
Staff	**Wolverton**—No. 2 *See page* 60.	1	373													
	Curve leading from Newport Pagnell line to up slow main line														10	
	CAMBRIDGE SOUTH TO BLETCHLEY No. 1.															
	Cambridge—South (L.N.E.)	—	—													
	,, Goods Yard	—	564													
	Lord's Bridge—Station	4	1399													
	Old North Road—Station	5	613													
	Gamlingay—Station	4	1142													
	,, Dennis' Siding	1	403													
	Potton—No. 2	1	213													
	Round Potton curve														45	45
	,, No. 1	—	315													
	Between Potton and Sandy (Deepdale curve, 27½ and 27 mile posts)														35	35
	Sandy—No. 2	3	497													
Token	,, No. 1	—	415			54										
Token	,, §Level Crossing	—	867													
Token	,, §Girtford Level Crossing	—	1406													
Token	**Blunham**—Station	1	224				*374 yards in rear of starting signal	Up loop	109	1 and 1 crow		1 and 1 crow		Sidings and *vice versa*		
Token	**Willington**—Station	2	490				*378 yards in rear of starting signal	Down loop	Level	1 and 1 crow		1 and 1 crow		Sidings		
Token							*237 yards in rear of starting signal	Up loop	300							
Token	,, Goldington (*Closed*)	1	992													
	In each direction through junctions at Goldington														15	15
Token	**Bedford**—No. 2	2	260													
	Bedford—No. 1	—	482							1 1 and 1 crow 2 crows		1 1 and 1 crow 2 crows		Through Sidings and *vice versa* Engine shed ,, ,,		
	,, §Kempston and Elstow Halt	1	295													
	Millbrook—Eastwood's Siding	1	1055				650 yards in rear of home signal	Up	163							
	,, §Kempston Hardwick Halt (Level crossing)	—	302													
	,, §Wootton Broadmead Halt	—	1528													
	,, Forder's Sidings	—	385							1 1 and 1 crow 1 crow		1 1 and 1 crow 1 crow		Through Sidings and *vice versa* Crossover		
	,, §Stewartby Halt and Green Lane Level crossing	—	1255													
	,, Station (Level crossing)	1	340													
	,, Brick Sidings	—	338													
	,, Marston Valley Brick Siding	—	955				500 yards in rear of home signal	Up	129	1 1 and 1 crow 1 crow		1 1 and 1 crow 1 crow		Through Sidings and *vice versa* Crossover		
	Lidlington—§Marston Level crossing	—	470													
	,, §Station (Level crossing)	—	715													
	Ridgmont—Station (Level crossing)	1	1478				338 yards in rear of distant signal	Up	129							
	,, §Husborne Crawley Halt	—	955													
	Woburn Sands—§Aspley Guise Halt	1	280													
	,, Station (Level crossing)	—	1627							1 and 1 crow 1 crow		1 and 1 crow 1 crow		Sidings and *vice versa* Crossover		
	Fenny Stratford—§Bow Brickhill Halt (Level crossing)	2	120													
	,, Station (Level crossing)	—	1598							1		1		Through		
	Bletchley—No. 4	—	1008													
P.B.	,, No. 5	—	692							1 2 crows 1 crow and 1 1 crow	 2 short 1 long	1 2 crows 1 and 1 crow 1 crow		Through Up goods loop to up slow Engines to loco. shed P. Way depot and *vice versa* Top yard sdgs. ,, ,, Crossover		
	From Bletchley to ¼ mile-post															25
P.B.	,, No. 1 *See pages* 61 and 62.	—	572													

Block posts on the Bletchley to Cambridge line, in 1957.
Cyril Gibbins

Bedford LNWR Station, in April 1914. The photographer is standing upon the platform built for the extended line to Cambridge in 1861. Until that time, all arrivals and departures were handled by the 'London' platform, as it was called, under the overall canopy. Bedford No. 2 signal box, on its original site, can be faintly seen behind the bridge support. In the foreground, one of the distinctive LNWR 90 degrees turning lamp ground signals can be seen.

L&GRP/Courtesy David & Charles

CHAPTER FIFTEEN

Bedford

Famous for its schools, the town of Bedford acquired residential advantages with many of the students living in the community of some 10,000 people. But it is to the developing industrial interests that the railway owes its beginnings.

Since the opening of the Ouse Navigation in 1689, the town's alternative transport for goods was by road wagons connecting with the Grand Junction Canal near Newport Pagnell. With the success of railways firmly established, a number of local business men, supported by the Duke of Bedford, wanted to put the town in direct railway communication. This became manifest with the opening of the Bedford Railway in 1846. It is worth mentioning that another scheme, if it had succeeded, would have affected Bletchley as the junction; this was the Wolverton–Newport Pagnell–Bedford Railway of 1844. As it lost ground to the Bedford Railway, it modified its proposals to forming a junction with the Bedford line at Ridgmont. However, the railway, as built, never proceeded beyond Newport Pagnell.

Support from George Stephenson and the Duke of Bedford must have counted a great deal in the Bedford Railway's favour, most of the land upon which the railway was built, including the Bedford Station area, being owned by the Duke of Bedford.

Chairman of the Company and Mayor of Bedford, T. J. Green, was concerned with the purveying of coals to the community. His enterprise in promoting the railway soon became manifest as during 1848, Bedford had received no less than 10,671 tons by rail. Trading in this valuable fuel was bound to be very competitive against the former conveyance at 11d (4½p) per cwt compared to 1s 9d (8p) per cwt. Although the railway had built a branch to the Ouse it was competition that the river would find impossible to withstand. Bedford was enriched further with the arrival of the Midland Railway in 1864, as the town was able to derive the benefits of coal gas with a new gasworks being built.

When the Bedford Railway opened for business in

As mentioned in the text, Bletchley received new, from the works, the first six of the last design by Ivatt for the LMS, the Class 4, 2-6-0 Mogul. This photograph shows No. 43005, with the 12.56p.m. Bletchley to Cambridge train on 15th April 1949, pausing at Bedford St. John's. The disproportionate appearance of a double chimney was not to remain, as these were all altered and additions to the class were fitted with a single chimney.

T. J. Edgington

November 1846, the scene at the station would have looked very different from the photographs in this book. Whilst the Cambridge extension was struggling to come about, there would not have been the London Road bridge. Whilst all the main station buildings were on the southern side of the line, facing the public house, the situation of open fields brought many complaints of the muddy footpath that led to the station. Obviously, since that time, a great deal of development has occurred, beginning with the station's goods facilities. These came to be built in an unusual position, on the branch to the Ouse Navigation and not alongside the main buildings, a logical arrangement that would allow exchange of traffic to take place with the river clear of the passenger part of the station. A second connecting line created, in effect, a triangle which diverted drainage to produce a pond for the station and locomotive shed water supply. The small two road locomotive shed, for one engine in use and one spare, survived for nearly eighty years, representing the paucity of those early days.

Popular use of the railway was intensified with the opening of that mid-century empyrean spectacle, The Great Exhibition of 1851. Excursions abounded; 6.20a.m. from Bedford on 23rd August became full to bursting point as its twenty five carriages set out for the capital. More carriages were added at Marston and Woburn, but still all of the people that wished to travel could not be accommodated. Another train was made up to follow and supply a good day for the populus and, no doubt, for the railway receipts.

Amongst early sidings to be agreed with the railway was a name still familiar in Bedford today; Franklin, who had a wagon repair business in the goods yard by 1871. Messrs Astell & Sons operated St. Leonard's Saw Mills on the Bedford side of the triangle in 1876, whilst Whittaker's Brewery and sidings were beneath the Ampthill Road bridge, opened in 1872, trailing from the original Ouse River branch. Roger's Siding, into the flour mill site, was added in 1886 which crossed in scissor arrangement over the Astell Siding to run alongside the mill. Development on the 'up' side of the station, the original station side, did not appear until the early days of the twentieth century. Two LNWR sidings were put in for Messrs B. Ward & Co., in 1905. A siding ran across the Elstow Road and was gated on each side. The siding on the other side of the London Road bridge was installed for Sterling Foundry Specialities Limited in 1922. Although these sidings were adopted by subsequent companies, they are the names on the first agreements made with the Railway Company.

The Midland Railway lodged a Bill, in 1855, for the Leicester to Hitchin Railway to make a London connection at Hitchin with the Great Northern. This was at first opposed by the latter company. Its opposition was based on the GNR's own protracted branch to Bedford from their main line at Sandy. To placate the GNR, the Midland Railway offered to form an agreeable interchange with the GNR traffic at Hitchin which appears to have found satisfaction. This line was opened on 8th May 1857 and its construction did create something of an oddity in the

British Railways standard locomotives. The 2-6-2 tank, No. 84005 is waiting to leave with the 3.35 p.m. for Bletchley, whilst the Class 4 waits in the middle siding with the 4.20 p.m. for the same destination. This scene was pictured on 7th November 1953.
T. J. Edgington

S.D.—82

London and North Western RAILWAY.

On SATURDAY AUGUST 2nd,

THE

9.10 p.m. Train,

BLETCHLEY TO BEDFORD

WILL BE

EXTENDED

TO

CAMBRIDGE

CALLING AT ALL

INTERMEDIATE STATIONS,

AS UNDER:—

DEPART.	P.M.	DEPART.	P.M.
BEDFORD	9 57	GAMLINGAY ...	10 32
BLUNHAM	10 8	OLD NORTH ROAD	10 40
SANDY	10 14	LORD'S BRIDGE ...	10 50
POTTON	10 26	CAMBRIDGE ... arr.	11 0

Euston Station, London,
July, 1884.

G. FINDLAY,
General Manager.

McCorquodale & Co., Limited, Cardington Street, London, N.W.

G. Howe Collection

Bedford LNWR Station, for the survey of their line brought them directly across the LNWR lines on the Bletchley end of the triangle. It was a feature similar to the American Grade crossing rather than British practice and, with the dense traffic of British lines, might have appeared risky. However, for its hundred and twelve years it was marred by only one accident. Its role diminished with the opening of the Midland Railway's new line to St. Pancras in 1868.

The accident revealed the shortcomings of signalling at the time and the arbitrary customs developed by LNWR footplate staff. It took place on 12th March 1875 involving the 7.15 p.m. passenger train from Bedford to Bletchley and the 6.45 p.m. Midland passenger train from Hitchin to Bedford which hit the rear coaches of the LNWR train. One passenger was killed and four injured, including the guard. During the inquest, the crossing was described as having a signal post with two semaphore arms on each side of it that were both 'homes' using the same rear lamp. This post was for 'up' and 'down' Midland trains and was situated in the south-west corner of the crossing. Also on the Midland line was a distant signal some 969 yards south of the crossing. In the north-west angle of the crossing was a post for LNWR trains. This also had two 'home' semaphores on each side of the post operating from one lamp. In the 200 yards from that signal to the end of the platform of Bedford Station there was no other signal. This lead to a tendency for LNWR drivers to either wait at the station until the crossing had been pulled off, as there was no platform starter, or, as in this case, after the guard had allowed the train to leave the platform, creep up to the crossing edge and wait for the signal to clear.

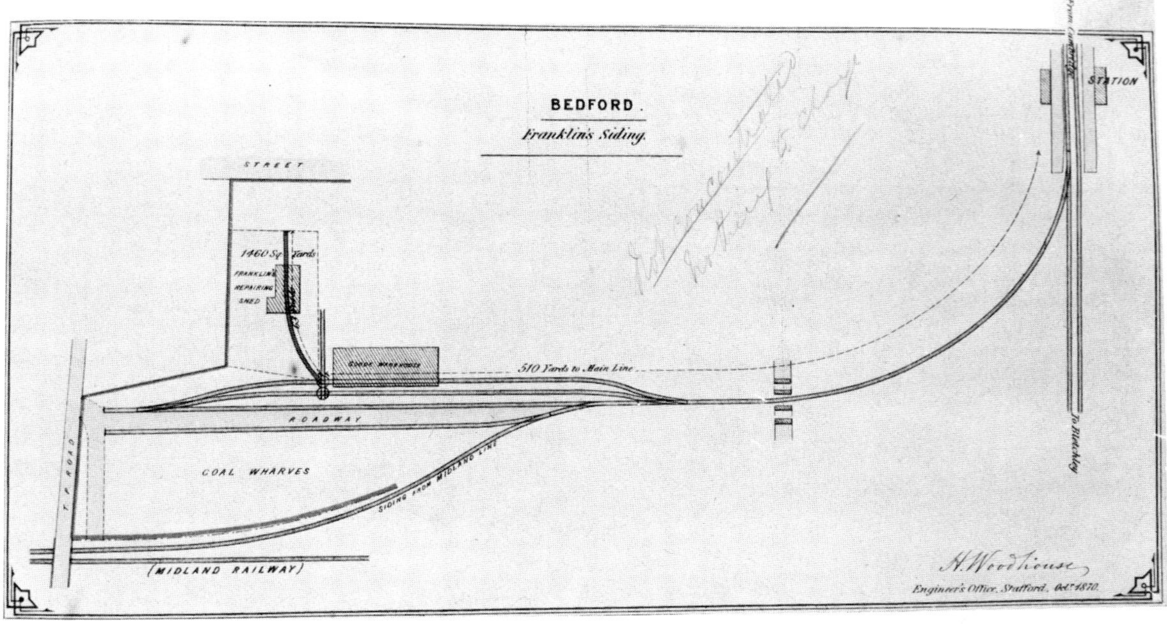
BEDFORD.
Franklin's Siding.
STREET
1460 Sq Yards
FRANKLINS REPAIRING SHED
GOODS WAREHOUSE
510 Yards to Main Line
ROADWAY
COAL WHARVES
SIDING FROM MIDLAND LINE
(MIDLAND RAILWAY)
STATION
H. Woodhouse
Engineer's Office, Stafford, Oct. 1870.

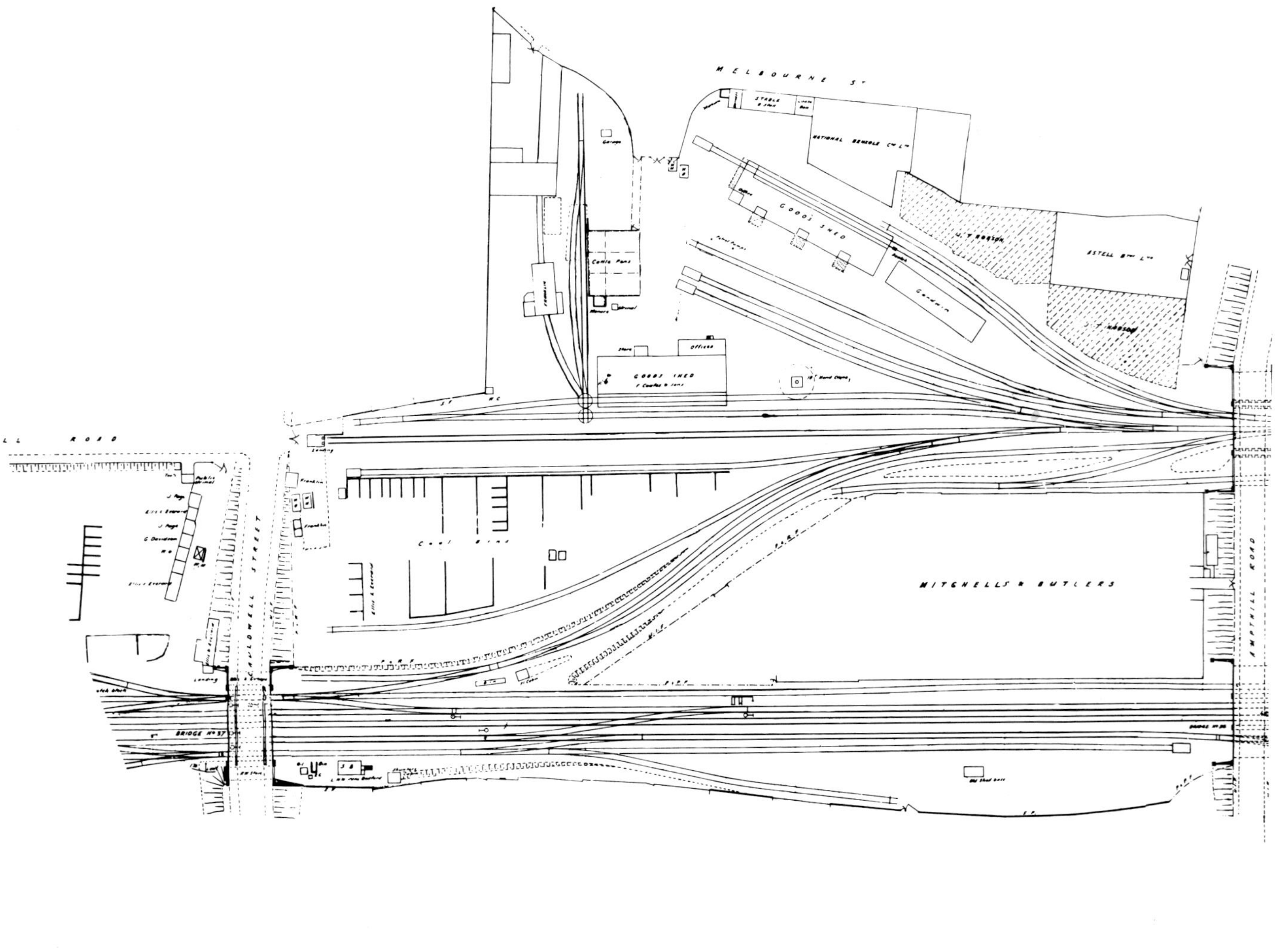
MELBOURNE ST
GOODS SHED
NATIONAL BENZOLE Co Ltd
ESTELL Bros Ltd
GOODS SHED
Coal Bins
MITCHELLS & BUTLERS
CAULDWELL STREET
AMPTHILL ROAD
BRIDGE No 57

The complete Bedford St. John's plan alongside the Leicester & Hitchin branch. A view of the location, in 1870, on the inset diagram, gives a good example of the changes and development as the station complex moved towards its peak of intensity which lasted well up to the end of World War II.

J. A. Turner Collection

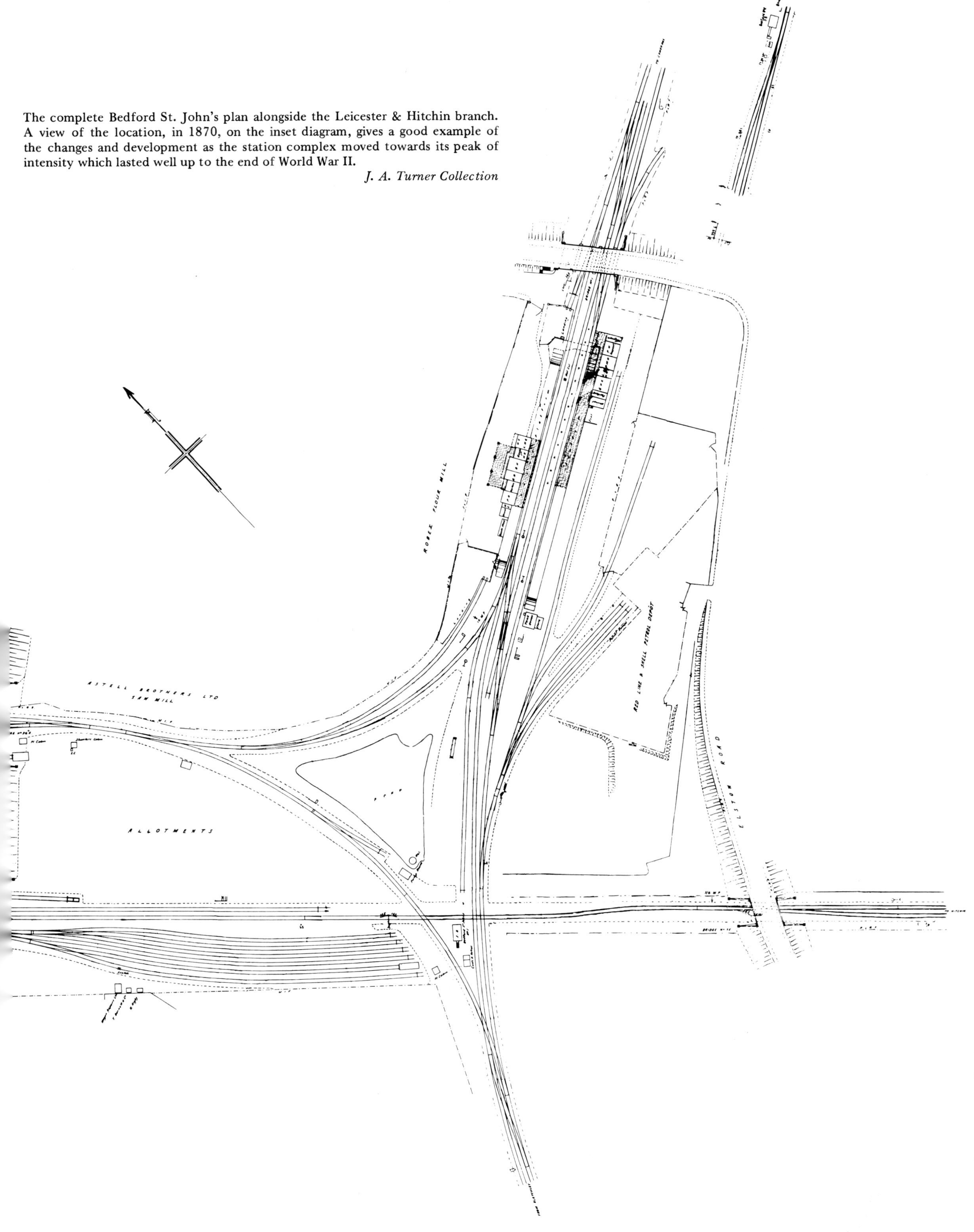

A view across the Bedford St. John's goods yard in the 1950s, with a Class G2, No. 49078, of Willesden shed, preparing to leave. Two large goods sheds were needed in the Bedford yard, the oldest, from the Bedford Railway and Ouse Navigation days, is the one on the left of the photograph.

Ian Hall

Signalman Bishop, who was in charge of the crossing's eight levers, which were scattered around in various positions alongside the lines, cleared the road for the Midland train from Hitchin. He saw the LNWR train in Bedford Station and was concerned to see it moving off. Obviously, it had been cleared to leave by the guard. Its approach did not lead him to believe that it was going to stop at the crossing whereupon he tried to attract the attention of the driver to make him aware that he had signalled the Midland train through. The hapless Bishop was unable to catch the driver's attention, as his position was on the opposite side from where the driver was standing. The driver was very soon to become aware that he was fouling the path of the oncoming train and tried to accelerate over the crossing. At the same time, the Midland driver was trying to brake his train for all he was worth, having first of all decelerated to a regulation speed of 12 m.p.h. for the crossing, and then down to 6 m.p.h. at the moment of impact with the last but one carriage of the LNWR train. It was in this shattered carriage that the Reverend W. Sprott was fatally injured. The Midland engine then left the rails and became buried up to its axles in ballast.

The badly sited LNWR starting signal, originally used before the Midland line was built, was strongly criticized at the enquiry which recommended that all the signalling should be brought into control within an elevated cabin and be interlocking.

The driver of the LNWR train John Perkins, was dismissed and faced Bedford Assizes on 26th July 1875, after having a verdict of manslaughter brought against him at the inquest. He pleaded that the weather conditions of falling sleet had hindered his vision and he was eventually fined £20. One of the peculiarities of coincidence was that the driver of the Midland train was also called John Perkins!

Of interest, is the type of engine involved and in use on the branch at that time. This was a 2-2-2 locomotive No. 127 named *Peel* with a single driving wheel of 6 ft. It was built in 1850 and rebuilt in 1864 being given the number 1886. It was finally scrapped in January 1878. The situation at the Bedford crossing fared rather better, as on 9th February 1877, a new signal box with 29 levers, (3 spares), controlled the new interlocked signals. A charge of £260 per annum was made to the Midland Company towards the signalling. The Hitchin line was singled by the Midland Railway in May 1911, with its diminishing importance from 1868, and the new main line route to St. Pancras, that avoided Bedford LNWR Station, crossed the branch near the 15 mile post. A footnote to the development of signalling was the introduction of the 'block' system throughout from Bletchley to Cambridge on 14th July 1880.

Relationships between the two companies at Bedford never developed sufficiently to enable agreement to be reached for the building of a joint station, although the Midland made use of the LNWR station before theirs was

A '3 Freight' 0-6-0, No. 43449, crosses the Bedford to Hitchin line on its way from Bedford St. John's to Ridgmont, giving a clear indication of the unusual level crossing.

Ian Hall

complete. Although such an arrangement may have brought an early end to Bedford St. John's, as it was named after 1924, it does seem a great pity that a joint station was not built before the Cambridge extension in 1862. The Mayor of Bedford petitioned strongly for it in 1861 and passengers complained, rightly so, of having to walk across the town, in all too English weathers, to change trains. It appears that the LNWR were somewhat grieved that, with the opening of the Cambridge route, passengers for Derby, Leicester and Manchester could change to the Midland line by agreement, to choose the shortest route, but this agreement did not apply if they had to change stations. Thus penurious differences were to spite the rational course and leave a legacy of discontent.

Until about 1880, the little more than basic LNWR four wheel coaches were in use on the Oxford to Cambridge route and were gradually supplanted by six wheel stock. Until 1906, these set trains were composed of three 32ft. vehicles with a 30ft. 6in. brake third at each end.

It was in 1906 that the new 'Bletchley sets' of bogie stock were introduced; three 50ft. vehicles in each set total of 36 vehicles in 12 trains. The first four sets had the cove roof profile but were identical to the 50ft. arc roof stock and were 9ft. wide over the guard's ogees. They were on bulb iron underframes with standard bogies of 8ft. wheelbase and lit by electricity. A further 7 three coach sets were added in April 1909, to the first four of 1906. These had a change in the higher roof profile with top light windows over the van sections that had on the other sets been plain. The underframe design was of steel channel section solebars and a detail change was a different design of torpedo ventilator on the roof.

Three of the sets were disbanded about 1912, the composite in each case being converted into a motor train vehicle and the brake ends dispersed to other sets. The remaining nine sets continued into LMS days until subsequent reduction and piecemeal alteration to 'Oxbridge' trains.

In 1908, there were six return passenger journeys from Bletchley to Bedford, Sandy and Cambridge; none of which were expresses. Three of the trains allowed for through working to Oxford on certain coaches.

With the outbreak of that great twentieth century catastrophe, World War I, the Bedford to Cambridge line was to witness an early dramatic turn of events. It was announced that on 24th December 1914, sixty nine troop trains would enter the Company's system from Bedford Midland starting in the early hours. Each train would be numbered B1 to B69 and the trains would run at intervals of twenty minutes. Drawn by Midland engines, they would carry LNWR pilots from Bedford to Cambridge where they would be handed over to the Great Eastern Railway who would return the empty stock to the Midland Railway via South Tottenham. Each train would be allowed ninety minutes to complete the journey from Bedford to Cambridge all other traffic being suspended during the operation. Although there was no report of the tonnage of each train, it was quite obviously a very large proportion of

E.P. ROSE & SON LTD
MILLINERY D
AND ALL
LADIES' WE
HIGH STREET, B
NORTHAMPTON

◁ A view of the three car articulated unit at Bedford St. John's in April 1938. This unit was considered appropriate for trial on the Oxford to Cambridge line with its large number of stations requiring sharp acceleration between stops. It was 184 ft. long and weighed 73 tons. An interesting method of articulation allowed the maximum coach length without excess overhang on curves and the prospect of fouling the loading gauge. This view shows the unit on trial. It did not enter passenger service until 12th September 1938, with three trains daily from Cambridge and two from Oxford. There were shorter Bletchley to Cambridge trips interposed with stops at Bedford and Sandy. With three stops over the 77 miles and a highest booked average speed of 53.3 m.p.h., the journey was completed in 1¾ hours, a smart improvement on 3 hours by steam locomotive. The train was not inserted on the regular advertised schedules, but was advertised on the handbill.

Details on the unit are as follows: Power is provided by six Leyland 125 b.h.p. oil engines, running up to a maximum of 2,200 r.p.m. Two engines are mounted beneath the floor of each carriage which drive the inner axles of the adjacent bogies. The only axles of the train that are not driven are the two at the extreme ends. Although it was regulated to a maximum speed of 75 m.p.h., a speed of 82 m.p.h. was reached between Euston and Tring on former trials. It was fitted with Westinghouse compressed air brakes, operated through individual cylinders on all wheels with Ferodo block linings.

It will be noted that, compared with the later photograph, seen in *Oxford to Cambridge Railway (Volume One)*, the valancing below solebar height was removed, probably to facilitate greater maintenance, and that windows were later protected with strong wire mesh, which rather spoiled the appearance of the front, which had a whimsical contrast with the traditional engine lamps mounted on the streamlined buffers.

Bedford Times

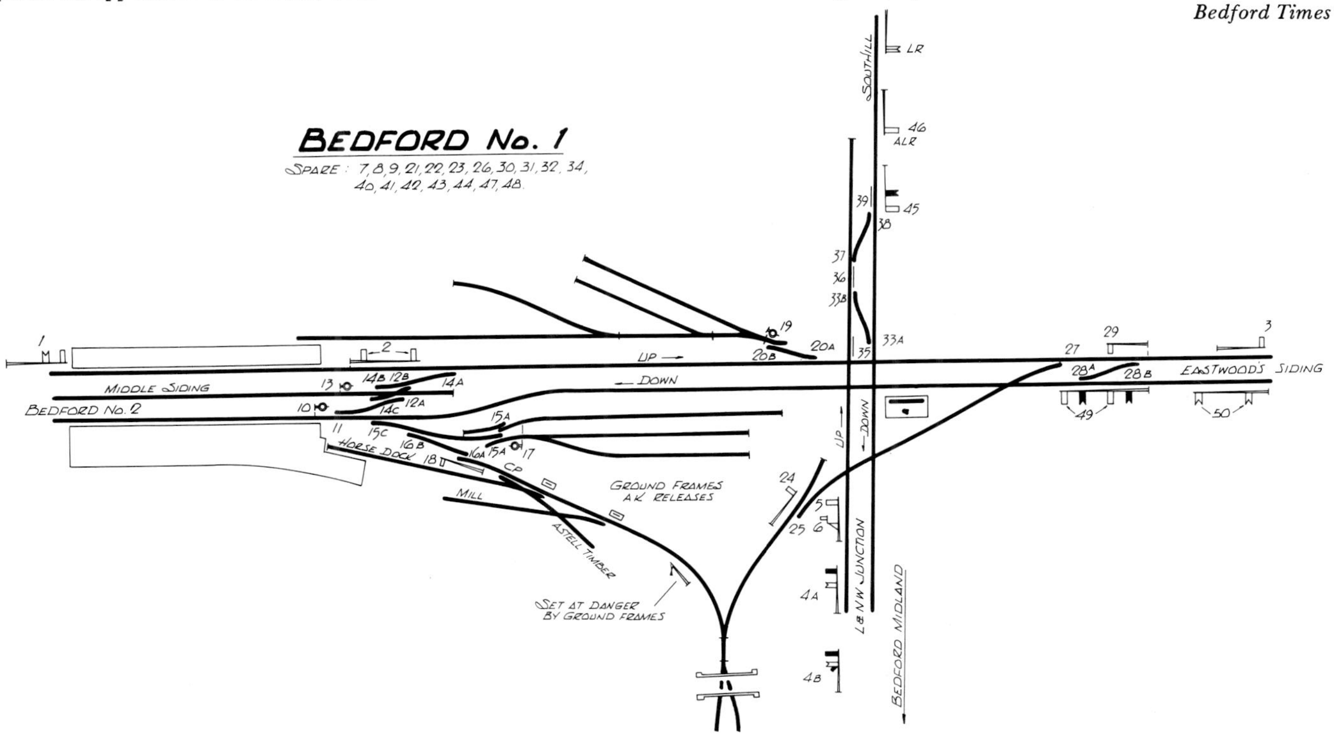

Another view, in August 1969, looking from alongside the centre storage siding towards Bletchley and the Bedford No. 1 signal box. The photograph illustrates how the water tank house obscures the view of the crossing signal, which caused LNWR drivers to move off towards the crossing, which brought about the accident of 1875. Note the bracketed arm, now visible at the end of the platform.

John Spencer

A visitor, this time from the other direction, as Cambridge B1, No. 61379, pulls away from a water stop at Bedford with an out-of-gauge load of concrete beams from the Anglia Concrete Co., Norwich, bound for the Bletchley flyover construction. The B1 is fitted with electric lighting.

Ian Hall

Kitchener's Army bound for France and their first Christmas of the war.

Shortly after the war, the Railway Executive moved towards amalgamation of all large and small railways into four large companies in the Amalgamation of Railways Act of 1921, which came into effect by January 1923. This brought the Cambridge line and the other station at Bedford into the same company, the London Midland & Scottish Railway. Wasting little time, the new company closed the small shed at Bedford in the same year but still retained the coaling facilities, whilst Bedford was suffixed with 'St. John's' in the following year.

It became obvious that the Bedford to Bletchley section of the cross-country route was the most successful for the motor train or push-pull working, even though the halts had been suspended during World War I. With their reintroduction, and the developing interests of the London Brick Company, they had a distinct advantage over their rural contemporaries on the Oxford line. At Wootton Pillinge, the halt was rebuilt as a station in 1932, eventually acquiring the name Stewartby. With the replacement of the less than successful railmotor, in 1926, the motor trains shuttled happily between the two towns with their LNWR coaches and 2-4-2, 4ft. 6in. 'motor tank' engines attaching the odd extra coach or van, parcels or cattle. When the ex-Midland Railway shed took this working over, with the closure of Bedford shed, it was operated by one of the Johnson 0-4-4 1P tanks with 5ft. 4in. driving wheels, together with men from the Midland shed. Coaches were stored, when not in use, in the middle siding at Bedford St. John's Station. The Johnson 1P tank engines lasted on this service for quite a long time until scrapping in the early 1950s. They were, however, supplanted to some degree after World War II, when the LMS introduced the new Class 4, 2-6-0 Mogul, the 43000 class. The first five of these came to Bletchley directly from the works, and were unique as only the first three engines appeared in the LMS style. They were to work the branch for a period of time and after their departure to other routes, the service was operated by Ivatt and Riddles 2-6-2 tank locomotives and, occasionally, by a Class 4, 4-6-0 standard type. By 1959, however, the 'motor trains' or push-pull, so affectionately regarded by all the locals, crossing keepers and signalmen down the line, were to cease and their well-known nightly sojourn, in the middle siding at Bedford, faded into history. Diesel multiple units replaced them. Although the pay train system, with guard/conductor issuing tickets on the train, survives as of the beginnings of 1905, now all of the stations are halts, even Bedford St. John's itself.

The decade of the 1930s saw a number of diversions in experimental trains on the branch. In 1932, the first experimental 'Micheline' was tried out. This was described in detail in *Oxford to Cambridge Railway, Volume One.* In 1935, another 'Micheline' appeared, rather more promising but not totally convincing and a description of this appears in the Cambridge section of this volume.

Another development, that was of purely British design, appeared on the line on 12th September 1938. This was a three car diesel unit which, in its way, was a precursor of the ubiquitous diesel multiple unit of twenty years later. In feature, it superseded it, with its aerodynamic bow front and pneumatic doors operated by the guard with separate passenger switches. Airy futurism of shiny tubular steel and moquette upholstery, these vehicles comprised 24 first class and 138 third class seats. This was the concept of Sir William Stanier and Derby's form of the train to be, had not the dead hand of war put an end to its prospects, along with the optimism of the design. During the short period of trials on the Oxford to Cambridge route, it was met with a great deal of excitement by its designers and the railwaymen that operated it. Its three double trips daily were not on the timetable, but were advertised by handbill with stops at Bletchley, Bedford and Sandy and it could cover the 77 miles in 1¾ hours, giving a daily mileage of 462.

During the war, it was put in store at Bedford only to emerge, like after the first war, to a changed world. The two end units were converted into self-propelled articulated units for use in the installation and maintenance of the overhead wires and equipment on the electrified lines.

Wartime traffic at Bedford included a special train that left Bedford St. John's at 7.50a.m. with civil service personnel evacuated from besieged London and who worked at Bletchley Park, but who lived in Bedford. Their returned working, unofficially named by the railwaymen as the 'Whitehall', left Oxford at 5.00p.m.

During restrictions of wartime, in blackouts and ponderous delays, not to mention cantankerous locomotives that had been too long since their last 'shopping' visit, it would be far less romantic and a great deal more miserable.

Amongst the more unusual visiting engines is this ex-Lancashire & Yorkshire 'Crab' replenishing its tanks as it journeys on with the morning Cambridge goods which, in 1955, was normally a 'Black Five' working. This mogul has wandered in its transports from Nuneaton shed.

Ian Hall

One goods working during this period was the 3.15 a.m. from Bletchley to Bedford and the isolated rural post of Gamlingay. It contained an assembled mixture of coal for Bedford, tariff van supplies and parts for the American tank assembly taking place in the brickworks. The 0-8-0, G2 class would have a good load as its exhaust echoed through the early hours from the Bletchley yard on to the branch. After the dangerous and difficult job of night shunting at various stations, the train would reach Gamlingay at 11.00 a.m., often with sixty five wagons behind with which to shunt the sidings for three to four hours. On its return, it would call at Belle Vue Sidings and collect more wagons to add to a probable twelve of vegetables already brought from Gamlingay. Ten more vegetable wagons would be picked up at Potton and more at Blunham. A further six would be collected at Willington, which would bring a train of forty six wagons rolling into Bedford St. John's. Here the guard would remarshall the train, sending the Belle Vue wagons to the Midland, along with twelve wagons of vegetables. Collecting a number of urgent livestock vans, the train would then make haste to Bletchley where it would be marshalled into three distinct sections; London, Birmingham (Curzon Street) and Bletchley sidings, to be dispersed elsewhere.

The size of the home food production taking place around Sandy can be appreciated by the sheer bulk of Welsh coal and anthracite, needed to heat the greenhouses, that was leaving Swanbourne Sidings daily in forty wagon loads.

During the war, a large ammunition store was built up at Lord's Bridge which brought many new workings to the line to the extent of keeping an ex-Midland 2F tank locomotive permanently held there to shunt each train into the depot as it arrived and, of course, prepare empties for return. The tank engine was replaced by 3F tender engine No. 3374 as shunting demands increased later in the war. Added to this, were the numerous troop and ambulance trains, all needing engines and crews, and Bletchley became hard pressed to supply all the power. This brought a supplementary batch of sorely needed G2, 0-8-0s. A further eight of these were supplied, which brought Bletchley's allocation to an all time record of seventy five engines.

After the war, the prosperity of brick and vegetable production continued with unending reliance on the G2, 0-8-0 (Super D) locomotives and Midland 4F 0-6-0 engines

An interesting diagram relating to the raising of the 'down' platform to standard height that also gives a good indication of the interior layout of the station buildings.
BR/OPC Collection

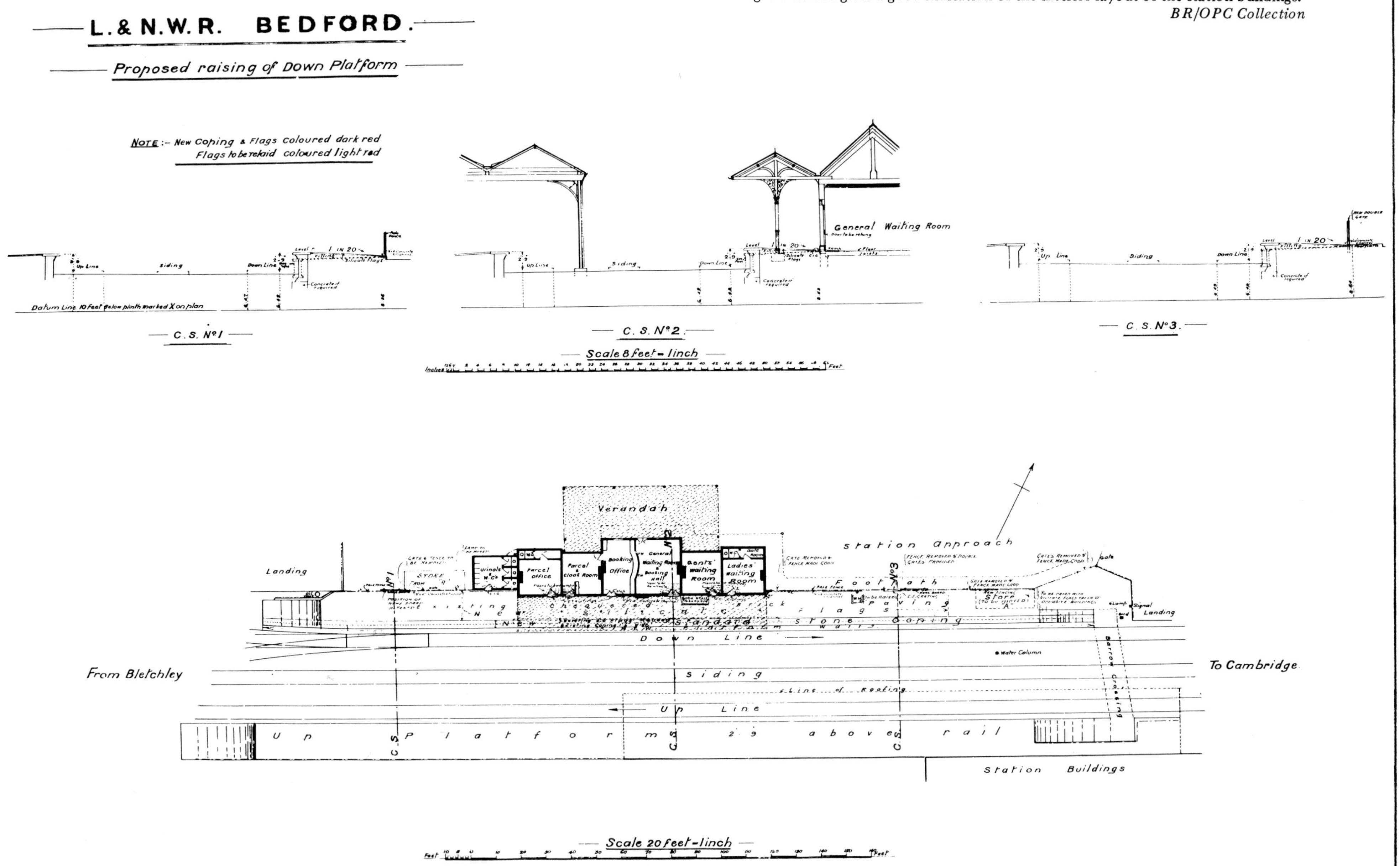

Different kinds of trunks with the arrival of a circus. Staff at Bedford St. John's make their acquaintance in the mid-1950s.

Ian Hall

assisted now by the Stanier workhorse, the '8 Freight'. Cambridge pick-up goods trains, working from the ex-Great Eastern shed, would be handled by J19, J20 and J39 classes with 'Black Fives' and Thompson B1s in charge of passenger and parcel trains that were not beyond picking up sugar beet and vegetable vans. Significant tonnages of cattle trains were also in evidence.

Having a major position on one of the busiest of the cross-country routes, with numerous sidings and connections, plus the Midland trains to Hitchin cutting across the station area in their odd fashion, Bedford St. John's has had a restless and engaging history of activity. From the first flush of sanguine optimism by its promoters, it had witnessed an expectation in commerce through the brick and vegetable industries that made it a focal point on the route between Oxford and Cambridge. Its decline, in latter years, reflects the changing profile of British Rail and industrial merchandising that is served from the road rather than from these once numerous sidings.

Class 2, 2-6-2T, No. 84020 is pictured on the Bedford push-pull service, when but a month old in 1953, at Bedford St. John's.

I. Simpson

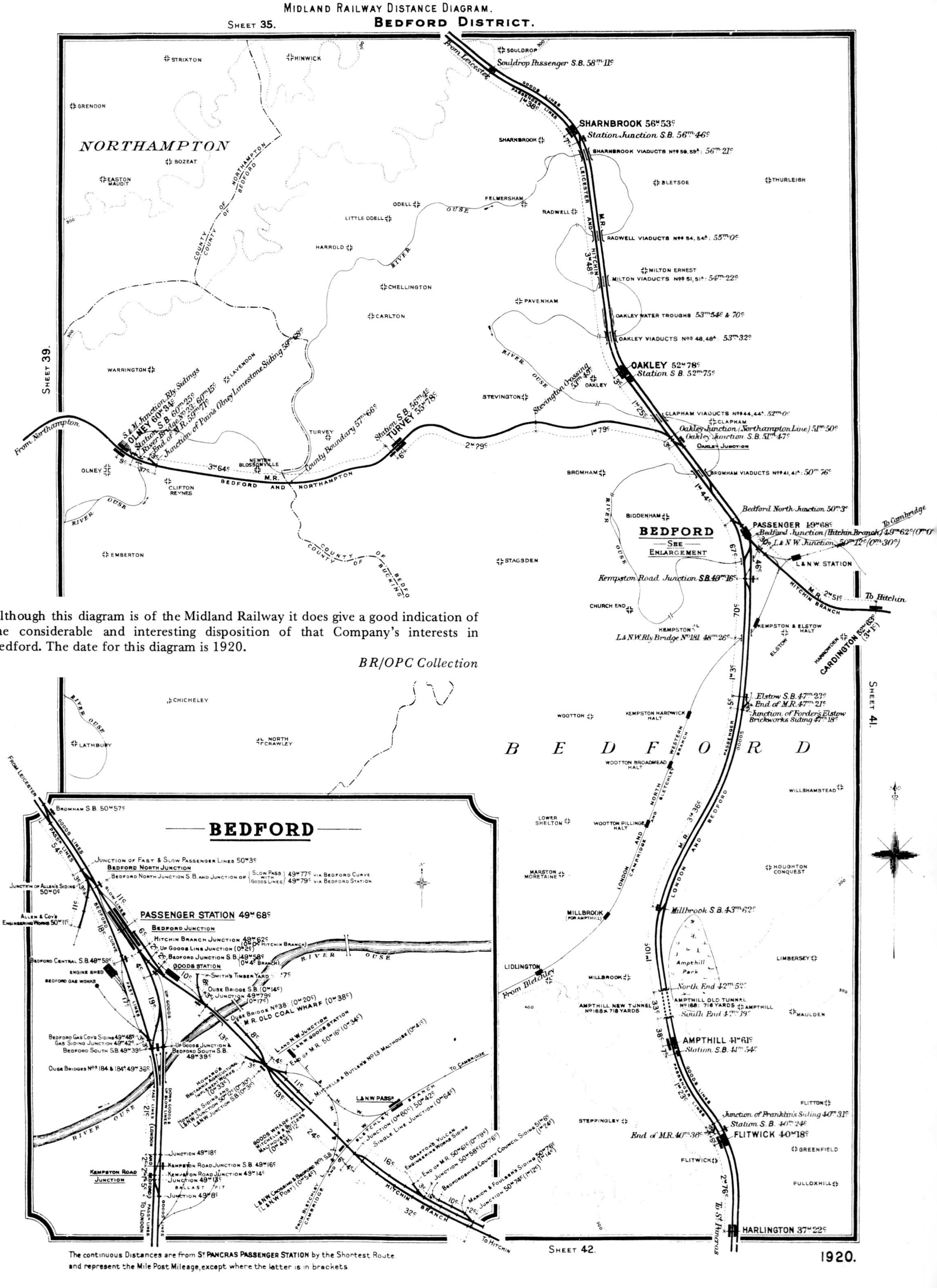

Although this diagram is of the Midland Railway it does give a good indication of the considerable and interesting disposition of that Company's interests in Bedford. The date for this diagram is 1920.

BR/OPC Collection

The situation of Bedford No. 2 box, removed to the Ouse River bridge No. 3 at the beginning of the war, to extend the double/single line junction, looking in the Cambridge direction. On many occasions, the single line staff slipped into the Stygian depths of the Ouse from the signalman's misplaced hand. A pouch and loop wire were introduced to alleviate this mishap.

A. Warrington

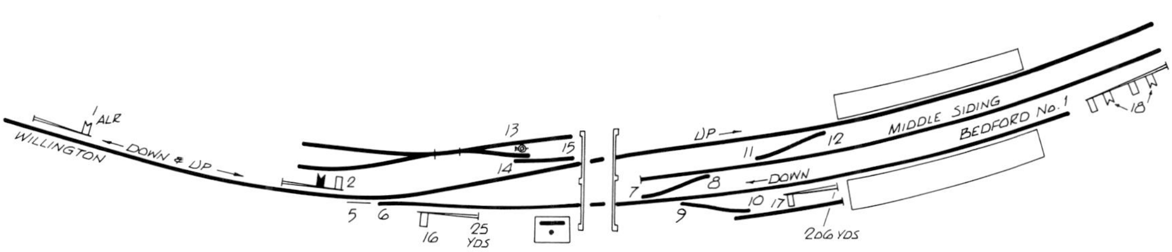

Bedford No. 2 box, when it was close to the station and situated on the other side of the London Road bridge. It was moved to bridge No. 3 location early in World War II.

M. Christensen

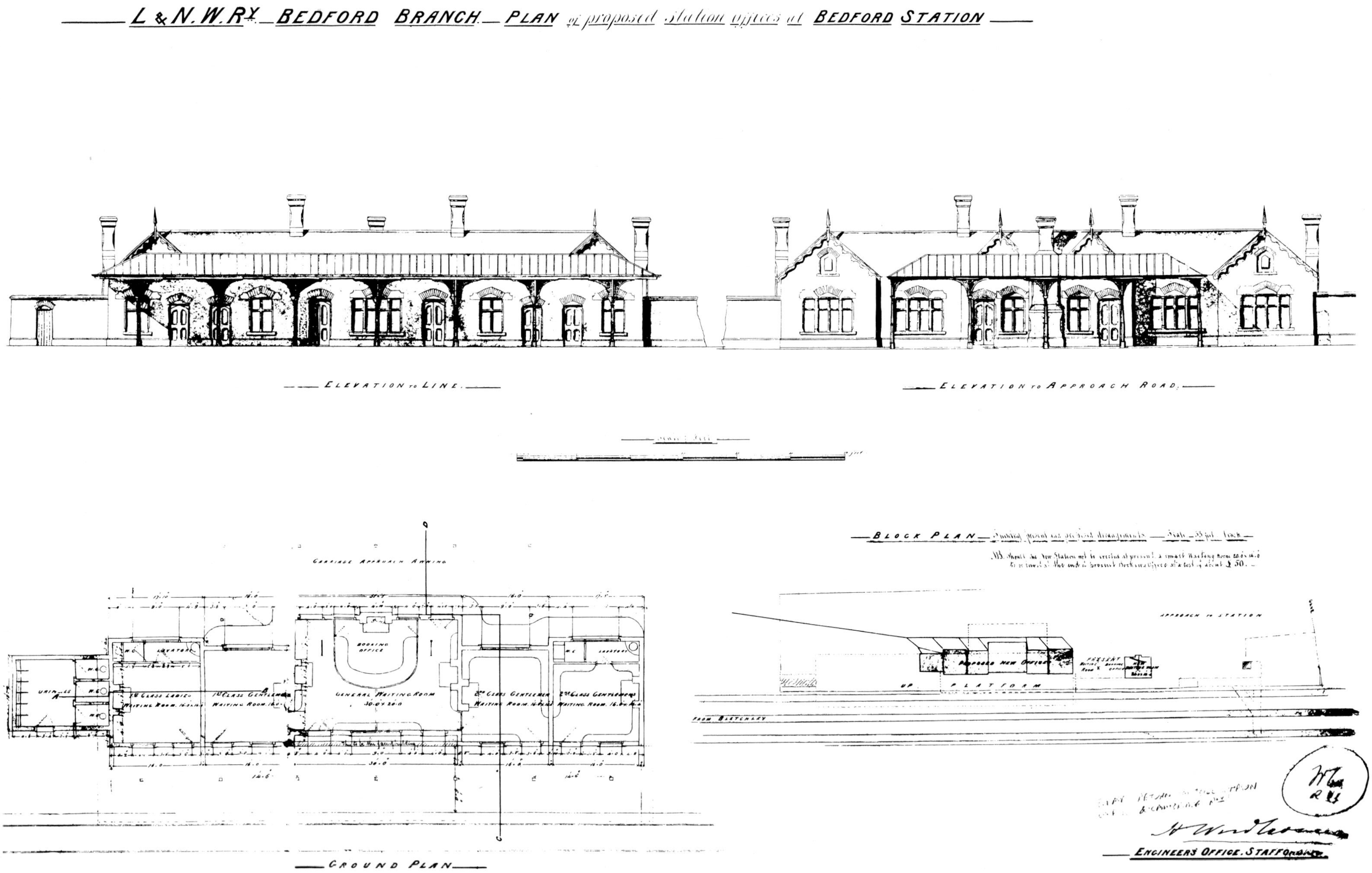

New buildings for Bedford LNWR Station with the development of the 'down' platform for through trains to Cambridge. Probable date; circa 1861.

J. A. Turner

Goldington Power Station engine; an 0-4-0 saddle tank.
John Spencer

A view looking back from the No. 4 bridge, to No. 3 in the distance, with Bedford beyond. The foreground points are for the 'loop' and siding for Bedford Corporation Newnham Siding on the 17 mile post.
Author's Collection

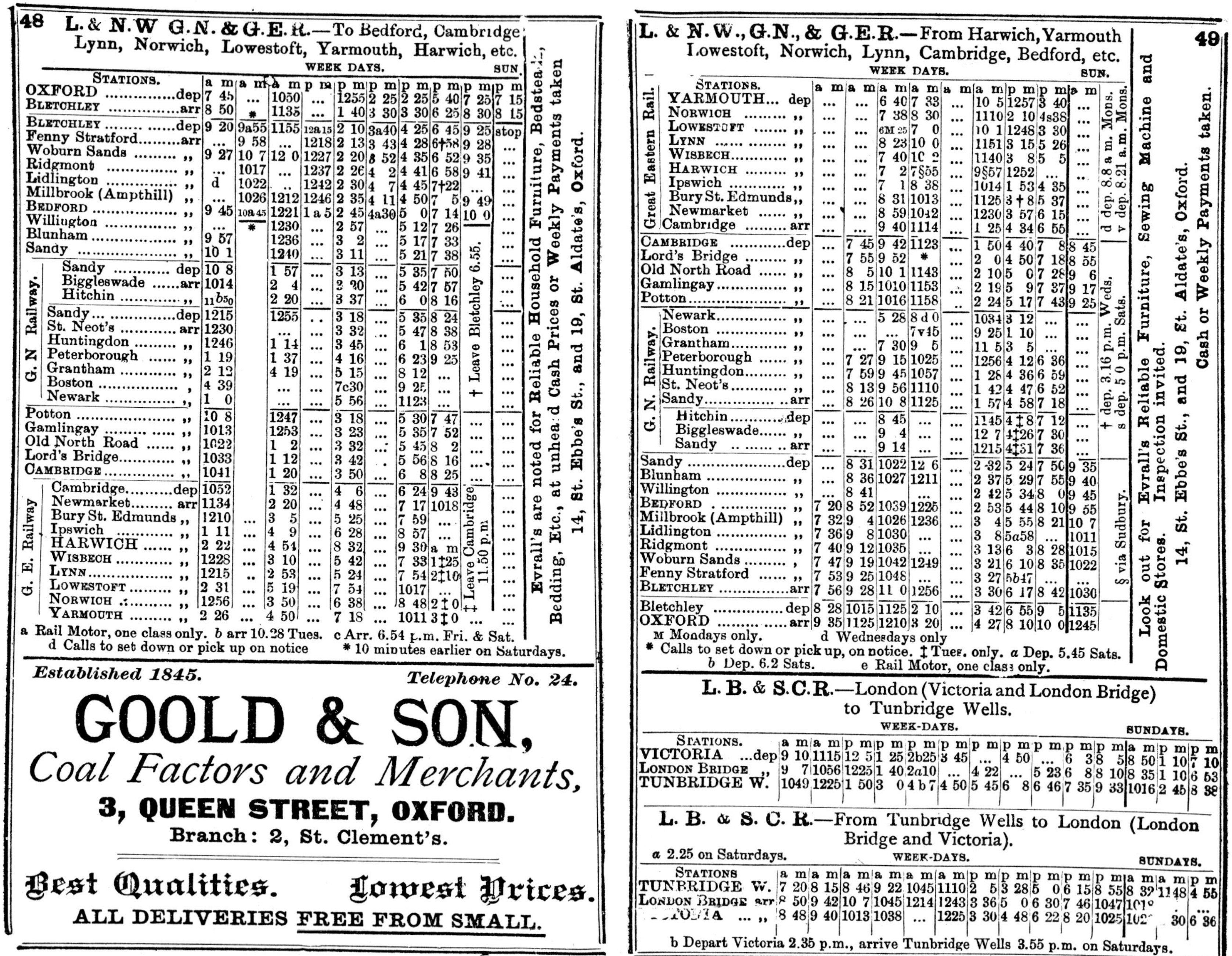

48

L. & N. W G. N. & G. E. R.—To Bedford, Cambridge, Lynn, Norwich, Lowestoft, Yarmouth, Harwich, etc.

WEEK DAYS. / SUN.

STATIONS.	a m	a m	a m	p m	p m	p m	p m	p m	p m	SUN. p m
OXFORD ....dep	7 45	...	1050	...	1255	2 25	2 25	5 40	7 25	7 15
BLETCHLEY ....arr	8 50	*	1135	...	1 40	3 30	3 30	6 25	8 30	8 15
BLETCHLEY ....dep	9 20	9a55	1155	12a15	2 10	3a40	4 25	6 45	9 25	stop
Fenny Stratford.........arr	...	9 58	...	1218	2 13	3 43	4 28	6†58	9 28	...
Woburn Sands .... ,,	9 27	10 7	12 0	1227	2 20	3 52	4 35	6 52	9 35	...
Ridgmont .... ,,	...	1017	...	1237	2 26	4 2	4 41	6 58	9 41	...
Lidlington .... ,,	d	1022	..	1242	2 30	4 7	4 45	7†22	...	...
Millbrook (Ampthill) ,,	...	1026	1212	1246	2 35	4 11	4 50	7 5	9 49	...
BEDFORD .... ,,	9 45	10a45	1221	1 a 5	2 45	4a30	5 0	7 14	10 0	...
Willington .... ,,	...	*	1230	...	2 57	...	5 12	7 26		...
Blunham .... ,,	9 57		1236	...	3 2	...	5 17	7 33		...
Sandy .... ,,	10 1		1240	...	3 11	...	5 21	7 38		...
G. N. Railway.										
Sandy .... dep	10 8		1 57	...	3 13	...	5 35	7 50	† Leave Bletchley 6.55.	...
Biggleswade ......arr	1014		2 4	...	3 20	...	5 42	7 57		...
Hitchin .... ,,	11b50		2 20	...	3 37	...	6 0	8 16		...
Sandy ....dep	1215		1255	..	3 18	...	5 35	8 24		...
St. Neot's .... arr	1230		...	...	3 32	...	5 47	8 38		...
Huntingdon .... ,,	1246		1 14	...	3 45	...	6 1	8 53		...
Peterborough ...... ,,	1 19		1 37	...	4 16	...	6 23	9 25		...
Grantham .... ,,	2 12		4 19	...	5 15	...	8 12	...		...
Boston .... ,	4 39		...	...	7c30	...	9 25	...		...
Newark .... ,,	1 0		...	...	5 56	...	1123	...		...
Potton .... ,,	10 8		1247	...	3 18	...	5 30	7 47	...	...
Gamlingay .... ,,	1013		1253	...	3 23	...	5 35	7 52	...	...
Old North Road ...... ,,	1022		1 2	...	3 32	...	5 45	8 2	...	...
Lord's Bridge............ ,,	1033		1 12	...	3 42	.	5 56	8 16	...	...
CAMBRIDGE .... ,,	1041		1 20	...	3 50	...	6 8	8 25	...	...
G. E. Railway										
Cambridge.........dep	1052		1 32	...	4 6	...	6 24	9 43	‡ Leave Cambridge 11.50 p.m	...
Newmarket......... arr	1134		2 20	...	4 48	...	7 17	1018		...
Bury St. Edmunds ,,	1210	...	3 5	...	5 25	...	7 59	...		...
Ipswich .... ,,	1 11	...	4 9	...	6 28	...	8 57	...		...
HARWICH ...... ,,	2 22	...	4 54	...	8 32	...	9 30	a m		...
WISBECH .... ,,	1228	...	3 10	...	5 42	...	7 33	1‡25		...
LYNN............ ,,	1215	..	2 53	...	5 24	...	7 54	2‡10		...
LOWESTOFT .... ,,	2 31	...	5 19	...	7 54	...	1017	...		...
NORWICH .... ,,	1256	...	3 50	...	6 38	...	8 48	2‡0		...
YARMOUTH .... ,,	2 26	...	4 50	...	7 18	...	1011	3‡0	...	...

a Rail Motor, one class only. b arr 10.28 Tues. c Arr. 6.54 p.m. Fri. & Sat.
d Calls to set down or pick up on notice * 10 minutes earlier on Saturdays.

Evrall's are noted for Reliable Household Furniture, Bedsteads, Bedding, Etc., at unheard Cash Prices or Weekly Payments taken 14, St. Ebbe's St., and 19, St. Aldate's, Oxford.

Established 1845. *Telephone No. 24.*

GOOLD & SON,

Coal Factors and Merchants,

3, QUEEN STREET, OXFORD.

Branch: 2, St. Clement's.

Best Qualities. Lowest Prices.

ALL DELIVERIES FREE FROM SMALL.

L. & N. W., G. N., & G. E. R.—From Harwich, Yarmouth, Lowestoft, Norwich, Lynn, Cambridge, Bedford, etc.

49

WEEK DAYS. / SUN.

STATIONS.	a m	a m	a m	a m	a m	a m	p m	p m	SUN. a m
Great Eastern Rail.									
YARMOUTH... dep	...	...	6 40	7 33	...	10 5	1257	3 40	...
NORWICH .... ,,	...	...	7 38	8 30	...	1110	2 10	4s38	...
LOWESTOFT .... ,,	...	...	6M25	7 0	...	10 1	1248	3 30	...
LYNN .... ,,	...	...	8 23	10 0	...	1151	3 15	5 26	...
WISBECH............ ,,	...	...	7 40	10 2	...	1140	3 8	5 5	...
HARWICH .... ,,	...	...	7 2	7§55	...	9§57	1252	...	...
Ipswich .... ,,	...	...	7 1	8 38	...	1014	1 53	4 35	...
Bury St. Edmunds ,,	...	...	8 31	1013	...	1125	3†8	5 37	...
Newmarket ...... ,,	...	...	8 59	1042	...	1230	3 57	6 15	...
Cambridge ....arr	...	...	9 40	1114	...	1 25	4 34	6 55	...
CAMBRIDGE ....dep	...	7 45	9 42	1123	...	1 50	4 40	7 8	8 45
Lord's Bridge .... ,,	...	7 55	9 52	*	...	2 0	4 50	7 18	8 55
Old North Road ...... ,,	...	8 5	10 1	1143	...	2 10	5 0	7 28	9 6
Gamlingay............ ,,	...	8 15	1010	1153	...	2 19	5 9	7 37	9 17
Potton............ ,,	...	8 21	1016	1158	..	2 24	5 17	7 43	9 25
G. N. Railway.									
Newark............ ,,	...	...	5 28	8 d 0	...	1034	3 12	...	...
Boston .... ,,	...	...	...	7v45	...	9 25	1 10	...	...
Grantham............ ,,	...	...	7 30	9 5	...	11 5	3 5	...	...
Peterborough ...... ,,	...	7 27	9 15	1025	...	1256	4 12	6 36	...
Huntingdon......... ,,	...	7 59	9 45	1057	...	1 28	4 36	6 59	...
St. Neot's............ ,,	...	8 13	9 56	1110	...	1 42	4 47	6 52	...
Sandy............ ..arr	...	8 26	10 8	1125	...	1 57	4 58	7 18	...
Hitchin............dep	...	...	8 45	...	...	1145	4‡8	7 12	...
Biggleswade...... ,,	...	...	9 4	...	...	12 7	4‡26	7 30	...
Sandy .. ..arr	...	...	9 14	...	...	1215	4‡31	7 36	...
Sandy ....dep	...	8 31	1022	12 6	...	2 32	5 24	7 50	9 35
Blunham .... ,,	...	8 36	1027	1211	...	2 37	5 29	7 55	9 40
Willington .... ,,	...	8 41		...	...	2 42	5 34	8 0	9 45
BEDFORD .... ,,	7 20	8 52	1039	1225	...	2 53	5 44	8 10	9 55
Millbrook (Ampthill) ,,	7 32	9 4	1026	1236	...	3 4	5 55	8 21	10 7
Lidlington .... ,,	7 36	9 8	1030	...	...	3 8	5a58	...	1011
Ridgmont .... ,,	7 40	9 12	1035	...	...	3 13	6 3	8 28	1015
Woburn Sands .... ,	7 47	9 19	1042	1249	...	3 21	6 10	8 35	1022
Fenny Stratford ...... ,,	7 53	9 25	1048	...	...	3 27	5b47	...	...
BLETCHLEY ....arr	7 56	9 28	11 0	1256	...	3 30	6 17	8 42	1030
Bletchley ....dep	8 28	1015	1125	2 10	...	3 42	6 55	9 5	1135
OXFORD ....arr	9 35	1125	1210	3 20	...	4 27	8 10	10 0	1245

d dep. 8.8 a.m. Mons. v dep. 8.21 a.m. Mons.
† dep. 3.16 p.m. Weds. s dep. 5 0 p.m. Sats.
§ via Sudbury.

M Mondays only. d Wednesdays only
* Calls to set down or pick up, on notice. ‡ Tues. only. a Dep. 5.45 Sats.
b Dep. 6.2 Sats. e Rail Motor, one class only.

Look out for Evrall's Reliable Furniture, Sewing Machine and Domestic Stores. Inspection invited.
14, St. Ebbe's St., and 19, St. Aldate's, Oxford.
Cash or Weekly Payments taken.

L. B. & S. C. R.—London (Victoria and London Bridge) to Tunbridge Wells.

WEEK-DAYS. / SUNDAYS.

STATIONS.	a m	a m	p m	p m	p m	p m	p m	p m	p m	p m	p m	SUN. a m	SUN. p m	SUN. p m
VICTORIA ...dep	9 10	1115	12 5	1 25	2b25	3 45	...	4 50	...	6 3	8 5	8 50	1 10	7 10
LONDON BRIDGE ,,	9 7	1056	1225	1 40	2a10	...	4 22	...	5 23	6 8	8 10	8 35	1 10	6 53
TUNBRIDGE W.	1049	1225	1 50	3 0	4 b 7	4 50	5 45	6 8	6 46	7 35	9 33	1016	2 45	8 38

L. B. & S. C. R.—From Tunbridge Wells to London (London Bridge and Victoria).

a 2.25 on Saturdays. WEEK-DAYS. / SUNDAYS.

STATIONS	a m	a m	a m	a m	a m	a m	p m	p m	p m	p m	p m	SUN. a m	SUN. a m	SUN. p m
TUNBRIDGE W.	7 20	8 15	8 46	9 22	1045	1110	2 5	3 28	5 0	6 15	8 55	8 32	1148	4 55
LONDON BRIDGE arr	8 50	9 42	10 7	1045	1214	1243	3 36	5 0	6 30	7 46	1047	[illegible]	[illegible]	...
VICTORIA ... ,,	8 48	9 40	1013	1038	...	1225	3 30	4 48	6 22	8 20	1025	[illegible]	[illegible] 30	6 36

b Depart Victoria 2.35 p.m., arrive Tunbridge Wells 3.55 p.m. on Saturdays.

The Railway Guide for the Oxford to Cambridge route with connections for the Great Northern and Great Eastern railways at Sandy and Cambridge.

Ted Evans Collection

The last station to be opened between Oxford and Cambridge, was Willington, in April 1903. Consequently, it typifys the LNWR construction techniques; station buildings of a standard modular type with rusticated weatherboarding, simply erected and ubiquitous on the Company's system. The signal box is of the last design by that Company, introduced in the first few years of the twentieth century, barge boarded with deeply overhanging eaves and large double finial. Greater visibility was obtained from the longer windows. This view of the station, looking north towards Blunham, is deceptive, giving the impression of double track when, in fact, it is the exceptionally long loop that is seen.

John Spencer

CHAPTER SIXTEEN

Willington

'Willington, the new railway station is about completed, the last thing noticable being the fixing of the lamps on the platform giving the name of the station. At first, trains will not stop there except when required. Persons wishing to alight must give notice at the preceding station, and when passengers wish to join the train it will be stopped by signal.' Thus reported the *Bedford Times* of the last station to be opened on the line from Oxford to Cambridge. This was on Friday, 1st May 1903, but a siding had been installed for goods, mainly vegetables, in September 1896. Villagers of Willington had petitioned, without success, for a station when the line opened and by now, as the subsequent halts proved, the railway companies were having to look harder for as much revenue as possible.

Simple modular timber framing and rusticated boarding, beloved of the mass production of Crewe, was Willington's belated acquisition. Solid brick and paved on the 'up' side with timber piling and planking on the 'down'. As the line from Bedford to Sandy was built and remained single, there was an exceptionally long passing loop at the station that went well beyond the station platforms. This was, in fact, extended to facilitate the burden of greater wartime traffic on 3rd August 1916. A short sixteen lever (4 spares) LNWR signal box was installed, of the last design of that Company, known as type 5 and introduced in 1903.

Looking back towards Bletchley, showing the siding that actually preceded the station beyond the platform. The odd change from brick to timber on the platform could well have been due to further extension, as many platforms were extended, especially during World War I. This view is during the 1950s under British Railways ownership. Enamel signs mix with the early LMS 'Hawkseye' board alongside the LNWR oil lamps and delightful gas lamps.

Lens of Sutton

A ground plan of the vegetable siding at Willington in 1900. A platform for the passenger station was added a few years later.

Courtesy of the Ordnance Survey

A mixture of electric train staffs alongside the Webb lever frame. On the left is the Bedford No. 2 to Willington section of the miniature electric train staff, whereas the Willington to Blunham section is of the heavier earlier design of instrumentation.

John Spencer

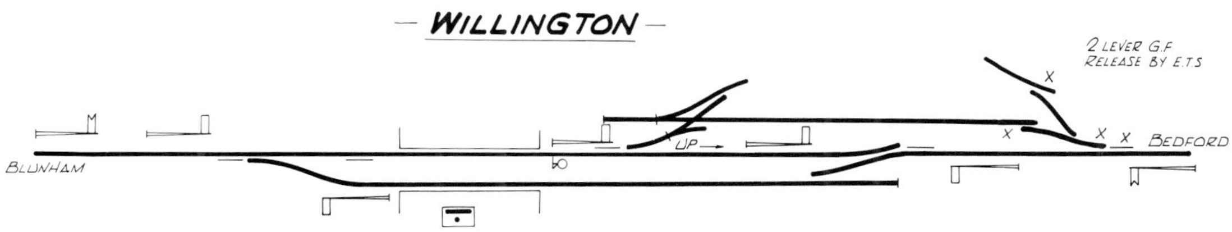

Willington siding and station, in August 1912, when the extraordinary long 'down' loop was put in, as was the timber platform on the side. The siding did, in fact, precede the station by seven years. It was released for use by the electric train staff.

M. Christensen

At Blunham, the first of the apparent standard design for the Bedford & Cambridge/LNWR Joint Committee Station appears. A substantial building of robust brick construction, platformed in Staffordshire paviors with stone edging. The loophole vented windows are in the lavatory block. Together with the matching goods shed, the entire station buildings made a pleasant analogous group. For country stations they were exemplary for their businesslike appearance, if not as picturesque as many. From the outset, there appears to be little compromise to cost. The appearance of two tracks, like Willington, is deceptive, as Blunham also possessed an extremely long passing loop.

Lens of Sutton

CHAPTER SEVENTEEN

Blunham

On a journey from Oxford to Cambridge, Blunham would be the first station where one would encounter the building style of the Bedford & Cambridge Railway, a style which is maintained with variations on each station thenceforth until Cambridge itself. It included strong gables in yellow gault brickwork with red brick dressings and string courses, a uniform arrangement with all the station buildings situated on the 'down' side, with the exception of Potton. The 'up' side had a series of curiously designed wooden shelters. Cursory by contrast, they appeared almost like an afterthought. Uniformity was maintained by the solid brick LNWR goods shed with round-topped louvred windows, a contrast with the Bedford branch where all were standard timber, even Bedford itself. The specification in the building of the later line was looked upon with concern by the local Company who saw the LNWR's influence in controlling the Joint Committee responsible for structures along the line. The Bedford to Sandy single line section is noteworthy in the history of the LNWR for the first introduction of the electric train staff, on 18th March 1888. Staff release instruments were installed on each side of the thirty lever frame in the Blunham signal box.

With longer trains running on the Oxford and Cambridge line, the platforms at Blunham, Gamlingay, Old North Road and Lord's Bridge were lengthened on 17th July 1907, whilst the loops at Blunham and Willington were extended on 3rd August 1916. The new installations included a new passing loop, between the 18 and 18½ mile posts, called Goldington, with its own signal box of thirteen levers and seven spares. This interposed a new staff section that appeared thus:

	Form	*Colour*
Between Bedford and Goldington	Round	Green
Between Goldington and Willington	Round	Blue
Between Willington and Blunham	Round	Red

Goldington loop and its signal box were closed on 7th November 1938 and station loops were extended again during World War II.

This view looks back in the Bedford direction with the goods shed abutting the back of the 'down' platform. It has the same style of signal box as Willington, but is rather longer as thirty levers are housed.

Lens of Sutton

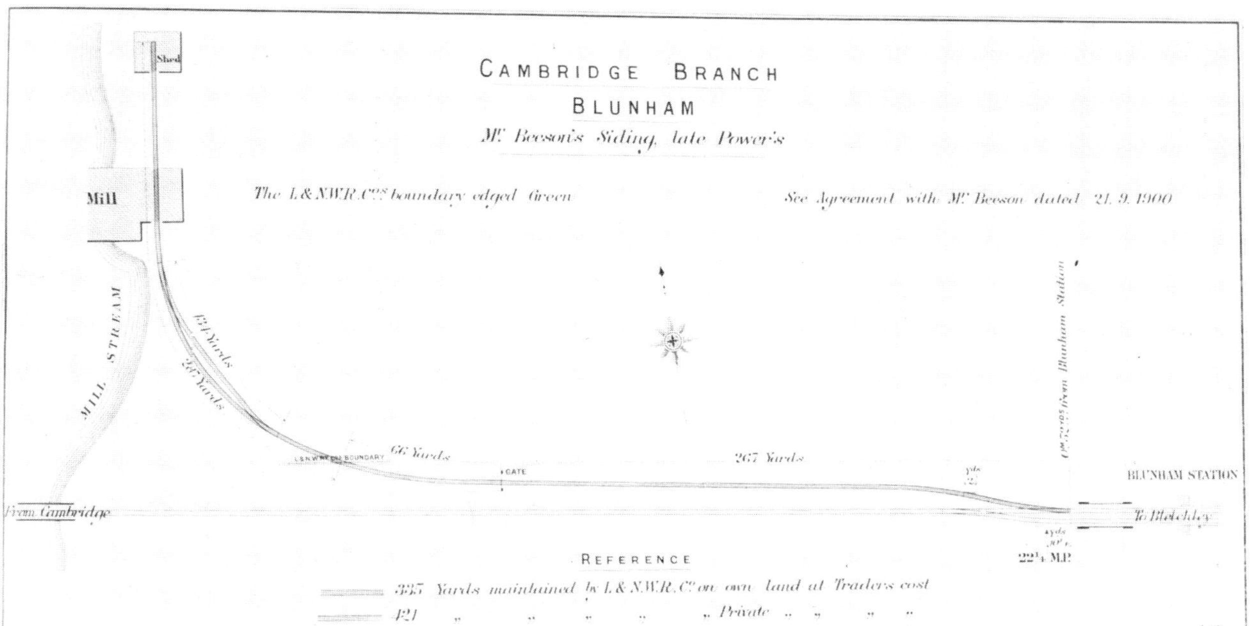

An interesting characteristic of Blunham Station was the long siding heading down to the linseed oil mill situated on the River Ivel. This covered over a third of a mile, to the stop blocks in the shed through a run round loop, and would have provided an interesting spectacle when in operation.

J. Pritchett Collection

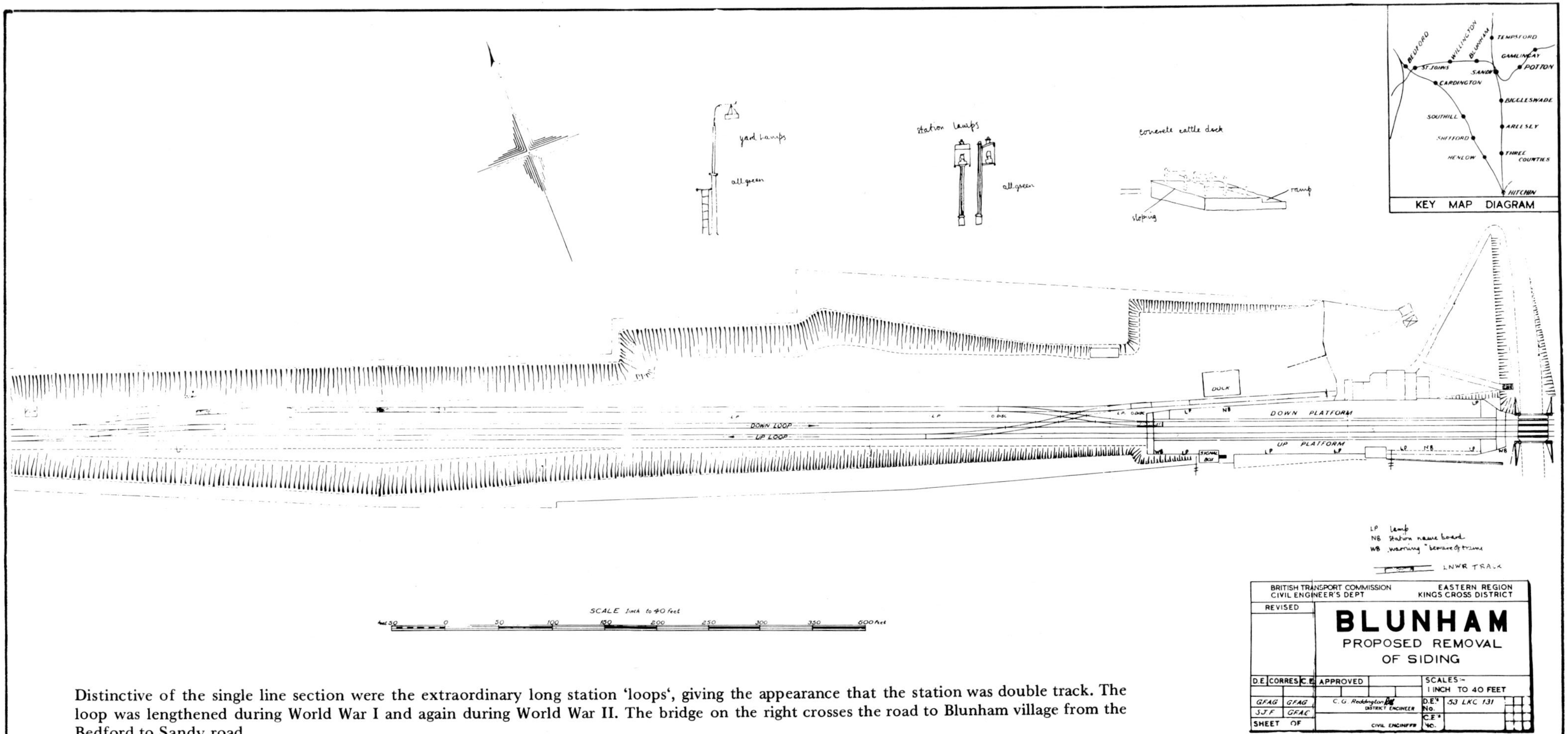

Distinctive of the single line section were the extraordinary long station 'loops', giving the appearance that the station was double track. The loop was lengthened during World War I and again during World War II. The bridge on the right crosses the road to Blunham village from the Bedford to Sandy road.

J. A. Turner

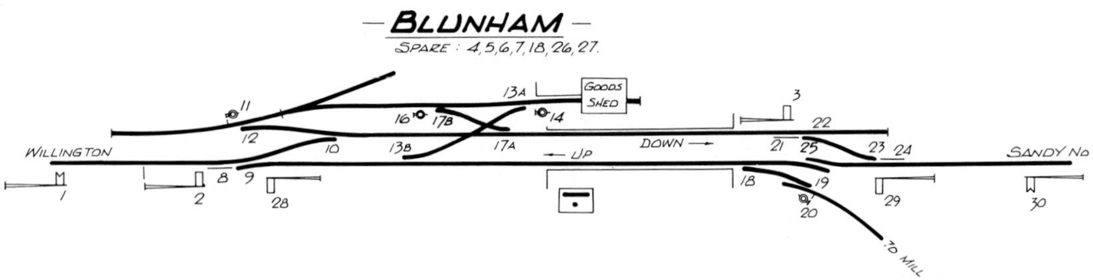

Blunham box, opened in 1879. A layout also with a long loop with the added interesting working of the long siding down to Power's Linseed Oil Mill

The interior of Blunham box. The staff instrument at the end of the frame is for the Blunham to Willington section.
John Spencer

The original lattice girder bridge, over a tributary of the River Ivel, that was strengthened during World War I.
J. R. Rounthwaite

At Sandy, the LNWR met the second neighbouring company since Bletchley; the Great Northern Railway, their celebrated main line from King's Cross reaching York and becoming part of the eventual LNER line to Edinburgh. This view, in the latter Company's days, was taken during the 1930s and shows No. 2750 *Papyrus* northbound with the famous 'Flying Scotsman'. The photograph gives a good indication of the disposition of the stations of both companies, with the GNR station on the right and the LNWR station over on the left, with a glimpse of the goods shed behind the footbridge. Sandy's reputation for well-kept flower beds and shrubberies is clearly justified. It is perhaps the greatest regret of the modern lineside view, that passengers can no longer delight in these highly personal manifestations of horticultural skill that added so much charm to an arrival, and were a palliative of delight for a weary and long journey.

Soole Collection (NRM)

CHAPTER EIGHTEEN

Sandy

Situated upon the alluvial banks of the River Ivel, appropriately named on the edge of the greensand, the town of Sandy developed the market gardening industry from its source spreading east and west. The Sandy to Potton Tramway, of Captain William Peel, had a good purpose in moving produce from his estates near the town to reach the London markets via the newly opened Great Northern Railway of August 1850. With the building of the Bedford & Cambridge Railway, this industry was given much greater support and came to depend, like the brickworks on the Bedford branch, on the railheads. Large amounts of coal to heat the greenhouses, timber for construction, manure from London stables and, perhaps, an even less agreeable cargo, – soot, were transported. Not quite so obvious to fructification were the wagon loads of old clothes used to retain moisture and ploughed into the fickle sandy loam.

Sandy looked like one station, but was, in fact, two, with two station masters until 1917, when the staff and responsibility for the station came under the GNR station master using the booking office on that side. A popular use of the station, by passengers from the university city wishing to go north by the GNR, was to join the train here rather than change stations at Peterborough. That was before the direct route north of Cambridge, via March and Spalding, was opened.

For goods there was an exchange siding between the two railways and their respective yards which, in 1900, handled 200 tons of potatoes. This was at a time when four trains of vegetables per week were going from the GNR yard down to London, whilst daily wagon loads, like those already described, were being taken along the Cambridge branch to Bedford, Bletchley and on to Birmingham and Manchester. From a population in pre-railway days of 1,000, Sandy had almost reached 3,000 by the turn of the century.

To enter the station from Bedford, the trains crossed over

Before reaching the station, the LNWR crossed over the GNR line and ran alongside on a gradient down to the station. This photograph, of 25th May 1935, shows the unusual passenger train loading of three coaches. The last one appears to be a repainted 42 ft. radial of the LNWR and is seen with two LMS non-corridor suburban brake/third and a composite. With a good head of steam, 'Precursor' class No. 5241 *Napoleon* brings the train into Sandy Station. This engine was introduced in March 1906 and withdrawn one year after this photograph was taken. A splendid line up of private owner wagons is held on the LNER line.

L. Hanson

the GN main line by an iron lattice bridge north of the station, an expense that the Bedford & Cambridge Railway would have preferred to have avoided, wishing to cross the main line on a crossing. The LNWR trains rolled down the 1 in 125 descent to the station and surrendered the train staff of the Blunham to Sandy section to Sandy No. 1 box, south of the platform. From that point onwards, the line was double to Cambridge. Here would be the visual delight of much cherished station gardens and platform shrubs that were neatly attended. In inclement weather one could regard, with some satisfaction, the airy glazed canopy and cast-iron columns with decorative quatrefoils and the 'B&C' legend cast into the brackets. Such dignified canopies were bestowed upon Sandy and Potton, the only minor stations to acquire anything like such glazed elegance between Oxford and Cambridge.

In the engineer's survey for the line, it was proposed that the two railways would have a connecting curve joining the lines north of the station which remained, penuriously or otherwise, unrealized. With the outbreak of World War II, this relic was to be swiftly brought into existence at the 23½ mile post and opened on 23rd June 1940. This was in accord with a new connection with the GWR at Oxford and with the LNER at Claydon, plus the restoration of another main line connection at Bletchley which enabled, in an emergency, trains to be diverted round the bomb-damaged rail network in London. The new curve at Sandy received its own box, 'Sandy LNER Junction'. A third Sandy box was situated south of the station and called 'Sandy No. 2'. This operated points and signals at the end of the yard and was sometimes switched out of the block, according to necessity.

Another interesting role for Sandy during World War II was the building of an RAF petrol supply depot at the 27 mile post, about two miles further down the line towards Cambridge. Connecting pipes, together with rail supplies from the outlet at Sandy, were sent to airfields throughout East Anglia. Petrol trains were operated as block trains to keep them out of marshalling yards for obvious reasons. The depot siding at Sandy had its own box called 'Sandy Heath', opened on 4th September 1942, which must have operated to tremendous intensity during the three months following the allied invasion of France in 1944, as 634 trains were distributed from Sandy at the rate of 7 trains each day for the three months.

Until shortly after the war, prodigiously loaded fruit and vegetable trains threaded the area until the effect of road competition was to tighten its grip and slow this traffic to the merest trickle by the 1950s.

During the LNWR period, a familiar 18in. Goods or 'Cauliflower' brings an appreciably well-loaded goods train up the long drag at Sandy to reach the cross-over bridge leading to Blunham and Bedford. The sheeted open wagons were a rather more common practice than is sometimes realized, with box vans being sparingly used.

L&GRP/Courtesy David & Charles

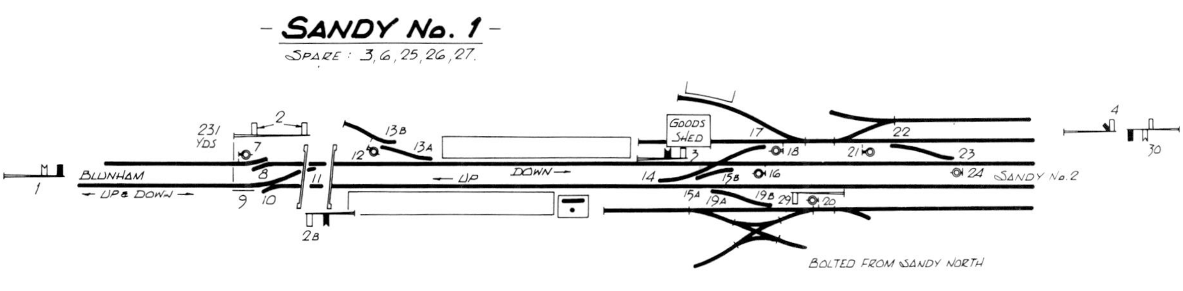

Sandy No. 1 box, controlling the LNWR side of the GNR station. Note the exchange siding points released by electric train staff from the GNR box.

M. Christensen

'Prince of Wales' class, No. 25797 heads a Bletchley to Cambridge train into Sandy LMS Station in the 1930s. The 'up' and 'down' lines operated as a loop as the line was single on the crossing bridge.

Soole Collection/NRM

The crossing of the GNR by the LNWR as seen from a rather more unusual angle, as a southbound coal train, hauled by a 2-8-0 Class O1 2 cylinder locomotive, (which were usually called 'Tangos'), passes below the crossing bridge. Of particular note are the LNWR signals above, that protect the public road crossing on the line at Sandy crossing. The roof of the keeper's house can also be seen. The siding alongside the engine and the road bridge both lead to Sandy Brickworks. This photograph is of the mid-1930 period.

Soole Collection (NRM)

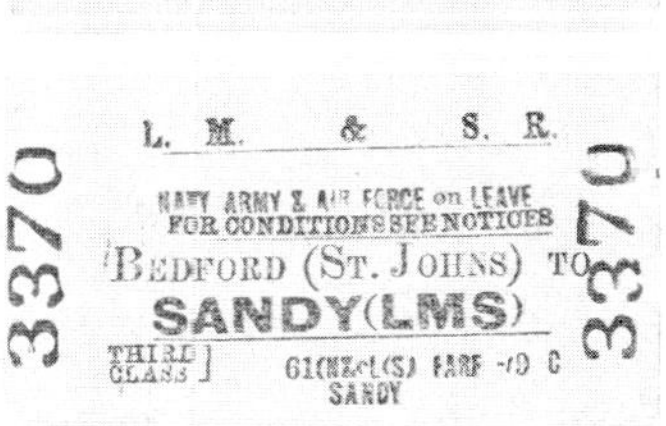

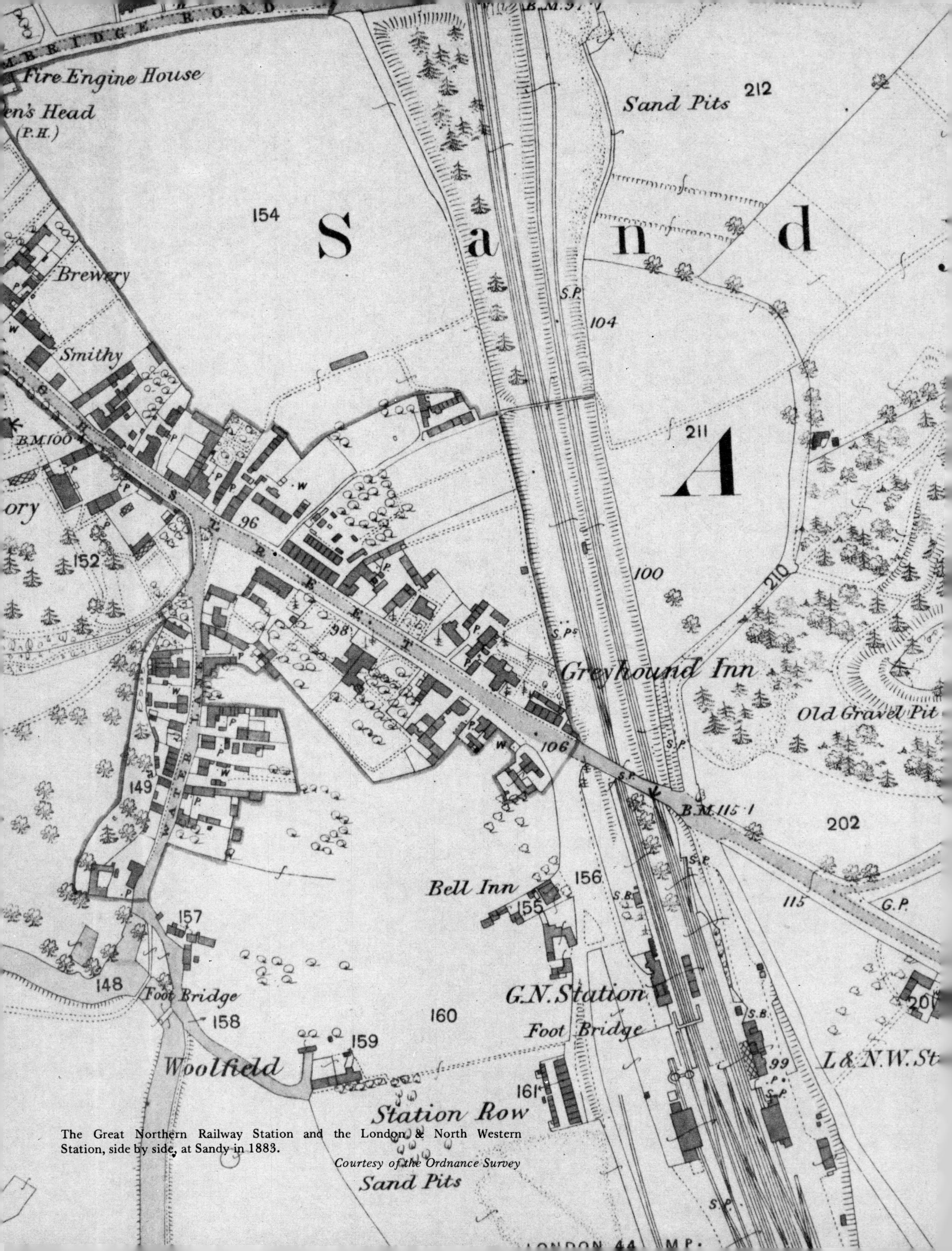

The Great Northern Railway Station and the London & North Western Station, side by side, at Sandy in 1883.

Courtesy of the Ordnance Survey

LNWR platforms Nos. 3 and 4 with that Company's style of signal box. Cast-iron and glazed canopies at Sandy and Potton bring an ornamental touch to the otherwise plain buildings at these two stations.

Lens of Sutton

Modest by proportion but might by endeavour, a member of the celebrated 'George the Fifth' class works out its twilight days on the Oxford to Cambridge route. This engine *Daschund*, or as latterly named *Bulldog*, (No. 956; LMS No. 5340) would probably have little difficulty with this unit from the Bletchley 'set', with additional full brakes, on the climb from Sandy to Blunham. Feats by this class of locomotive, with more than four hundred ton trains, on the main line, became legend. The probable date of this photograph is the early 1930s.

Lens of Sutton

An excellent standard shot of the situation between the two companies at the south end of the station. The 'Queen of Scots' Pullman is obviously in the charge of an Ivatt Atlantic. The Great Northern goods shed is situated on the right, with just a little of the LNWR goods shed being visible over the roof of the signal box on the left. Between them, are the connecting lines over which much traffic was interchanged. Upper quadrant signals have displaced some somersault signals on the, now, LNER lines, whilst a surviving LNWR lower quadrant, nods approval for a 'Prince of Wales' to bring on its goods train. In the misty distance, the hipped roof of Sandy No. 2 box, which controlled the entrance and usage of the goods yard, can be seen. Its opposite co-ordinator, on the GNR side, can be seen just behind the last car of the train.

Soole Collection (NRM)

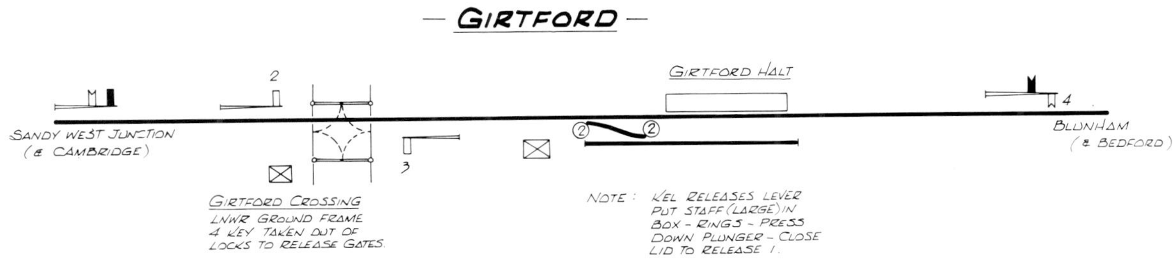

An interesting arrangement close together; the crossing and the vegetable siding at Girtford. The former dates from the opening of the line, whereas the halt's short life commenced in 1938.

M. Christensen

An oddity of the line was the introduction, in 1938, of this short platform called Girtford Halt, at the 23¼ mile post. A short life, even by 'halt' standards, for with the outbreak of war, the halt was subsequently closed in 1940. The gentleman on the platform, Mr G. Webb, an accomplished local railway historian, is not expecting a train to stop, as the photograph was taken by a local railway photographer when the halt was derelict.

J. R. Rounthwaite

Potton No. 1 box which replaced the original Saxby type box first used *(see photograph on facing page)*.
J. Waldock

Potton Station in the mid-1950s. Reconstruction of the 'down' platform, with its curiously-styled timber shelter, can clearly be seen.
Author's Collection

Potton Station and staff, circa 1900, photographed from the 'down' platform. An interesting point in this photograph is the early signal box on the platform. This is one of the Saxby type 2 standard boxes built for the LNWR. This could well be the pattern for the earliest boxes on the line, which were built before the absolute block system was introduced in 1880.

L. Impey

CHAPTER NINETEEN

Potton

Potton's first railway was, of course, the Sandy & Potton Tramway which closed with the building of the Bedford & Cambridge line in 1861. The settlement of Bedford workers in Potton had increased the tiny village into a considerable community of 2,000 people by that year.

Beside the merchandising of coal and vegetables, Potton also had two soot landings in the yard for handling considerable tonnages of this commodity from London, Liverpool, Manchester and Sheffield.

Fortunately, by courtesy of Mr George Howe, a number of old waybills and invoices have been discovered concerning transactions carried out by the first station master of Potton, Mr. Wilson, between 1864 and 1866. They give an interesting insight of the day to day transactions of the time.

In August 1864, large consignments of cucumbers left for London, whilst apples and onions were sent to Preston at £1 15s 10d (£1.79) per ton and £1 1s 0d (£1.05) per ton respectively. In September, grain was sent to Luddendenfoot, in Yorkshire, whilst potatoes were sent to Leamington at 13s 4d (67p) per ton. November and December saw potatoes and onions leave Potton for Norwich and Bolton at 14s 2d (71p) per ton from station to station. All the aforementioned vegetables show the heaviest tonnages from Potton with sundry other vegetables in smaller loads. A cargo that was quite unique to the area was a material called 'coprolites' which appears to be a fossilized dung that was found in appreciable amounts near the surface, on three sites between Sandy and Potton. The fructal qualities of this material appear to have caused its demand from as far away as Newcastle upon Tyne to Market Harborough, Ipswich and West Bromwich. One contract, for Wolverhampton, was for 1,500 tons at 9s 2d (46p) per ton .

Amongst traffic received, in addition to the aforementioned soot, were the very large consignments of manure for growers and farmers. Much of this came from London stables and an esoteric amount from London Zoo. One farmer, Mr Blundell, received 8 tons 19 cwt 1 qtr on 13th September 1862, speedily taking advantage of the new railway. A local draper received trusses of trousers and other cloths from Bolton, Bradford and Manchester (London Road), whilst the local ironmonger received seven shovels and boxes of nails from Wolverhampton, with stoves and seventy bundles of iron and steel from Birmingham. The same day the local builder received twenty six ridge tiles.

Pride of Potton Station is the cast-iron canopy, a distinction shared with Sandy, which no other small station, between Oxford and Cambridge, can claim. A little of the lattice footbridge can be seen on the right and behind that, the larger water tank house, the only locomotive supply between Sandy and Cambridge.

Lens of Sutton

Four licencees received their ale from Allsopp's of Burton. Coal for Mr Robert was brought from Atherstone, Coalbrookdale, Springs Branch (Wigan), Shipley, Notts. via the Midland and Doncaster via the GN at Sandy. Consignments were entered in monthly tonnages and arrived along three Company routes. The first month of the line's opening saw 97 tons 1 cwt delivered to Potton from Bedford LNWR whilst the Midland supplied 53 tons 10 cwt and the GN, via Sandy, 19 tons 14 cwt. The use of coal for heating greenhouses would maintain some of the demand. The highest tonnage came in the following November with 181 tons 19 cwt, 175 tons 4 cwt and 45 tons 16 cwt respectively.

Facing the coal wharfs, Beart's Brick Company had a siding for a large sand-pit. It was situated 312 yards from the station in the Gamlingay direction on the 'down' side. This was opened in October 1870 and it is possible that the sand was used for facing the bricks.

With the drastic changes in material handling, the mundane sack in coarse brown jute, belonging to the world of the plodding dray horse and village carrier, had faded from the scene. Produced in enormous quantities, they became, themselves, a source of business with large sack hire depots at Northampton (LNWR) dispersing variable quantities to stations in the area. The Potton station master was instructed to put up a placard advertising sack hire. The use of this service can be clearly illustrated by a letter that he received from Sutton village, nearby, on 12th October 1866.

> 'Dear Mr Wilson,
>
> My team will be at Potton Station tomorrow morning the 13th with some barley. I want 90 more sacks to fill with barley. Will you oblige me with that number of sacks tomorrow morning.
>
> Yours truly,
>
> William E. Masters'

It appears that operating as goods agent and station master, Mr Wilson had plenty to occupy his waking hours at Potton Station.

From the point of view of the locomen, Potton also had a special significance as it was the only station between Sandy and Cambridge where they could top up the water tanks. The container on top of the water tank house was economically replenished by a natural well in the station master's garden. A steam pump, operated by a member of the station staff, would bring the water up.

A view towards Gamlingay and Cambridge, from the Potton platform. Some of the delicacy of the cast iron-work in the brackets can clearly be seen.

Lens of Sutton

A smartly turned out new wagon for James Abbot. Unfortunately, the builder's sign 'Built by W. Rigley & Sons Ltd., Bulwell, Notts.' does not venture to the point of the highly praiseworthy distinction of the Gloucester Carriage & Wagon Co., by including details of the colour scheme. We are, therefore, left with the insoluble tones of a black and white photograph to ponder on what it may have been.

G. Howe

A view of *Shannon's* original home, the engine house of the Sandy & Potton Tramway, now used as a vegetable store. Though bricked in, the archway is clearly visible.

Author's Collection

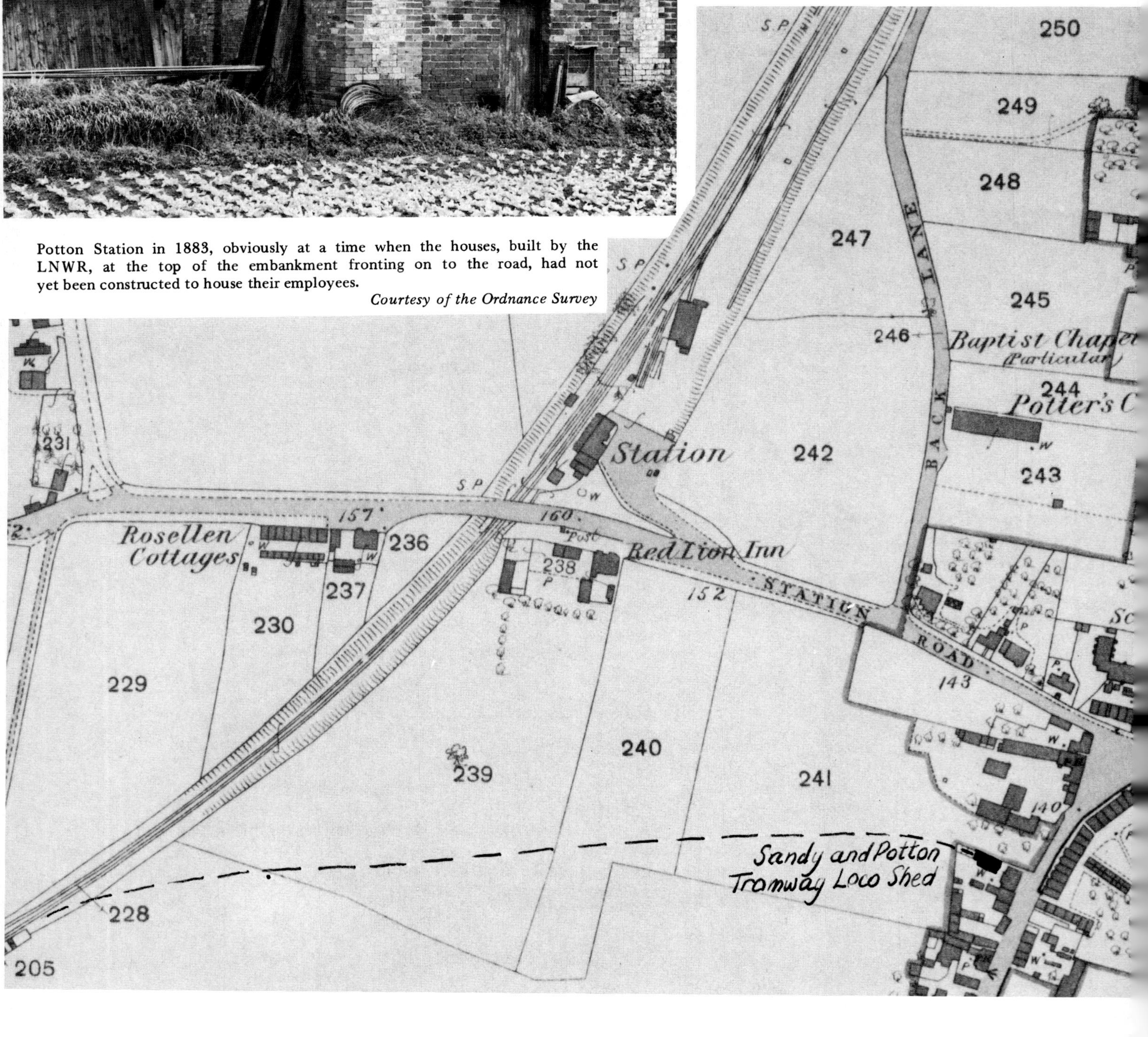

Potton Station in 1883, obviously at a time when the houses, built by the LNWR, at the top of the embankment fronting on to the road, had not yet been constructed to house their employees.

Courtesy of the Ordnance Survey

A side view of the building that has obviously received a different roof from that originally constructed. The yellow gault and dressing of red brick is still distinctive and must have looked very pleasing to the eye when the building was new.

Author's Collection

Whatever else may be said of the 0-4-0WT *Shannon*, she has certainly had a long, eventful, wayward and providential life. Her good fortune did not run out as it so often did for many locomotives, as she was rescued, firstly, by the GWR in 1946, after being withdrawn from service, and placed on a plinth at Wantage Road Station. With the closure of that station, she was rescued, yet again, and restored to steam by the noble efforts of the Great Western Society at Didcot. I think that it is fair to say that their efforts have retained, for all to see, a unique and priceless representative of the early days of railways.

It was something of a golden beginning for *Shannon*, named after the frigate commanded by Captain William Peel, builder of the Sandy & Potton Railway. The opening day of this little railway, of just over three miles in length, was during a glorious heat wave, with jubilant crowds and celebrations thronging the Bedfordshire town of Potton from sunrise to sunset. Hauling the celebratory first train was *Shannon*, newly purchased from George England & Co., Hatcham Ironworks, New Cross, London, for £800 and she inspired words of admiration from the assembled populus.

From the eventful day, in 1857, life was to be rather more mundane, but variable. Service on the Sandy & Potton Railway was not destined to be a long vocation for, as the text describes, the small line was overtaken by the much more ambitious Bedford & Cambridge Railway, and was therefore closed down in 1961. *Shannon* was bought by the larger company and sold to the contractor for the line, Joseph Firbank, to work on construction. A second locomotive from the same builders, a 2-2-2 engine named *Little England*, and older than *Shannon* by six years, also took up its labours on the building of this line.

With the opening of the Bedford & Cambridge Railway, the fortunes of *Little England* are not certain but *Shannon* passed into LNWR ownership and was anonymously numbered 1104 and later 1863 in the duplicate list. She was then put to work on the tortuous Cromford & High Peak Railway, in August 1863. From the Derbyshire peaks, she was brought into Works service at Crewe, which must have been, for her, a very contrasting role. Ensconced within the milieu of construction she may well have worn out her days, had it not been for another completely different occupation. This was to work just under 3 miles of line from Wantage Road (GWR) to Wantage Town; The Wantage Tramway. For that employment she was sold for £365 in May 1878, to surroundings not dissimilar to those in which she had first served, along a short length of railway. For the Wantage Tramway, she was No. 5, and known, unofficially, as *Jane*.

After the closure of the Wantage Tramway, in 1945, the GWR purchased the engine for £100, restoring it and placing it in its monumental position at Wantage Road Station. From there, she was rescued, as mentioned earlier, by the GWR Society and in 1975 must have felt, if engines feel anything at all, as if reliving that golden beginning, senior in years but smallest in stature, she steamed amongst giants in bright sunshine at the Shildon Cavalcade which celebrated the 150th anniversary of the first public passenger railway; The Stockton & Darlington Railway.

Obvious alterations from her earlier days are the buffers that stand proud of their beam to meet the standard height requirements, and the addition of a cab which would certainly not have been on the engine originally.

Author's Collection

The hatted and the hatless Potton Station staff, in 1920, assembled with Mr James Sinfield, station master of that time. There is an odd feeling of two different periods between the men standing and those sitting. Those pictured are: (back row) left to right: David Whitfield, signalman; Arthur Munns, goods checker; Herbert Waldock, goods porter; Arthur Quiney, signalman; Bert Hill, signalman; Fred Wilson, goods foreman; Albert Clerk, drayman; (front row) left to right: Jack Webb, goods clerk; Mr Barker, chief clerk; James Sinfield, station master; Alec Baker, passenger clerk; and Emmlyn Powwell, goods clerk.

J. Webb

The Potton staff, photographed about 15 years later, in the 1930s. Noticeably, less staff is required which reflects the changing nature of railway employment since before World War I. With LMS ownership came the famous 'Hawkseye' board which can be seen behind the group. Station master A. Cullam, this time wearing a peaked cap, is seated second from the right alongside J. Webb who is pacifying the station dog. On the back row, from left to right: John Page, clerk/relief signalman; Jack Gilman, passenger clerk; and on the front row, from left to right: Jack Twelves, signalman; Jack Webb, goods clerk; A. Cullam, station master and Bert Hill, signalman.

B. Hill

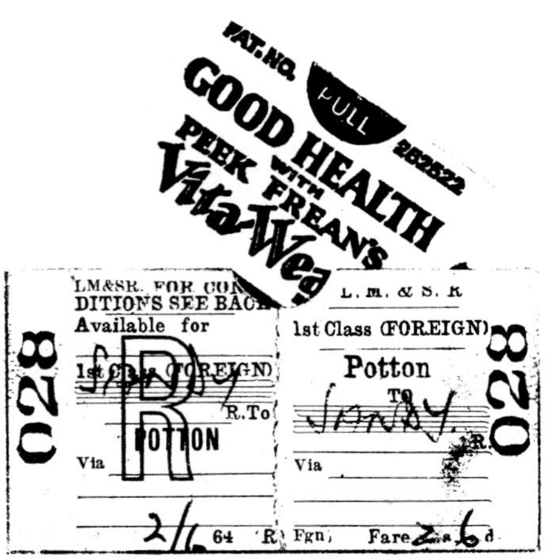

The entrance to Potton Station, a few years before the passenger service ceased. There is a mild polychromatic quality in the stone dressings and variegated string courses. Straight and round-topped windows, with louvred ventilators, provide a variety of angled shapes.

John Spencer

Cast into the ironwork, the legend of the Bedford & Cambridge Railway is evident one hundred and twenty years later.

Author's Collection

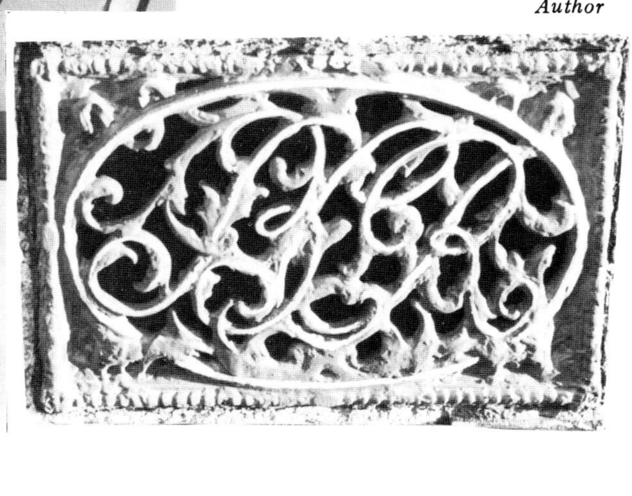

An example of the finesse of the buildings on the Bedford & Cambridge line. Even a small ventilation grille carries the legend 'BCR', cast in script letters.

Author

A view towards Sandy at Potton. On the platform is the familiar LNWR type 4 box, whilst on the roadway above, to the right, are cottages built by the LNWR for their employees working at the station.

Lens of Sutton

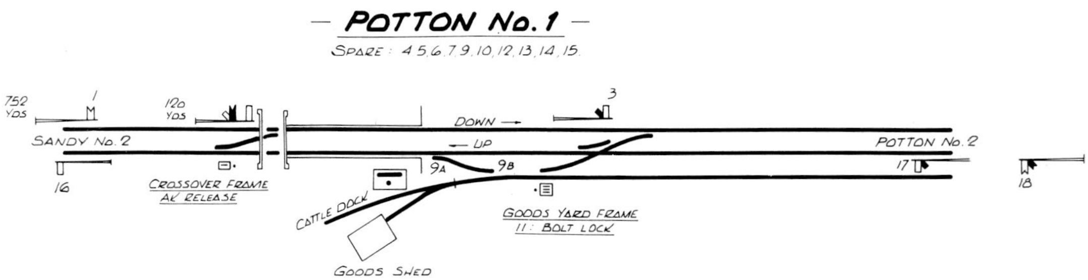

Potton No. 1 yard and crossover road for the 'up' and 'down' lines. The ground frame bolt was unlocked from No. 1 signal box.

M. Christensen

British Railways Board

PUBLIC NOTICE

Transport Act — 1962

Withdrawal of Railway Passenger Services

The Eastern, London Midland and Western Regions of British Railways hereby give notice in accordance with Section 56(7) of the Transport Act, 1962, that they propose to discontinue all railway passenger services between OXFORD and CAMBRIDGE (and from the following stations):—

ISLIP
BICESTER (LONDON ROAD)
LAUNTON
MARSH GIBBON & POUNDON
CLAYDON
VERNEY JUNCTION
WINSLOW
SWANBOURNE
FENNY STRATFORD
BOW BRICKHILL
WOBURN SANDS
ASPLEY GUISE
RIDGMONT
LIDLINGTON
MILLBROOK
STEWARTBY
KEMPSTON HARDWICK
BEDFORD ST. JOHN'S
WILLINGTON
BLUNHAM
POTTON
GAMLINGAY
OLD NORTH ROAD
LORD'S BRIDGE

It appears to the Board that the following alternative services will be available:—

Existing services by road

Bus Operator	Route No.	Serving
Premier Travel Ltd.	1	Cambridge—Lord's Bridge
Premier Travel Ltd. / Percival's Motors Ltd.	39	Cambridge—Oxford
Eastern Counties Omnibus Co. Ltd.	118	Cambridge—Lord's Bridge—Old North Road
	119 120	Cambridge—Lord's Bridge
Associated Motorways	4A 26 26A	Cambridge—Bedford
United Counties Omnibus Co. Ltd.	63 140 142	Bedford—Kempston Hardwick
	128	Cambridge—Bedford
	141	Blunham—Bedford—Kempston Hardwick—Ridgmont—Aspley Guise—Woburn Sands
	158	Bedford—Stewartby—Marston Moretaine (for Millbrook)
	159	Bedford—Marston Moretaine (for Millbrook)
	160	Bedford—Woburn Sands—Bow Brickhill—Fenny Stratford—Bletchley
	161	Bedford—Stewartby—Marston Moretaine (for Millbrook)—Lidlington—Ridgmont
	162	Bedford—Stewartby—Marston Moretaine (for Millbrook)—Lidlington
	175	Cambridge—Lord's Bridge
	176	Sandy—Willington—Bedford
	177	Willington—Bedford
	181	Bedford—Marston Moretaine (for Millbrook)—Lidlington
	190 195	Gamlingay—Potton
	194	Gamlingay—Potton—Sandy—Willington—Bedford
	66 166 376 386 387 394 395 396 397 398	Fenny Stratford—Bletchley (Bletchley Town Services)
	346	Winslow—Padbury—Buckingham
	377	Fenny Stratford—Bletchley—Swanbourne—Winslow
United Counties Omnibus Co. Ltd. 131 / City of Oxford Motor Services Ltd. 70	joint service	Bedford—Buckingham—Bicester—Islip—Oxford
City of Oxford Motor Services Ltd.	98 102	Marsh Gibbon—Launton—Bicester
	96 97	Bicester—Oxford
Red Rover Omnibus	—	Winslow—Padbury—Buckingham
Charlton-on-Otmoor Services	—	Bicester—Islip—Oxford

Additional services proposed

The existing alternative road services as shown above are being reviewed and the introduction of "limited stop" services in certain areas at present served by the rail passenger trains s also being investigated.

Any users of the rail service which it is proposed to discontinue and any body representing such users may lodge an objection in writing within six weeks of 20th February 1964 i.e., not later than 3rd April 1964, addressing the objection to:—

The Secretary, Transport Users Consultative Committee for the East Midlands Area, 44 Friar Gate, Derby
if the objection relates to closure in the Counties of Oxfordshire and/or Buckinghamshire

or

The Secretary, Transport Users Consultative Committee for the East Anglia Area, 47 Glisson Road, Cambridge
if the objection relates to closure in the Counties of Bedfordshire and/or Cambridgeshire.

If any such objection is lodged the service cannot be discontinued until the Transport Users Consultative Committee has considered the objections and reported to the Minister of Transport, and the Minister has given his consent to the closure under Section 56(8) of the Transport Act, 1962.

The Committee may hold a meeting to hear objections. Such a meeting will be held in public and any persons who have lodged an objection in writing may also make oral representations to the Committee, if they so wish.

If no objections are lodged to the proposal the service will be discontinued on 15th June 1964.

PUBLISHED BY BRITISH RAILWAYS (LONDON MIDLAND REGION)
STAFFORD & CO. LTD., NETHERFIELD, NOTTINGHAM

THE SANDY & POTTON

to help preserve a line for steam operation in the South-East Midlands

Enquiries to the Membership Secretary, c/o Barclays Bank Limited, 2 High Street, Sandy, Bedfordshire

or

The Membership Secretary, Junior Section, 24 Hazel Grove, Stotfold, Hitchin, Herts.

THE SANDY & POTTON STEAM RAILWAY SOCIETY

The Bedford to Bletchley Rail Users' Association

Since 1846 the Railway line between Bedford and Bletchley has served well the thousands of shoppers, schoolchildren, workers etc. living along its 16 mile route.

Since 1959 this service has repeatedly been under threat of closure, and is now again in desperate need of investment and promotion.

The BEDFORD TO BLETCHLEY RAIL USERS' ASSOCIATION has been formed to help co-ordinate improvement and promotion of this vital rail link and thus secure its retention for the future.

If you are a regular user of this service or in agreement with the aims of the Association, please join us without delay. We can only make progress to help secure a future for this rail service by having a large, growing membership. All members receive 4 copies of the Association's Newsletter each year.

Three examples of historical publications that reflect the conflicts described in the final chapter of this book. A Beeching closure notice; a brave attempt to retain and restore a section of the line at Potton, and a handbill publicizing the resolute and tireless efforts of the BBRU to keep the trains running and, more importantly, well used.

A distant view of Potton, at Potton No. 2 box. A type 4 box controlling the yard at Potton.

R. Powell

This sunlit view, looking towards Bedford, was taken around 1900 as three yardmen pause in their work in the doorway of the goods shed. Behind them, a wisp of smoke denotes that the steam pump, for bringing water from a well in the station master's garden, is working at its task beneath the water tank. The unmistakable height of an LNWR signal is clearly seen above the bridge and housetop, in its position controlling access to the station. The cottages, themselves, are of a standard type built for LNWR employees.

Mrs Cox

The view towards Cambridge, at Gamlingay, in LNWR days, possibly just before World War I. Trees in summer fullness, the ivy-fronted brickwork of the station buildings and a few milk churns, reflect the distinctly rural feeling of the line once beyond the township of Potton.
National Monuments Records

CHAPTER TWENTY

Gamlingay

From Potton onwards to Cambridge, the line takes on a distinct rural character, the stations being more openly spaced and sidings far fewer. Gamlingay is the first of these with its small village in open surroundings. It is situated shortly before the two mile climb of 1 in 150 to Hayley Wood.

Just before the 30 mile post on the Potton side, a brick siding was opened in 1870 called Dennis's Brick Siding. Points trailing from the 'up' side crossed the 'down' and through a gate on to the site. The arrangement had its own signal box on the 'up' side. This box retained its name although the siding itself passed through different ownership, eventually becoming known as Belle Vue Brickworks Siding by January 1909 and lasting until 20th April 1936.

A glance back towards Bedford, over half a century later, in August 1966. Gamlingay is little changed, save for the LMS and British Railway signs, apart from being, perhaps, a little overgrown. Note the LNWR oil lamps still in use and fixed to cast-iron fluted columns. One lamp has been detached and placed on the ground near to its column, by the sign in the foreground.

John Spencer

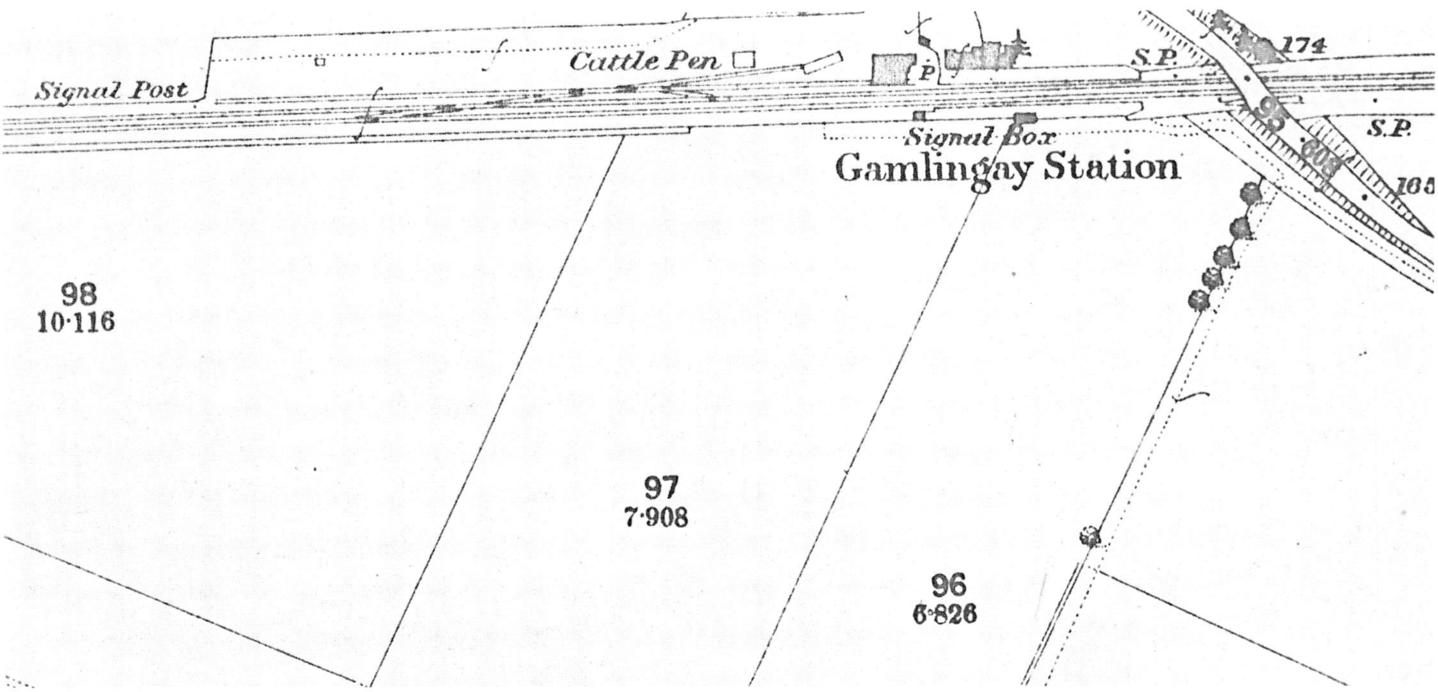

A ground plan of Gamlingay Station in 1900.

Courtesy of the Ordnance Survey

From the 'down' platform, a good view is seen of the all-timber and slate shelter on the 'up' side. Note the change of platform edging which suggests a probable extension, or replacement, of the timber of an early platform.

Lens of Sutton

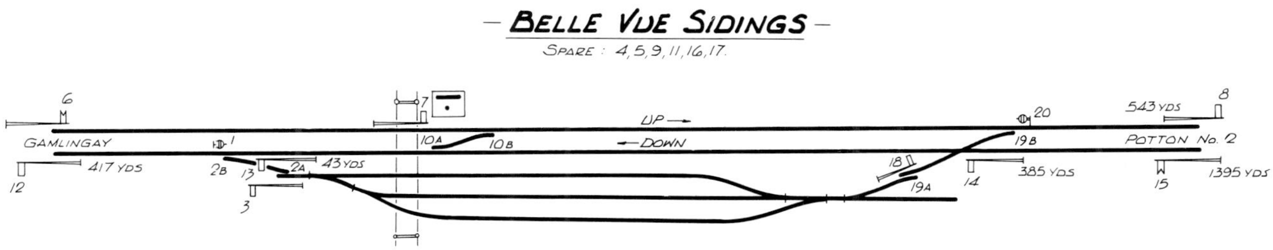

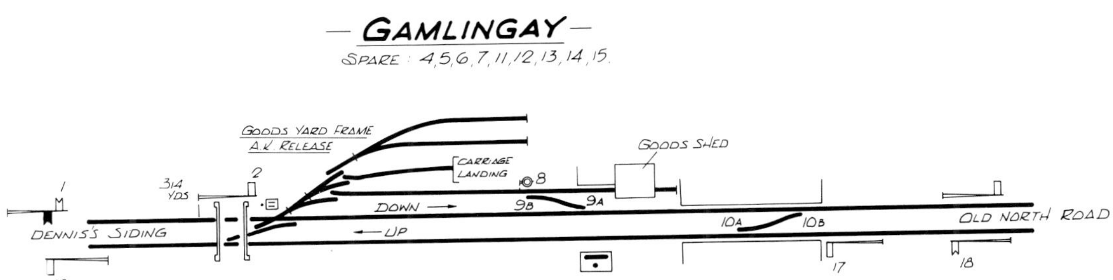

A Gamlingay diagram with the Annett's key release for the use of the sidings.

M. Christensen

Ivy-veined station buildings at Old North Road in 1900. A line of staff assemble in order of height and probable status. The station master, with buttonhole, imposes a slightly greater distance between himself and those in his charge. Of particular interest is the small hut situated on the site of the eventual lever frame signal box. This would have contained train indication instruments but all points and signals must, at that time, have been operated in the open.

Cambridge Libraries

The station, seen from beneath the Old North Road bridge, in August 1966. The platform was rebuilt sometime during the 1940s. Note the oil lamp above the gradient post, which is an obvious reminder of the long climb, (see gradient profile), to Hayley Wood in the Bedford direction.

John Spencer

A rather more animated view, in LNWR days, at Old North Road, as a 'Precursor' calls with a loose-coupled freight. It is likely that the train's eventual destination would be Bletchley.

National Monuments Records

CHAPTER TWENTY-ONE

Old North Road

The Old North Road Station stands alongside its namesake that recalls the antiquity of a time when this road was the principal northern route compared to the present Great North Road or A1.

A siding from the 'down' line had a ground frame that was operated by Annett's key from the signal box. A siding nearly half-way between Old North Road and Lord's Bridge was opened on 24th July 1911 and at first was called Toft Siding, after the nearby village. It later took another village name and became known, in 1912, as Toft & Kingston Siding. This siding handled a great deal of sugar beet and hay and during World War II a large quantity of timber. The key to unlock this siding was, in fact, issued from Lord's Bridge signal box.

Flowers, shrubs and herbaceous borders tended by the signalmen and other members of the station staff. A wishing well, behind the gas lamp, completes this display, in the summer of 1966. A comparitively recent reminder of the gentle art of ageing stations.

John Spencer

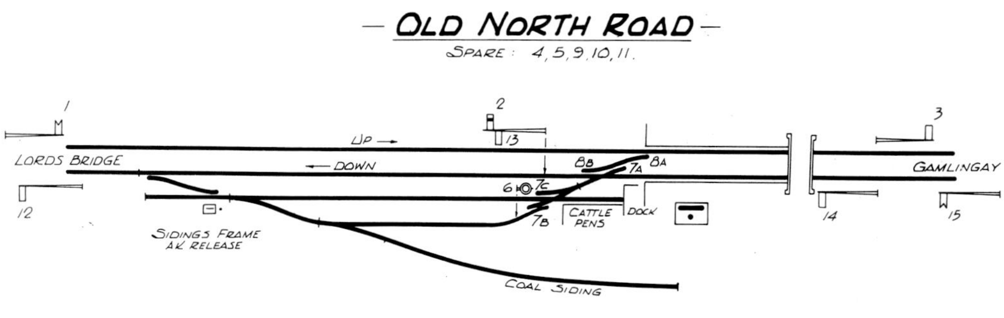

An Old North Road signalling diagram.

M. Christensen

A neat group of buildings, seen from the station approach, in March 1965, with the goods shed on the left. The type 5 LNWR signal box and station entrance under the canopied doorway are on the right.

R. Powell

Old Road North Station in 1883, looking little different from its appearance at the time of its closure.

Courtesy of the Ordnance Survey

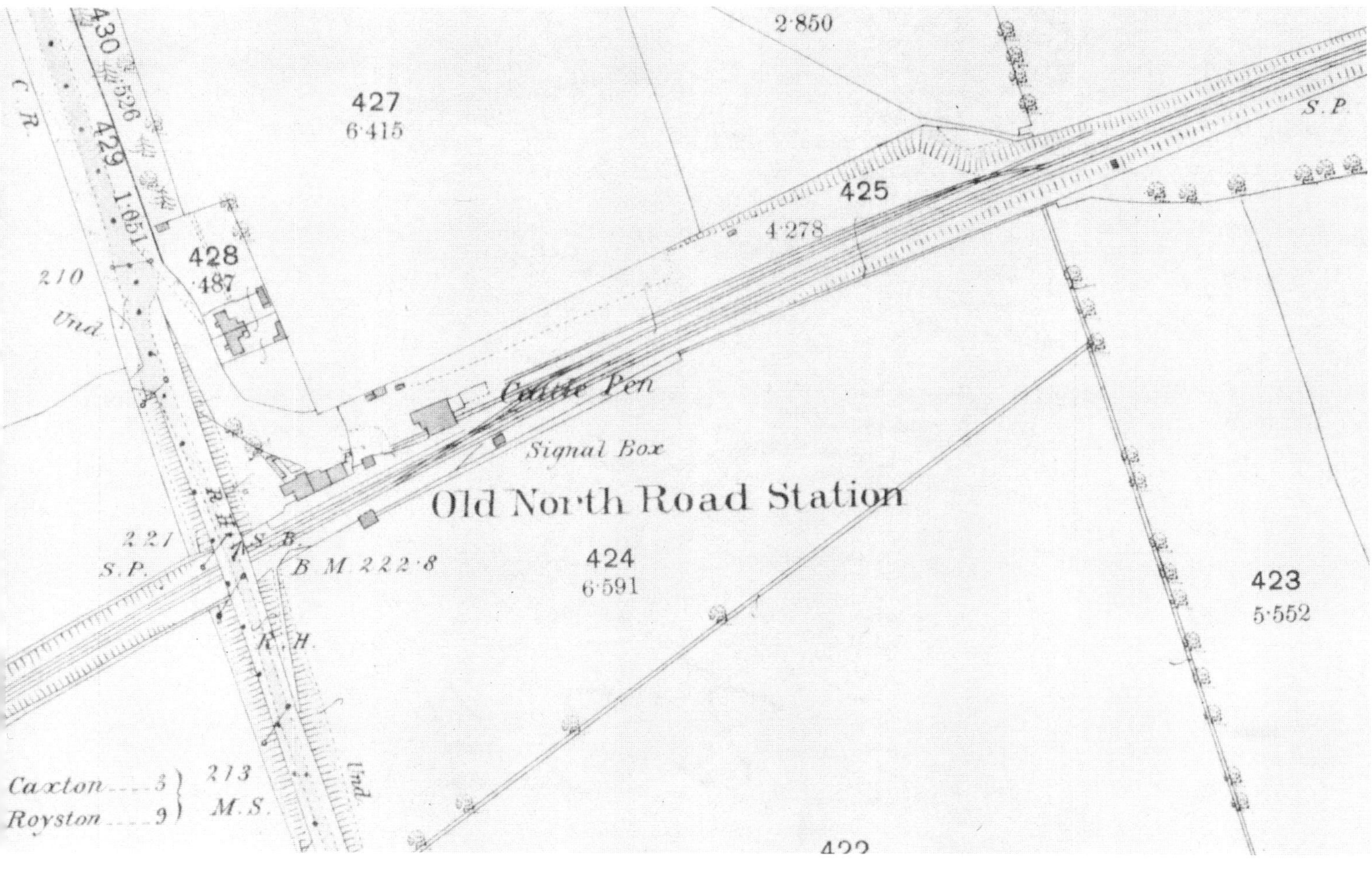

Eager to be off, this 'Precursor' pauses at Lord's Bridge with a Cambridge to Oxford passenger train, circa 1920. Tall trees against wide open skies, typify the Cambridgeshire landscape.

National Monuments Records

Lord's Bridge in the winter snow of 1902. There is an interesting comparison between the neighbouring stations of Lord's Bridge and Old North Road with the LNWR type 4 signal box situated between the station buildings and the goods shed. This was likely to have replaced a signalman's hut shortly after 'block' working was introduced on the line. The eventual box at Old North Road became a later version of type 5, introduced after 1904.

Cambridge Libraries

CHAPTER TWENTY-TWO

Lord's Bridge

Lord's Bridge Station is situated in the flat open Cambridgeshire countryside, almost at the 41 mile post, with a sprinkling of small villages around. Its yard siding was released by key from the signal box. An interesting user of this siding, during the 1920s, was the station porter who had entrepreneurial abilities by continuously adding to his collection of orchards. Railwaymen are traditionally associated with allotments and horticultural activities, but this employee expanded his interests until he owned a considerable acreage. This created the novel situation of the station master enquiring of his subordinate each week as to how many wagons he would require for fruit in the following week.

By the outbreak of World War II, the station was dealing with trains very much in contrast as they handled the live ammunition of the RAF in their sidings with the ex-Midland tank engines moving them respectfully on and off the site.

Between Cambridge and Lord's Bridge, this 4-6-0 'Experiment' class steps out with an 'up' fitted freight towards Bedford and Bletchley, during the 1930s.

Soole Collection (NRM)

Lord' Bridge Station in 1883. Note the two small signal boxes that were replaced by the type 4 structure.

Courtesy of the Ordnance Survey

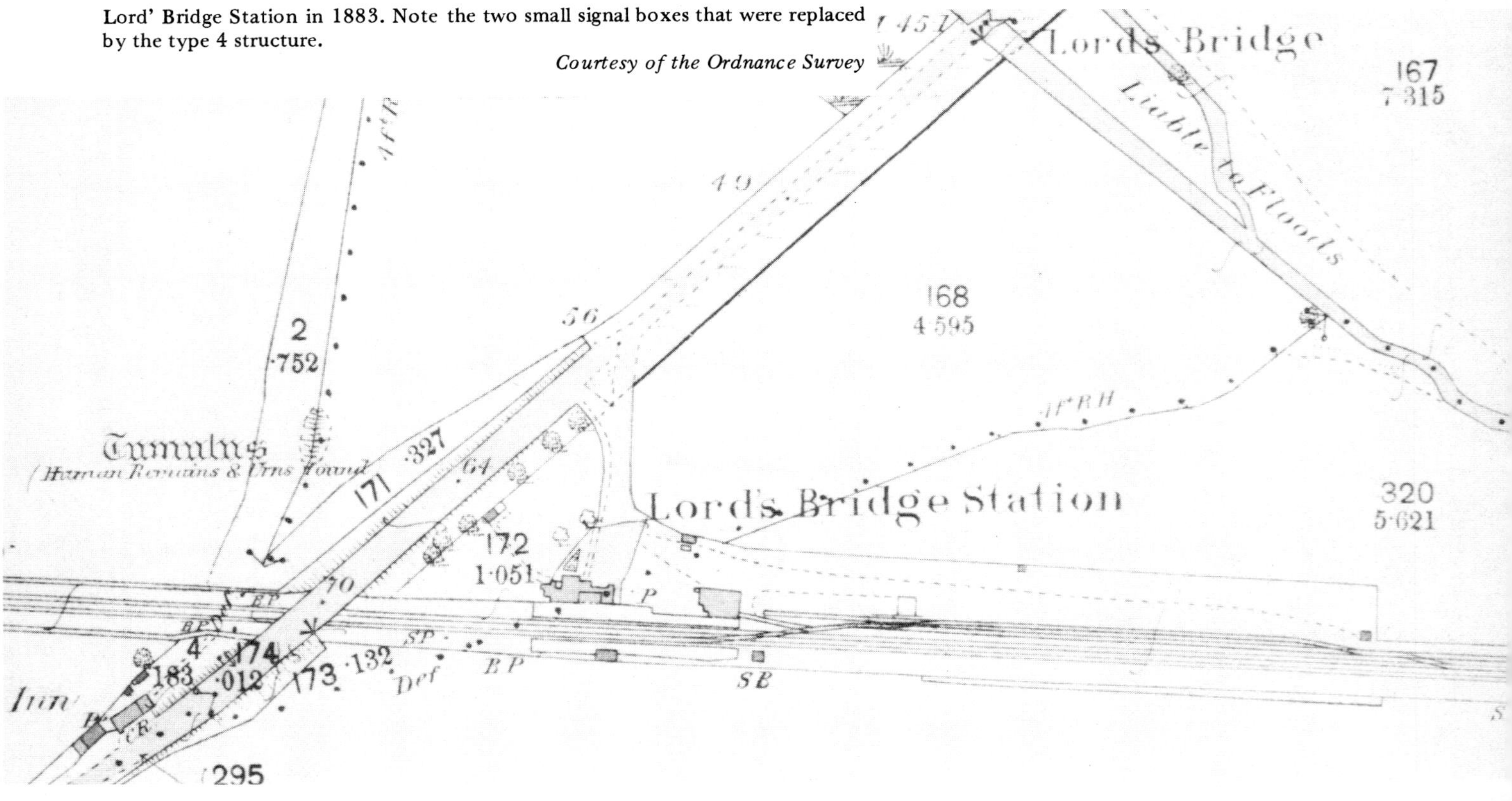

Shortly before closure, in 1967, a November sun brightens the last days of the 'down' platform canopy and rose-brambled window. Of particular interest is the bench seat, which is similar in style to a church pew. A surviving LNWR oil lamp clings to the one roof column.

John Spencer

A Lord's Bridge signalling diagram.

M. Christensen

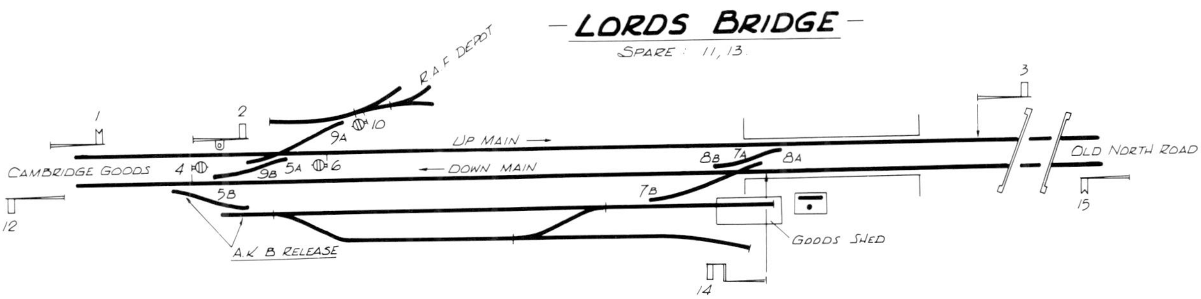

J. Spencer

S.D.—49

LONDON & NORTH WESTERN RAILWAY

CHURCH OF ENGLAND

TEMPERANCE FETE

AT

ST. IVES.

On Thursday, July 10th,

A SPECIAL TRAIN

WILL BE RUN TO

ST. IVES

AS UNDER:—

FROM	Starting at a.m.	Fares for the Double Journey. Third Class.	First Class.
BLETCHLEY	9 0	6/4	12/8
WOBURN SANDS	9 10	5/11	11/10
MILLBROOK (for Ampthill) ...	9 24	5/4	10/8
BEDFORD	9 40	4/7	9/2
BLUNHAM	9 50	4/0	8/0
SANDY	10 0	3/9	7/6
POTTON	10 7	3 5	6/10
OLD NORTH ROAD	10 17	2/8	5/4
LORD'S BRIDGE	10 27	2/1	4/2

Available for Return by Train leaving St. Ives at 8.55 p.m.

Tickets not Transferable, and available on day of issue only.

CHILDREN UNDER TWELVE YEARS OF AGE, HALF-FARE.

For all information as to Excursions on the London and North Western Railway, apply to Mr. E. M. G. EDDY, District Superintendent, Euston Station, London.

Euston Station, London, July, 1884. **G. FINDLAY**, General Manager.

McCorquodale & Co., Limited, Cardington Street, London, N.W.

G. Howe Collection

Cambridge Libraries

CHAPTER TWENTY-THREE

Cambridge

Like Oxford University, Cambridge was very guarded to the new opportunities of travel that the arrival of the railway would bring. The Eastern Counties Railway was the first to arrive on 30th July 1845 and their Act included, for the sake of the university, the provision; 'No person was to be picked up or set down within three miles of Cambridge between 10.00 a.m. and 5.00 p.m. on a Sunday, except when a train was running late; moreover, university officials were empowered to enlist the co-operation of the railway staff in identifying members of the university on the station and if any such did not hold the degree of Master of Arts or Bachelor of Medicine or Civil Law, would order the Company not to carry him for 24 hours even if the fare had been paid. Any failure to comply or attempt at evasion, dropping passengers between stations, (which was known to have taken place at Port Meadow, Oxford), made the Company liable to a fine of £5 to be made payable to Addenbroke's Hospital or some designated charity. Although the clauses remained effective when the Bedford & Cambridge Railway reached Cambridge in 1862, they were the substance of ideology rather than enactment and faded with time.

The southern bay of the station was the first of the two to be built to accept LNWR and GNR trains; the northern bay was added for the Midland Railway trains from Huntingdon along with the Newmarket branch. Cambridge became a nodal point for traffic to converge to reach the counties of East Anglia which made the indigenous Eastern Counties Company highly defensive of its position.

Many race specials with their string of horse-boxes were run from Bletchley for the Newmarket racecourse and these usually ran through the crowded station and on to the Newmarket branch. In 1910, there were eight meetings during the year, bringing a large number of these horse-boxes to the station to be carefully shunted to and from LNWR trains, with their priceless quadrupeds groomed and poised within.

Cambridge itself expanded with the arrival of the railway

Although this 1935 view of the 'Micheline' railcar is the intention of the photograph, it gives a good view of the situation of the bay, which is little changed from 1862. Great Northern pride is maintained in LNER guise by the presence of one of the famous Atlantics standing in the bay, with a Hitchin and King's Cross train. Behind, are the 'Homepride Flour Mills', with crenellated tower which stands on the site of graneries on the map of the station.

Soole Collection (NRM)

Cambridge south, with the LNWR goods yard and locomotive shed on the southern side of the Hills Road. The GNR goods shed and coal yard are on the opposite side of the road behind the row of houses. The sidings to the granary that became the Spiller's Flour Mill and those on the opposite side of the station with the large goods shed, are those of the GER. On this survey, of 1883, the locomotive facilities for the GER are practically as modest as those of the LNWR, although the former developed to a greater extent in subsequent years.

Courtesy of the Ordnance Survey

A Bletchley engine, quite eclipsed by the mechanical artistry of that Great Northern locomotive engineer, Patrick Stirling. His famous 'Single' No. 1 is photographed with a King's Cross to Cambridge excursion on 24th August 1938. The Bletchley train, with fireman Bill Buchanan climbing on to the footplate, is the apogee of Midlandization, with the profile of the LNWR being totally supplanted by both engine and coaches.

National Railway Museum

as did towns elsewhere, doubling its population from 24,453 by the time of World War I and reaching more than 92,000 a hundred years after the opening of the Bedford & Cambridge line. A corn exchange was opened in 1876 and a cattle market in 1885. Printing and scientific instrument making were fostered by the university. Later came plastics, chemicals and the production of agricultural machinery.

After covering 46 miles, the line from Bletchley joined the Great Eastern line at a junction just before the Hills Road bridge, almost in the station. In the bay, the LNWR trains used the opposite face of the main platform whilst the GNR used the platform on the town side. Facilities for LNWR passengers existed in the main station buildings, although offices and booking facilities were situated for the GNR next to their own platform entrance and exit. Direct London trains were, of course, operated by the Great Eastern Railway to Liverpool Street and the Great Northern Railway to King's Cross. It was the LNWR that provided the cross-country route connections terminating finally with access to the Great Western at Oxford and the West of England.

Goods traffic was handled independently by all the companies with the exchange taking place through the extensive sidings of the indigenous Company. The LNWR goods depot was opened alongside the Hills Road on 7th July 1862 and improved sidings were added in 1926. A small locomotive shed, with its turntable, was situated nearby.

With the expansion and demand of the railway, the station at Cambridge underwent periods of extensive rebuilding. As the first station, an impressive block of double arcades by Francis Thompson, that held the trains on one side and the arriving and departing carriages on the other, became too restrictive. An 'up' platform was laid in, temporarily, from 1850 to 1863 when the familiar long platform of 1,254 ft. was built with its bays at each end for the other companies. This new platform was built across the path of the original rails and was covered with a long cantilevered awning. Station premises were altered to create a new inward and outward parcels office with a much enlarged booking hall, new waiting-rooms and lavatories.

Signalling for the LNWR trains was controlled in the environs of the station by GER boxes at Hills Road Junction (77 levers) and Cambridge South, the latter just before the bay. An LNWR box was situated at the entrance to their own goods yard and locomotive facilities and later another box was built for the sidings on the 45 mile post at Trumpington. The goods yard box was replaced, because of wear, by an LMS box on 11th March 1944.

Locomotive stabling ceased at the Cambridge depot in October 1935, leaving one engine there on stand-by; this became an LNER duty. Turntable facilities and the water column were still used by visiting locomotives, but any coaling of engines was encouraged by the Bletchley shed foreman to be done on the LNER depot that had a mechanical hopper style plant and could obviate coaling back at Bletchley.

During the 1930s, the Oxford and Cambridge route continued in the role of testing ground for innovations in traction and stock that had developed from LNWR days, due, largely, to the close proximity of Wolverton. A vehicle mentioned in *Oxford to Cambridge Railway (Volume One)* in detail was the 'Micheline' railcar, a prototype, ideal in concept although less than satisfactory in practice. In the latter part of the decade a futuristic looking three car diesel multiple unit was tried between the 'Oxbridge' termini. A second 'Micheline' design was experimented with in the mid-1930s on the LMS main line between Euston and Leighton Buzzard. In February 1935, it completed the 40.2 miles in 42½ minutes, with a maximum recorded speed of 66m.p.h. This was, in fact, a further extension of the 'Micheline' idea of using pneumatic tyres, for the system devised on the 1932 car had rather more success on the continent and the company doubtless felt it worth persevering with this design. They also had the interest of a British manufacturer as the two cars built were constructed by

'Precursor' class locomotive, *Etna*, makes an eruptive display in this lively start from the Cambridge bay platform, for Bletchley. An assortment of stock comprises the normal three coach train with LNWR horse-boxes, an ex-Midland van and LMS suburban stock.
Soole Collection (NRM)

A view of the station from the Hills Road bridge early this century. Cambridge Station, with the Oxford train's bay to the left, is in the centre of the picture with the main Great Eastern goods facilities on the right. Leading towards the Spiller's buildings are the lines of the Great Northern goods facilities.

Cambridge Libraries

'Waterloo' class 2-4-0 locomotive, *Sphinx*, stands in the bay at Cambridge, with an Oxford train, in 1889. An interesting glimpse of early GER stock can be seen in the train behind.

L&GRP/Courtesy David & Charles

A view of the LNWR junction, with the original Eastern Counties main line, in early LMS days. Engines on the right of the photograph are standing in front of the very modest two road engine shed. Beyond them are the goods yard sidings.

S. P. W. Corb

A 'Waterloo' class locomotive *John o' Groat* replenishes its water supply at Cambridge shed, before its return to Bletchley, in 1913.

Kellend Collection (BRC)

Cambridge Station front, looking from the south, at around the turn of the century.

Cambridge Libraries

Armstrong Siddeley Co. Ltd., at their Coventry factory and from the outset, great care was taken to reduce the pay load/net weight ratio which created some interesting, if rather expensive, construction methods. It followed more closely the method of construction used for aircraft, rather than locomotives, with tubular framing on to which aluminium panels were bolted, with every part being carefully weighed to make sure that it would not exceed the specifications. The result was that, in working order, the weight was no more than 6¼ tons. On the narrow rim of rail, the carrying capacity of a pneumatic tyre was little more than a ton, so the weight was distributed amongst eight axles of sixteen tyres and pay load ratio in the car was 46 per cent. The earlier French-built 'Micheline' was driven by a 240b.h.p. Hispano Suiza engine. For this car, however, the Armstrong Siddeley Company developed a special 12 cylinder 'V' type OHV engine of 13 litres capacity which developed 275b.h.p. at 3,000r.p.m. and weighed only 1,000lb. Mechanical transmission drove on one of the two eight wheeled bogies. Although successful, the engine did have some problems in service and to continue, the experiment was replaced by one of the former designs.

The first appearance of the unit must have proved even more startling than the earlier machine, as it was painted in bright red and cream with the driver in a raised conning tower, as the guards position had been on early carriage stock, giving an unrestricted view of the entire train. In the case of the driver, this was to enable him to remain in this same conning tower cab whichever direction the train was going. After the driver's area, there was a luggage compartment and a lavatory, with the remainder being the passenger saloon. This was entered by double sliding doors in the centre of the body. Accommodation was normally for 48 passengers with an extra eight folding seats in the luggage compartment.

It was decided, after the aforementioned trial, to try out the appeal of the railcar with the public on the Oxford to Cambridge route, but it would not be advertised in the timetable as it would be something of an impromptu arrangement. With an unrestricted view ahead, comfortable seating and suspension on a gliding noiseless journey, the vehicle was warmly applauded by the everyday rail traveller who hoped to see more of them on inter-city routes. The eventual introduction of the units in a proper service, between Rugby and Coventry via Leamington and Nuneaton, received a lukewarm reception from the running department. An earlier pronouncement, that had horrified the designers, was their insistence that standard draw gear must be fitted, and this was mercifully prevailed upon. After such meticulous construction, the prospect of adding half a ton of excess on each end would quickly, and ignominiously bring 'Micheline' on to its immobile rims. During running, the light construction was an advantage in the high acceleration and braking performance reaching 50m.p.h. in 30 seconds or 900 yards and reducing the same speed in 9 seconds over 250 yards. Tyre section was in the shape of a horseshoe with a supplementary solid inner tyre. This would sustain support in the event of a collapse of the inflated section. In the event of this happening, an alarm would sound in the driving cab. Tyre life was not exemplary and at about 25,000 miles, wear would be caused, mostly on points and crossings. Like a road vehicle, it carried its spares, although the prospect of a driver stopping to change a wheel at the side of the track must have appeared a little eccentric to the railway officials.

By 1937, the appeal of the craft had not gained much ground with the running department of the LMS, or any other railway company in Britain, for that matter, even though there were many pleasing aspects of the idea that was not only before its time but introduced, like the diesel of the period, to become a victim of the time. For with the darkening portent of war, the company of Armstrong Siddeley would have to put aside its interests in experimentation and concentrate on rearmament, which left the second 'Micheline' design to be returned to Micheline at Stoke-on-Trent, to be eventually reduced to scrap in 1945. It was a most undeserving end to the fine efforts of the design and production teams that had worked on it, and it was worthy of a better fate.

In the 1950s, the Eastern Region of British Railways was extended to take in the Bedford to Cambridge line, up to and including Willington Station. This brought a change of paint to the station signs, with white letters on a dark blue ground, the only noticeable change up to closure. Cambridge, itself, received the customary face-lift during the up-dating of the image of British Rail. The striking quattrocento arcade, with college arms, was glazed for refreshment rooms and was improved by the removal of a short nondescript canopy. A busy commuter service to London ensures not only the old Great Eastern route, but the Great Northern route from the bay as well, although former passenger facilities there are now only parcel facilities.

Having brought in a train from Bletchley, on 20th May 1938, LMS 4F, No. 4077, idles in the bay platform at Cambridge prior to returning.
H. C. Casserley

A typical branch line LNWR locomotive, one of the 5ft. 6in. 2-4-2 tanks, is seen on shed, in 1905, at Cambridge. The immaculate condition of No. 1165 reflects a period when the footplate men took immense pride in how their engine appeared when out on the line. It is also fair to say that the men could identify strongly with their engines as they would be required to work the same locomotives for very long periods. This association was, of course, lost with the inception of the common user system.
L&GRP/ Courtesy David & Charles

Passing the fixed distant for Cambridge goods yard signal box, another engine of the Whale era, the 'George V' class, is seen here with a horse-box and cattle wagons on its way to Bletchley in the 1930s.

Soole Collection (NRM)

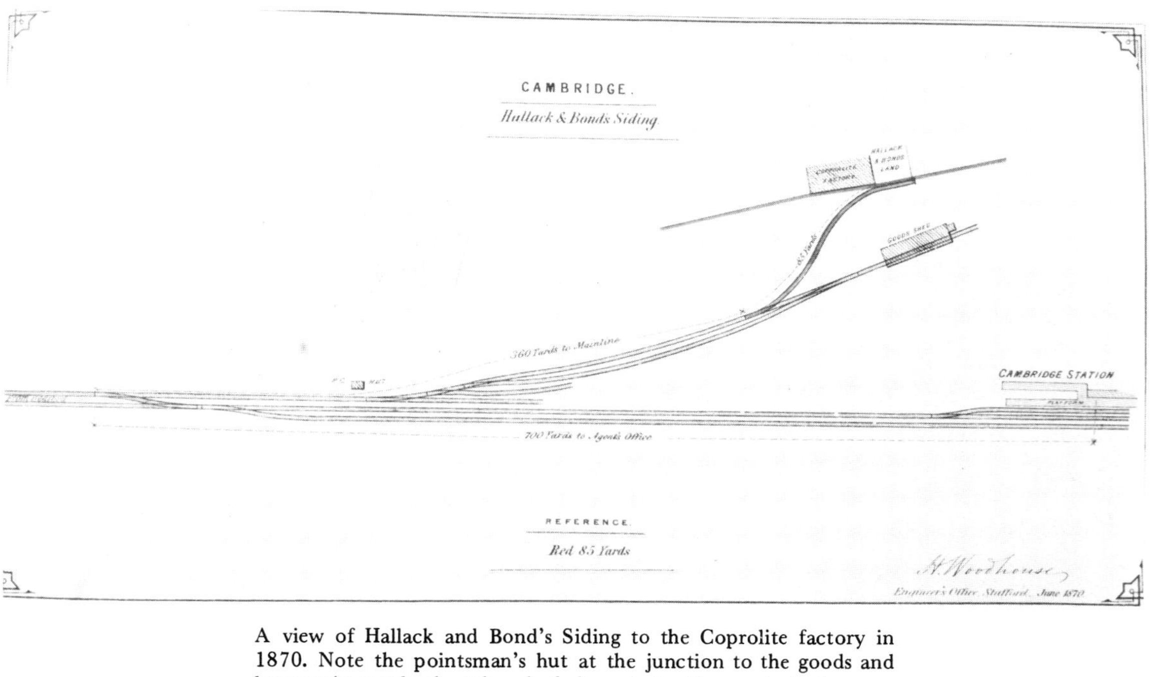

A view of Hallack and Bond's Siding to the Coprolite factory in 1870. Note the pointsman's hut at the junction to the goods and locomotive yards, the other shaded area being the goods shed.

J. Pritchett Collection

The LMS three car diesel unit, No. 80000, stands on the siding alongside the ex-LNWR goods yard at Cambridge in 1939. This should be compared with the earlier photograph at Bedford St. John's and the alterations mentioned, such as the removal of the streamlined casing beneath the solebar and the heavy mesh on the cab windows.

Cambridge Libraries

This passenger timetable of 1939 has a unique distinction as it shows the times of the trains for the very short-lived Girtford Halt, situated between Blunham and Sandy.

John Spencer Collection

A thin line between the hour and minute figures indicates p.m.

Table 62

BLETCHLEY, BEDFORD AND CAMBRIDGE.

WEEK DAYS.

					SO	SX					SO	SO		SO		SO	SX	
London (Euston) ......dep.			6A50		7 35	7 35		9 30		10T40	12|5	12|5	12|15		1SO55	2|7	2|7	3|6
Liverpool (L. St.) ...... "	10G0		11NS50		2MX30	2MX30		8 15					9 40		11 15		12 0	11SO55
Manchester (L. Rd.) ...... "	10G30		12g0					8D10					10 10		11 10		12 0	11SO50
Birmingham (N. St.) ... "	12G20				7 30	7 30		8 45					11c30		12|30			2|5
Rugby ...... "	2G45		3H34		8 23	8 23	8 42	9 38					12|52		2N13			3M14
Northampton (Castle) ... "	4MO12		7 8		8 52	8 52	9 0	10 14					1|5		2N43			3|47
Oxford ...... "					7 24	7 24	8 45	10 45			11 52		11SX52		1|55			3|15
Bletchley ......dep.	7 4	7 20	8 6	8 25	9 36	9 41	10 0	11 40		12|2	1|23	1|35	1|50		3|24	3|55	4|0	4|33
Fenny Stratford	7 6	7 22	8 8	8 27	9 38	9 43	10 2	11 46		12|4	1|25		1|52		3|26	3|57	4|7	4|35
Bow Brickhill			8 11	8 30			10 5			12|7			1|55			4|0	4|10	
Woburn Sands	7 13	7 28	8 15	8 35	9 44	9 49	10 9	11 52		12|11	1|31	1|42	2|1	2|50	3|32	4|4	4|14	4|42
Aspley Guise			8 18				10 12			12|14			2|4	2|52		4|7	4|17	
Husborne Crawley							10 15						2|7	2|55		4|10	4|20	
Ridgmont	7 18		8 22		9 48	9 53	10 18			12|18	1|36		2|10	2|58	3|37	4|13	4|23	
Lidlington	7 22		8 26		9 52	9 57	10 21			12|21	1|39		2|13	3|1	3|40	4|16	4|26	
Millbrook	7 27		8 30		9 56	10 1	10 25	12|2		12|24	1|43		2|18	3|5	3|44	4|20	4|30	
Stewartby			8 34				10 28		Through Train—Oxford to Cambridge.	12|27		1|57	2|21	3|8		4|23	4|33	
Wootton Broadmead							10 31					2|0	2|24	3|11		4|26	4|36	
Kempston Hardwick			8 38				10 33			12SO31		2|2	2|26	3|13		4|28	4|38	
Kempston and Elstow							10 37					2|6	2|30	3|17		4|32	4|42	
Bedford (St. John's) ...... arr.	7 37		8 45		10 6	10 11	10 41	12|12		12|36	1|53	2|10	2|34	3|21	3|54	4|36	4|46	4|59
Bedford (St. John's) ...... dep.	7 40		8 50		10 9	10 15		12|15			1|55				3|56			5|2
Willington	7 46		8 56		10 15	10 23		12|21			2|1				4|2			5|8
Blunham	7 51		9 1		10 21	10 29		12|26			2|6				4|7			5|13
Girtford Halt	7 54		9 4	One Class only.	10 24	10 32	One Class only.	12|29		One Class only.	2|9	One Class only.	One Class only.		4|10	One Class only.	One Class only.	5|16
Sandy (Junction with L.N.E.) ...	8 0		9 8		10 31	10 37		12|33			2|14				4|15			5|24
Potton	8 7				10 39	10 44		12|40			2|21				4|22			5|31
Gamlingay	8 12				10 44	10 49		12|45			2|28				4|27			5|36
Old North Road	8 21				10 54	10 59		12|54							4|36			5|44
Lord's Bridge	8 33				11 4	11 10		1|3							4|45			5|53
Cambridge ......arr.	8 43				11 14	11 20		1|13			2|52				4|57			6|3

WEEK DAYS—continued.

	SO	SX	SO	SX	SO	SX	SX	SO	SO		SO	SX	SO	SO
London (Euston) ......dep.	3|6	4|10	4|10	5|32	5|32	6|6		6|6		8L0	7|15	8|0		9|55
Liverpool (L. St.) ...... "				2|10	2|55					4 Z5		5|30		5|30
Manchester (L. Rd.) ...... "				2|30	2|40					4Z30		6|15		5|45
Birmingham (N. St.) ... "				4|0	5|0	5|0				7|5	7|55	7|55		9|8
Rugby ...... "				5|34	5|55	5|43		6F8		8L18	8|41	9|0		10|5
Northampton (Castle) ... "				5|54	6|12	6|12		6F43		8|35	9|18	9|31		11|10
Oxford ...... "				5|30	5|30	5|30	5|30	5|30	7|0		7|0	7|0		
Bletchley ......dep.	5|0	5|35	6|5	6|45	7|20	7|24	7|30	7|36	8|45	9|30	10|0	10|10		11|59
Fenny Stratford	5|4	5|37	6|7	6|47	7|22	7|26	7|32	7|38	8|47	9|32	10|2	10|12		12|2
Bow Brickhill	5|7	5|40	6|10	6|50	7|25		7|35		8|50	9SX35	10|5	10|15		
Woburn Sands	5|11	5|44	6|15	6|54	7|29	7|32	7|39	7|44	8|54	9|39	10|9	10|19		12|8
Aspley Guise	5|14	5|47	6|18		7|32		7|42		8|57		10|12	10|22		12B12
Husborne Crawley	5|17	5|50	6|21				7|45		9|0		10|15	10|25		
Ridgmont	5|20	5|53	6|24		7|38	7|37	7|48	7|48	9|3		10|18	10|28		12 15
Lidlington	5|23	5|56	6|27		7|41	7|40	7|51	7|51	9|6		10|21	10|31		12 18
Millbrook	5|27	5|59	6|31		7|45	7|44	7|55	7|55	9|9		10|25	10|35		
Stewartby	5|30	6|2	6|34		7|48		7|58		9|12		10|28	10|38		12 25
Wootton Broadmead	5|33	6|5	6|37				8|1		9|15		10|31	10|41		
Kempston Hardwick	5|35	6|7	6|39				8|3		9|17		10|33	10|43		
Kempston and Elstow	5|39	6|11	6|43				8|7		9|21		10|37	10|47		
Bedford (St. John's) ...... arr.	5|43	6|15	6|47		7|57	7|54	8|11	8|6	9|25		10|41	10|51		12 34
Bedford (St. John's) ...... dep.						7|58		8|8	9|30				H|16	
Willington						8|4		8|14	9|36				11|22	
Blunham						8|9		8|19	9|41				11|27	
Girtford Halt	One Class only.		One Class only.	One Class only.	One Class only.	8|13	One Class only.	8|22	9|44	One Class only (SX).	One Class only.		11|31	
Sandy (Junction with L.N.E.) ...						8|18		8|27	9|50				11|35	
Potton						8|25		8|34	9|57				11|42	
Gamlingay						8|30		8|39	10|2				11|47	
Old North Road						8|39		8|48	One Class only.					
Lord's Bridge						8|48		8|57						
Cambridge ......arr.						8|58		9|7					12|11	

SUNDAYS.

London (Euston) ......dep.		10 30	12|30	2|6		5|20	7|30
Liverpool (L. St.) ...... "		11†50	9 45	10 40			4|25
Manchester (L. Rd.) ...... "		12† 0	9 35	10 45			4|20
Birmingham (N. St.) ... "		8 20		12|50			6|0
Rugby ...... "		9 39	12|48	3|5			7|35
Northampton (Castle) ... "		10 13		3|25			8|7
Oxford ...... "			12|10			3|45	7|5
Bletchley ......dep.		12|6	2|6	4|19		6|50	9|35
Fenny Stratford		12|8	2|8	4|21		6|52	9|37
Bow Brickhill				4|24		6|55	9|40
Woburn Sands		12|14	2|14	4|28		7|0	9|44
Aspley Guise				4|31		7|3	9|47
Husborne Crawley							
Ridgmont		12|19	2|19	4|36		7|8	9|52
Lidlington		12|22	2|22	4|39		7|12	9|55
Millbrook		12|25	2|25	4|43	One Class only.	7|16	9|59
Stewartby				4|46		7|19	10|2
Wootton Broadmead							
Kempston Hardwick				4|51		7|24	10|7
Kempston and Elstow							
Bedford (St. John's) ...... arr.		12|35	2|35	4|58		7|31	10|14
Bedford (St. John's) ...... dep.	9 55	12|38	2|39		5|56	7|41	
Willington	10 1	12|44	2|45		6|2	7|47	
Blunham	10 6	12|49	2|50		6|7	7|52	
Girtford Halt	10 9	12|52	2|53	One Class only.	6|10	7|55	One Class only.
Sandy (Junction with L.N.E.) ...	10 13	12|56	2|57		6|14	7|59	
Potton	10 20	1|3	3|5		6|22	8|7	
Gamlingay	10 25	1|8	3|10		6|27		
Old North Road	10 33	1|17	3|19		6|36		
Lord's Bridge							
Cambridge ......arr.	10 49	1|33	3|35		6|52		

(In the "5\|20" Sundays column, the vertical note "One Class only." is printed beside the Liverpool–Northampton departures.)

†—Saturday night.
A—On Saturdays depart London (Euston) 7.0 a.m.
B—Calls to set down only.
c—On Saturdays, except August 5th, departs Birmingham 11.45 a.m. Change at Coventry and Rugby.
D—On Saturdays dep. Manchester (L. Rd.) 8.5 a.m.
F—Not after September 9th.
G—On Sunday nights departs Liverpool 11.55 p.m. and Manchester 12.0 night. On Mondays depart Birmingham 12.30 a.m. and Rugby 3.35 a.m.
g—Sunday nights excepted. On Friday nights departs Manchester (Vic.) 12.35 a.m.
H—Mondays excepted. On Saturdays dep. 3.49 a.m.
L—On Saturdays departs London (Euston) 7.16 p.m., Rugby 8.23 p.m.
M—On Saturdays departs Northampton (C.) 3.7 p.m.
MO—Mondays only.
MX—Mondays excepted.
N—On Saturdays depart Rugby 2.20 p.m., Northampton 2.48 p.m.
NS—Not on Sunday nights.
SO—Saturdays only. SX—Saturdays excepted.
T—On Saturdays departs London (Euston) 10.35 a.m.
Z—Via Birmingham.

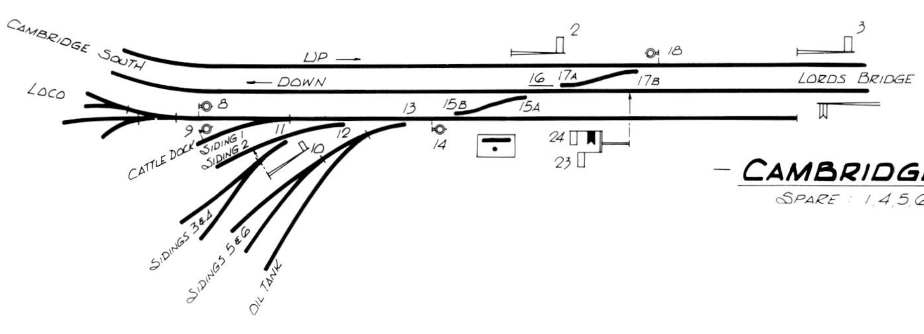

— CAMBRIDGE GOODS YARD —
SPARE: 1,4,5,6,7,19,20,21,22,25.

A thin line between the hour and minute figures indicates p.m.

CAMBRIDGE, BEDFORD AND BLETCHLEY.

Table 62

WEEK DAYS.

Station	One Class only.		One Class only.				One Class only.	
Cambridge dep.				7 42		9 28		11 5
Lord's Bridge				7 50		9 36		11 16
Old North Road				8 0		9 46		11 26
Gamlingay				8 9		9 55		11 35
Potton				8 14		10 0		11 40
Sandy (Junction with LNE)				8 25	9 27	10 8		11 48
Girtford Halt				8 29	9 30	10 12		11 52
Blunham				8 33	9 34	10 16		11 56
Willington				8 38	9 39	10 22		12 1
Bedford (St. John's) arr.				8 46	9 47	10 30		12 9
Bedford (St. John's) dep.	6 25			8 48	9 50	10 33	10 55	12 12
Kempston and Elstow							10 57	
Kempston Hardwick	6 30				9 55		11 1	
Wootton Broadmead							11 4	
Stewartby	6 35						11 7	
Millbrook	6 39			8 56	10 2		11 11	12 21
Lidlington	6 43			9 0	10 6		11 15	12 25
Ridgmont	6 48			9 4	10 10		11 20	12SO31
Husborne Crawley							11 22	
Aspley Guise							11 28	
Woburn Sands	6 54	7 37	8 45	9 10	10 17	10 49	11 30	12 34
Bow Brickhill	6 58	7 40	8 48				11 34	
Fenny Stratford	7 1	7 43	8 51	9 15	10 22		11 37	12 39
Bletchley arr.	7 5	7 47	8 55	9 19	10 26	10 56	11 46	12 43
Oxford arr.		9 51		11 10			1 0	2 22
Northampton (Castle) "		8E19		10 3	11 15	12SO9	12C17	1 40
Rugby "		8E49		11 2	11 51	12J23	12C46	1H54
Birmingham (New St.) "		9 54		11V21	1h14	1N25		3 10
Manchester (L. Rd.) "		12D18		2W 5	3SO37	3J20	3FO20	5b25
Liverpool (Lime Street) "		12D21		2A41		3J25	3FO25	5 21
London (Euston) "	8 35	9E14	9 55		11 20	12R 0	1 44	

Station	One Class only.	SX One Class only.	SO One Class only.		SO One Class only.	SX One Class only.	SO	SO One Class only.	SX One Class only.
Cambridge dep.				2 5			3 37		
Lord's Bridge				2 15					
Old North Road				2 25					
Gamlingay				2 34			4 2		
Potton				2 39			4 7		
Sandy (Junction with LNE)				2 52			4 17		
Girtford Halt				2 56			4 21		
Blunham				3 1			4 25		
Willington				3 6			4 30		
Bedford (St. John's) arr.				3 14			4 38		
Bedford (St. John's) dep.	12 55	2 45	2 50	3 17	4 0	4 32	4 40	5 6	5 17
Kempston and Elstow		2 47	2 52		4 2			5 8	5 19
Kempston Hardwick		2 51	2 56		4 6	4 37		5 12	5 23
Wootton Broadmead		2 54	2 59		4 9			5 15	5 26
Stewartby	1 2	2 57	3 2		4 12	4 42		5 18	5 29
Millbrook	1 6	3 1	3 6	3 25	4 16	4 46	4 48	5 22	5 33
Lidlington	1 10	3 5	3 10		4 20	4 49	4 52	5 26	5 37
Ridgmont	1 15	3 10	3 15	3 33	4 25	4 54	4 57	5 31	5 42
Husborne Crawley		3 12	3 17		4 27	4 56		5 33	5 44
Aspley Guise		3 16	3 21		4 31	5 0		5 37	5 48
Woburn Sands	1 21	3 20	3 25	3 39	4 35	5 3	5 3	5 41	5 52
Bow Brickhill	1 25	3 24	3 29		4 39	5 7		5 45	5 56
Fenny Stratford	1 28	3 27	3 32		4 42	5 10	5 8	5 48	5 59
Bletchley arr.	1 32	3 31	3 36	3 46	4 46	5 14	5 16	5 52	6 3
Oxford arr.	3 3			5 16					
Northampton (Castle) "	2 29			4T44	5 39	6 8	6 8		
Rugby "	3 12			5 1	5 49				
Birmingham (New St.) "	4a47			6T25	7 27				
Manchester (L. Rd.) "	6a19			8 5	8 48				
Liverpool (Lime Street) "	6a24			7 45	8 52				
London (Euston) "	2a41			4T50		6 55	6 55		7 5

WEEK DAYS—continued.

Station		SO One Class only.	SX One Class only.	SO One Class only.		SO One Class only.	SO One Class only.	SX One Class only.	SO One Class only.	One Class only (SX).	SO	SO	SO One Class only.
Cambridge dep.	4 42				6 26							10 0	
Lord's Bridge	4 53				6 34							10 8	
Old North Road	5 4				6 44							10 18	
Gamlingay	5 13				6 53							10 27	
Potton	5 18				6 58							10 32	
Sandy (Junction with LNE)	5 27				7 7							10 39	
Girtford Halt	5 31				7 11							10 43	
Blunham	5 35				7 14							10 47	
Willington	5 40				7 23							10 52	
Bedford (St. John's) arr.	5 52				7 31							11 0	
Bedford (St. John's) dep.	5 56	6 9	6 25	6 53	7 36	7 48	8 20	8 22	8 58		10 34		11 5
Kempston and Elstow		6 11	6 27	6 55									11 7
Kempston Hardwick		6 15	6 31	6 59			8 26	8 27			10 39		11 11
Wootton Broadmead		6 18	6 34	7 2			8 29	8 30			10 42		11 14
Stewartby		6 21	6 37	7 5		7 57	8 32	8 33	9 5		10 45		11 17
Millbrook		6 25	6 41	7 9	7 45	8 1	8 36	8 37	9 9		10 49		11 21
Lidlington		6 29	6 45		7 49	8 5		8 41	9 13		10 53		11 25
Ridgmont		6 34	6 50		7 54	8 10		8 46	9 18		10 58		11 30
Husborne Crawley		6 36	6 52			8 12		8 49	9 20		11 0		11 32
Aspley Guise		6 40	6 56			8 16		8 52	9 21		11 4		11 36
Woburn Sands	6 14	6 44	7 0		8 0	8 20		8 56	9 28	9 50	11 8		11 40
Bow Brickhill		6 48	7 4			8 24		9 0	9 32	9SX53	11 12		11 45
Fenny Stratford	6 18	6 51	7 7		8 5	8 27		9 3	9 35	9 56	11 15		11 48
Bletchley arr.	6 22	6 55	7 11		8 9	8 31		9 7	9 39	10 0	11 19		11 52
Oxford arr.		8 40	8 40			10 26		10 26			One Class only.		
Northampton (Castle) "	7 14	7 46	7 56		9SX4	10 0		9 52					
Rugby "	7 45	8 2	8 48		9SX32	10 45		10 43					
Birmingham (New St.) "	8 47	9 48	9 48			11 57		11 59					
Manchester (L. Rd.) "		1 35	1 35		1NS35	3Su42		2 58					
Liverpool (Lime Street) "		1 5	1 5		1NS5	3Su45		5 55					
London (Euston) "	8B42	8 50				11 9		10 40		11 38			4Su59

SUNDAYS.

Station		One Class only.		One Class only.		One Class only.	One Class only.
Cambridge dep.	11 31		2 43		5 53		8 35
Lord's Bridge							
Old North Road	11 46		2 58		6 8		8 50
Gamlingay	11 55		3 8		6 17		8 59
Potton	12 0		3 13		6 22	8 15	9 4
Sandy (Junction with LNE)	12 8		3 21		6 29	8 21	9 12
Girtford Halt	12 12		3 25		6 34	8 25	9 16
Blunham	12 15		3 29		6 37	8 28	9 20
Willington	12 20		3 34		6 42	8 34	9 25
Bedford (St. John's) arr.	12 28		3 42		6 50	8 41	9 33
Bedford (St. John's) dep.	12 37	2 46		5 50	6 54	8 45	
Kempston and Elstow							
Kempston Hardwick		2 50		5 55		8 50	
Wootton Broadmead							
Stewartby		2 55		6 0		8 55	
Millbrook	12 45	2 59		6 4	7 3	8 59	
Lidlington	12 49	3 3		6 8	7 7	9 3	
Ridgmont	12 54	3 8		6 13	7 12	9 8	
Husborne Crawley							
Aspley Guise		3 12		6 17		9 12	
Woburn Sands	1 0	3 16		6 21	7 18	9 16	
Bow Brickhill		3 20		6 25		9 20	
Fenny Stratford	1 5	3 23		6 28	7 23	9 23	
Bletchley arr.	1 9	3 27		6 32	7 27	9 27	
Oxford arr.	2 59	6 33			8 35		
Northampton (Castle) "		5 29			8 45	10 35	
Rugby "	2 22	6 4			9 16	11 5	
Birmingham (New St.) "	3 21	8 2			10 39	12§13	
Manchester (L. Rd.) "	5 0	9 40			1§10	2§58	
Liverpool (Lime Street) "	5 5	9 32				3§18	
London (Euston) "	2 35	5 5		8 40	9 41	11 12	

§—Mon. morn. **A**—On Sats., July 22 to Aug. 26 inclusive, arr. Liverpool (LS) 2.54 p.m.

a—On Saturdays arrives Birmingham 4.6 p.m., Manchester (L.Rd.) 6.35 p.m., Liverpool (Lime St.) 6.43. London (Eus.) 2.37 p.m.

B—On Sats. arr. London (Euston) 7.50 p.m.

b—On Saturdays arrive Manchester 5.30 p.m.

C—Fridays only. On Saturdays arr. Northampton (C.) 12.36 p.m., Rugby 1.32 p.m.

D—On Fridays, July 21st, 28th, August 4th and 11th, also on Sats. arrives Manchester (Lon. Rd.) 12.26 p.m., On Saturdays arrives Liverpool (Lime St.) 12.27 p.m.

E—On Sats. arr. Northampton (C.) 8.27 a.m., Rugby 8.56 a.m., London (Eus.) 9.34 a.m.

FO—Fridays only.

H—On Saturdays, also July 28th, August 4th and 7th, arrives Rugby 2.10 p.m.

h—On Saturdays arr. Birmingham 1.7 p.m.

J—On Fridays arrives Rugby 12.46 p.m., Saturdays 12.44. On Saturdays arrives Manchester (Mayfield) 3.53 p.m., Liverpool (Lime Street) 3.49 p.m.

N—Mondays only. On Saturdays arrives Birmingham 1.55 p.m.

NS—Not on Sundays.

R—12.10 p.m. on Saturdays.

SO—Sats. only. **SX**—Sats. excepted.

Su—Sundays only.

T—On Sats. arr. Northampton 4.26p.m., Birmingham 6.35 p.m., London (Eus.) 4.5 p.m.

V—On Sats. arrives Birmingham 11.42 a.m.

W—Sats. excepted. On Sats. until September 2nd arrive Manchester (Vic.) 2.28 p.m. On Saturdays, commencing Sept. 9th, arrives Manchester (L. Rd.) 2.36 p.m.

Once numerous throughout the country, isolated ground frames are now as rare as the sidings which they once served. This two lever frame, at Trumpington near Cambridge, was photographed in October 1950.

M. Bland

Between turns to Cambridge from Bletchley, LMS 2-6-0 locomotive No. 3001 rests on the storage road of the now closed two road LNWR shed at Cambridge on 6th May 1948.

M. Bland

On the carriage and van storage siding, behind the bay platforms, 'Prince of Wales' class No. 25722 waits between duties on 20th May 1938.

H. C. Casserley

A Cravens two car unit waits at platform 8 at Bletchley, with the 15.10 for all stations to Bedford St. John's on 22nd October 1981. The Bedford and Cambridge platform was reduced, from a similar length, to that of the main line platform with the installation of the 25kV electrification in the early 1960s.

Author's Collection

CHAPTER TWENTY-FOUR

Modern Times

With the publication of the new British Railways modernization plan in 1955, the Oxford to Cambridge Railway seemed to have hopeful prospects. Large capital sums were to be invested in effecting what the war years had begun, for it was through the advent of war, that the various freight connections, already mentioned, were put in hand. It seemed, therefore, in the reasoning of the time, that what worked well in war, may work even better with the experience of less hasty planning and modern traction and rolling stock. With this regard, it was announced that a large new mechanised marshalling yard would be built at Swanbourne and that a new flyover, costing £1,500,000, would be built at Bletchley to carry the flow of this freight traffic clear of the newly electrified main line. Construction of this began on 29th September 1956. In the same year, the old lattice bridge at Sandy was replaced by a new and stronger concrete and plate girder bridge. The wartime spur, between Blunham and Tempsford, would also play an important part, with a new westward spur from the Midland line, at Bedford, connecting with the cross-country route, whilst other connections, back along the line after Bletchley, were at Claydon and Oxford itself.

Although the plan seemed logically based on the success of wartime, it was, in fact, extending an outmoded merchandising system, for goods conveyancing was moving away from the marshalling yard system built up by the old pre-grouping companies and into 'block' train systems with much of the smaller piecemeal loads and livestock starting to be conveyed by road. It was a realization that overtook this grand scheme in mid-construction, for the flyover was built but the yard at Swanbourne remained stillborn on the planning board. The flyover was completed on 15th January 1962, but the tracks that had been planned to accept some eight trains per day, never saw a fraction of that total, and by 1981, a single working each day for four days of the week was just keeping the rust off the rails. As a result of the new flyover, the Cambridge route had now acquired another single line section through Fenny Stratford forming a junction from the flyover just before the A5 road bridge.

The scheme had been something of a hiatus for the Oxford to Cambridge route, for the passenger service first came under review for closure in May 1959. The number of passenger trains had been reduced and British Railways looked to ending in steam without the introduction of diesel traction. Reaction to this, and the strength of feeling about the service, must have surprised even British Railways, girded to defend Governmental edicts for

A view from the southern parapet of the Hills Road bridge where a diesel multiple unit can be seen crossing the junction of the LNWR to GER metals. Lines into the Cambridge goods yard are visible on the right, although the site of the small locomotive shed was on the immediate right, now replaced by a row of staging.

R. Powell

The turmoil of modernization. A photograph, taken high up from one of the construction cranes, shows the pier supports for the new flyover in position. Bletchley No. 1 box and the carriage shed can be seen through the sheerlegs of the crane. Both the box and carriage shed were subsequently demolished. The train in the photograph is carrying out an interesting operation with the suburban set from Euston, which has finished its duties for the day. It is being taken along the 'up' fast line to be returned through the station on the 'down' slow line until it reaches a point between Bletchley Nos. 2 and 3 boxes north of the station. At that point, it will be shunted on to the middle long siding, to be held for use, until the following morning.

BR/OPC Collection

The entrance to modern Bletchley Station, in 1982, with the bridge and lifts like an assembly of boxed-in chutes. Glazing on the bridge would have added much to the appreciation of the electrified main line vista for the travelling public.

Author's Collection

economies. Effective opposition was polarized by the speed with which the local authorities reacted. In July 1959, a conference was called at Bedford, of all the County Borough and Rural District authorities, including Cambridge and Oxford, to form the strongest possible opposition to the closure of these lines. British Railways recoiled for the time being, conceding to arguments that the local service would be greatly improved by acceleration with the new diesel multiple units. Derby lightweight units were, therefore, introduced on 2nd November 1959.

Reaction had been sufficient to find only cursory mention of a few modifications on the route in the Beeching Plan, published in March 1963. That was until the following December, when closure was belatedly included and battle was joined once more.

Sunday passenger services were withdrawn in November with the coup de grace, complete closure, planned for the following February. Opposition to this was successful in bringing a suspension of the closure pending a public enquiry, in July 1964, with the East Anglian and East Midland Transport Users' Consultative Committees (TUCC).

Bletchley's population was 3,300 at the time of the first closure attempt, and was expecting to achieve a minimum total of 24,000 by the late 1960s, with proposals for an entirely new city in the same area, by 1981, of 70,000 and by the year 2000, a population of 250,000. The Bedford Committee argued strongly that there would be gradual increase all along the section between Bletchley and Bedford which it felt the Railways Board was totally ignoring. British Railways reacted with figures that the gross annual earnings of the passenger service were £102,200 against direct terminal, track and signalling expenses of £80,600, and movement expenses of £119,100; a total of £199,700 bringing an annual deficiency of £97,500. Notwithstanding, local authorities still pressed hard that the loss of the service would cause great expense and hardship to the community. Neither were the local authorities alone in their fight, for on Tuesday, 4th February, railway employees at Bletchley held a meeting where the strongest arguments were put forward against closure.

With a new Government in 1964 came a new Transport Minister who consented closure, only when a satisfactory bus service alternative had been provided; this was in 1965.

The alternative buses proved to be a bone of contention. Applications were made by the United Counties Omnibus Co. Ltd., and the City of Oxford Motor Services to the East Midlands Traffic Commissioners in October 1965. After a hearing, in December, licences were granted for the following August, with the exception of the Bletchley to Bedford section which, it was concluded, would not be adequately served. A plague of bus cancellations in the district was not helping the case for the alternative transport. However, with the granting of licences to the bus companies for the Oxford to Bletchley and Bedford to Cambridge sections, British Railways was able to post closure notices for these sections. This was to be 31st December 1967, but as this was a Sunday, the actual last train was scheduled to run on the 30th, Saturday night.

Unfortunately, a black and white photograph cannot allow an appreciation of No. 73014 in Brunswick Green livery. Construction of the flyover has obviously been completed in this 1964 view. Note the water column and barrow crossing, at the position of the original length of the Cambridge line platform.

John Spencer

After a battle that had been fought well by railwaymen and local councils, supported by the public at large, the inevitable closure day arrived when enthusiasts joined the melancholy train of a two car diesel multiple unit set, Nos. E56454 and E51296, leaving Bedford at 9.26p.m. for Cambridge. The return journey, the last scheduled passenger train on the line, left Cambridge at 10.30p.m. This was another two car unit, Nos. M79136 and M79657. In view of the fact that track lifting was to soon follow along this section of the line, it incurred special sympathies. Like any other cherished branch line, it reflected the experience and scenes with which people felt securely associated, a companionable way for the regular traveller. Detonators at Potton cracked their sharp percussive echo through the dark countryside. There was a sound of ritual dissent beneath the glazed canopy, where the letters, B&C, in cast iron, bore a legend to the last of three companies' lines and the first to cease.

Goods traffic on the line began its descent from a wartime peak to the post-war decline with the closing of Girtford Siding on 1st November 1951 and Toft's Siding on 13th July 1952. From then onwards, it was a piecemeal decline with Sandy officially closing on 4th February 1963, whilst Willington, Blunham and Lord's Bridge all closed on 13th July 1964. Gamlingay and Old North Road lasted until April of the following year. Greatest resistance was again to be found at Potton, which held off closure until 1st January 1966. The last regular freight train traversed the branch in April of the same year, leaving only a short occasional working up to Blunham Mill, which finished in December 1966.

All goods yards on the Bedford to Bletchley section, with the exception of Bedford St. John's, closed on 17th July 1967. This yard closed on Monday, 10th August 1970.

Track lifting for the Cambridge extension began in earnest on 13th August 1968, with two exceptions in prospect. The first of these was for a section between Potton and Gamlingay, pending negotiations for a preservation scheme by the Sandy & Potton Steam Railway Society. A much shorter section was to be retained at Lord's Bridge for the Mullard Radio Astronomy Observatory. Unfortunately, the former section of 5¼ miles could not be purchased by the Society owing to lack of funds and was lifted. The chagrin to their brave cause was the A603 (B1042) bridge over the line at Potton which was becoming quite unsafe and would require extensive and costly repairs. Sandy wartime curve was lifted by April 1966.

These closures did not leave the Bedford line unscathed for, in addition to the loss of goods and parcels facilities, every station became an unstaffed halt from 15th July 1968. Responsibility for them all down as far as, and including Bow Brickhill Halt, came under the supervision of the Area Manager based at Bedford Midland Station.

Even this tenuous arrangement was not to remain unsullied or allowed to drift into complacency as the *Bedford Times* of March 1971 pointed out, for as the main station buildings and water tower at Bedford St. John's were demolished, British Rail posted notices to the effect that all passenger services would cease in the following October. This brought opposition en masse as before. Hearings were held with East Anglian and East Midlands TUCC's in July with advice to the Transport Minister, pointing out the hardships caused by rail closure in the following September. A ludicrous example of the journey between Lidlington and Bletchley stated that a modest journey time of twenty minutes would, in fact, involve an overnight stop; a two day journey in reality. Once more, the Minister gave consent only when the bus service supplanted, satisfactorily, the existing rail service, and closure was suspended until that was achieved. In July 1972, the United Counties Omnibus Co. Ltd. applied to the Traffic Commissioners for a licence which they were granted in the following November. Whereupon British Rail advertised in the *Daily Express* that four of the line's stations would be sold for auction in the following month. Closure was to become effective on 31st December 1972. Once more, what appeared like un fait accompli was stayed by the sheer tenacity of local councils and public opinion, which took a consolidated shape with the formation of the Bedford Rail Users' Association. This is a dedicated band of enthusiasts who are willing, in all kinds of weather, to stand or distribute leaflets and impart information to support the retention of the railway service. British Rail were grasping the nettle! Closure was once more postponed pending appeal by the local interests and against the conditions of the road licences. The upshot of this debate was

In leisurely contrast, a diesel multiple unit 'Paytrain' crosses the Grand Union Canal on a Saturday afternoon, under the watchful eye of Fred Bateman, Area Supervisor.

Author's Collection

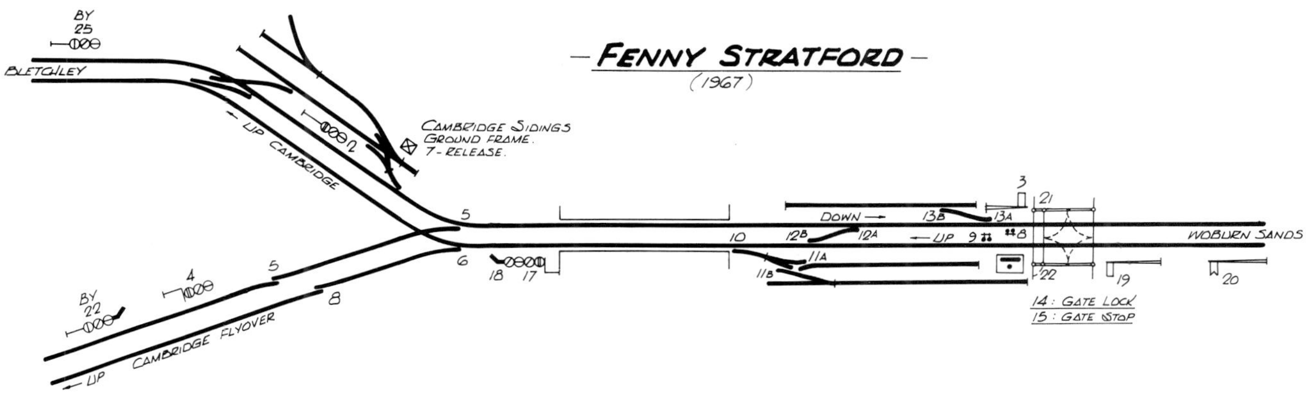

Alterations at Fenny Stratford, to the single line working, did not take place immediately after the flyover was opened, but with the removal of the sidings. A new diagram of 1967 was followed by the modifications on the other diagram for November 1972.

M. Christensen

Aspley Guise Halt, with its raised platforms, looking in the Bedford direction.

M. J. Lewis Author's Collection

A diesel unit arrives at Woburn Sands in July 1966. Woburn gasworks buildings are still evident with its siding on the right. The entrance to the goods yard is indicated by the loading gauge on the left.

John Spencer

The distant chimneys of Marston Valley Brickworks (LBC) are in perspective for this single car unit, seen on its way to Bedford St. John's, as it leaves Lidlington. The brickworks were demolished in 1981.

John Spencer

The modern 'Fletliner' service is something of a marvel in handling and hauling power, compared to early days of large brick tonnages that were loose-coupled behind LNWR 0-8-0s straining on the climb to Ridgmont. Even this train, having its pre-packed load assembled at Stewartby, would require all the exertions of a pair of Class 25 diesel locomotives.

London Brick Company

that the service was to survive into a changing mood of British Rail and Government thinking, as it became grant aided per annum, this being renewed during another closure crisis in 1974. The Government's inclination to give greater emphasis on rail as a public service, and not the threadbare Beeching adage of ruthless profitability, may now see this line playing a unique role in the developing new suburbia of Milton Keynes.

Interestingly, a study, made at the instigation of the Milton Keynes Development Corporation, of the existing passenger service in 1974, showed that in 1964, a total of 979,000 people used the line with Woburn Sands being, by far, the station most heavily used.

With regard to freight movements, one factor with likely consequences was the prospective closure of the Market Harborough to Northampton line, which would have left the Bedford line as an alternative freight link.

It was the unglamorous, but essential, matter of freight that was to bring an eleventh hour twist to this line's fortune. This came, once more, from the line's great benefactor, the London Brick Company, who signed a contract with the Greater London Council in April 1973 to accept 1,200 tonnes of rubbish, daily, in the reclamation of old clay pits to be filled and restored to farmland. This contract, for twenty years, is worth £10 million to British Rail who would operate block trains from the special handling depot at Hendon to Stewartby. Additional sidings were installed at Stewartby together with the new overhead lifting equipment taking the yellow, with blue letters, 'Easidispose' containers from the train and placing them on to vehicles that would tip them at the pit edge. Trains run at one or, sometimes, two per day in the charge of Classes 45, 46, 47 or 56 locomotives, and are routed from the Bedford end of the line, having travelled along the ex-Midland Railway route. This inherent benefit from the brick-making industry, supplants the decreasing volume of brick traffic by rail, and ensures the life of the line for at least the duration of the contract.

Besieged as it may have been, the line still retains popular use, although the station at Bedford has a most unsaintly appearance, and is something of an anti-climax after the residual charm of the small country halts at Bow Brickhill, Aspley Guise and Kempston Hardwick, whilst the half-timbered Gothic design of Fenny Stratford, Woburn Sands, Ridgmont and Millbrook are left to retain, as best they can, the dignity of fading splendour.

As the forays between British Rail and the Ministry of Transport engaged the opposition of local councils, Railway Trade Unions and public protest, the line went about its daily business. The familiar three coach motor train or push-pull unit shuttled back and forth between Bletchley and Bedford with a regular 2-6-2 tank in charge, one of the class, No. 41272 proudly bearing a plaque on the side stating that it was the 7,000th locomotive to be built at Crewe, a heavy responsibility for the humble tank. In the latter days of the Cambridge line's life, ex-Great Eastern and LNER engines took up many of the passenger rosterings, with Classes D16, B12 and B1 locomotives fulfilling the roles.

An eccentric working from Bletchley to Ridgmont and back was often hauled by a 'Black 5', 'Patriot', or even a 'Jubilee' class, Nos. 45507 and 45586 having been seen on this duty. 'Patriot' No. 45503 *The Royal Leicestershire Regiment* came off its Euston train on 10th July 1957 and after taking water, was allocated the 3.30p.m. to Bedford with the return passenger working at 5.15p.m. to Bletchley. Pick-up goods trains along the line were usually hauled by Nos. 48898 and 44447 with '8 Freights' also working the

Each a glimpse. The London-bound Class 45 has just left Bedford Midland and passes over the line and a Cravens two car unit at the 15 mile post at Cow Bridge. Alterations have, in fact, changed the scene a great deal since the early years of the nineteenth century, when a small hump-backed bridge, so named, carried the rough unmetalled road over a tributary of the Ouse. This road was diverted to some degree with the building of the Bedford Railway in 1845/6. However, much more alteration took place with the construction of the new Midland route to St. Pancras in 1867, as this is carried on bridges. The site of Kempston & Elstow Halt was immediately on the other side of the bridge, where a little of the roof of the crossing house can be seen, just in front of the engine, in this view taken in July 1970.

John Spencer

After damage by fire, in the 1970s, the Bedford LNWR type 5 box was rebuilt in this flat roof style.

Author's Collection

The ominous posters, displayed by the British Railways Board, are notifying the public of the closure and of the alternative United Counties bus service for passengers. This was the penultimate notice of 1971, which was followed, in 1974 by another attempt at closure. However, the line still bravely resists.

K. Bristow

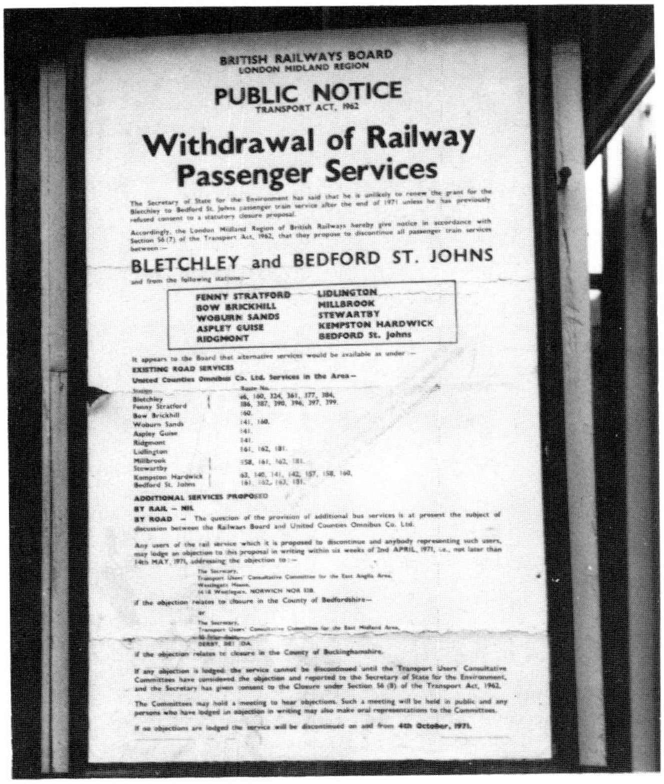

Driver Sid Stevens exchanges the tablet at the former Bedford LNWR box, after leaving the single line section of the Hitchin route on the Midland line. This line was singled in 1912 after being relegated to a route for local services with the opening of the new Midland main line route. It was closed to passengers on 1st January 1962 and closed completely on 14th April 1969.

Ian Hall

Bedford St. John's, on 16th May 1981, now simply a terminus halt. The line on the right was for Goldington Power Station but is now no longer used. Behind this is the enlarged installation that was originally Roger's Flour Mill. No sidings now remain on the 'up' side of the station for the oil depot, which transfers supplies by road haulage. The three car diesel multiple unit in the platform is, in fact, on a Railtour special, 'The Oxbridge Rambler' which was organized by Oxford Railway Publishing Company Limited, and was not a regular class of unit seen on the line. The use of this 'up' platform in latter years has a certain irony, insomuch as it is the original Bedford Railway platform.

Author's Collection

A Class 31 diesel locomotive brings an 'up' engineer's train through Willington on 11th September 1964.
R. Powell

heavy brick trains. Steam working from the Bletchley end was no longer possible after July 1965 when the depot was closed, with coal and water softening plants being demolished. Rails that had felt the intensive use of LNWR, LMS and British Railways engines were lifted after more than one hundred years, ending a successive dynasty for generations of Bletchley families.

By November 1959, the halts along the line had been rebuilt to longer timber platforms and raised to a standard height to facilitate the new cars. There were, however, some exceptions, for the halt at Husborne Crawley, with its signalman's cabin and keeper's house, disappeared completely, along with the defunct Ministry Depot Siding, as a new bridge was built to elevate the road over the line for its eventual connection with the M1 motorway.

The first diesel units to go into service were the Derby lightweights, operating through to Cambridge. These were later replaced with the long term familiar Cravens units which soldiered on for nearly twenty years until their replacement, with the Class 104 Birmingham RCW sets brought from the North of England, began in late 1981.

It is conceivable that the last regular steam working seen on the Oxford to Cambridge Railway was the coal train working to Goldington Power Station. By 27th July 1971, there were three trains returning each day, hauled by a Class 47 diesel, from the power station. The isolated structure of Bedford No. 2 signal box was demolished in October 1970, most of its duties having ceased in the previous January.

In July 1971, the Eastern Counties and United Counties Omnibus Companies withdrew their replacement bus services for the line to Cambridge from Bedford, as they stated they no longer received financial aid from the local authorities to run them.

It is difficult to be certain about the future of the passenger services as present loadings are 9 per cent down on the rest of British Rail, whilst the closure of the brick-works may have some effect.

Certainly the popularity of the line is by no means in doubt, having survived the Beeching holocaust and more recent purges. It appears to possess a hardy and endemic will to survive. Apparently, the founding will of those men of Bedfordshire is not lightly to be put off by the successive generations of its inheritors.

One change that, at the present time, seems to be in little doubt, is that the one hundred and thirty five years of manned crossings will come to an end with the installation of half-barrier automatic crossings.

Alterations at Sandy came about with the prospect of introducing the alternate fast freight plan, centred on Bletchley. To this effect, a steel plate girder bridge was built, costing £150,000, to replace the old lattice type. It was brought into use on Sunday, 27th October 1957 but, with the cessation of passenger services in 1968 and the dwindling goods traffic thereafter, its use had ceased by the late 1960s and it was removed completely in June 1975. This view, of the construction period, was taken in August 1957.

M. Christensen

If diesels are entitled to develop legends like steam locomotives, the Class 55 'Deltic' locomotive would certainly be amongst that number. It is now twenty years since they replaced the famous LNER classes of steam locomotive, and during that time they have inherited the tradition of the East Coast Main Line to Edinburgh, in a way that had not, at first, been expected. Sandy, of course, was a good place to see them come sweeping into view, as can be seen in this photograph of a 'Deltic' passing beneath the Bedford to Cambridge line. By now, the plate girder had replaced the older lattice construction. The house, keeper's cabin and 'up' signal still survive on the far side of the bridge at Sandy crossing.

R. Powell

A good view of the single line curving over the GNR at Sandy, as a diesel multiple unit leaves Sandy with a Bletchley train from Cambridge (11.22a.m.) in April 1964. A fragmentary glimpse of Sandy crossing over the new bridge is also afforded.

C. F. Burton

A Class 24 BR Sulzer diesel locomotive is another type now committed to memory. A member of this class rolls through Sandy with a Bletchley to Cambridge fitted freight, on 30th July 1965. The passing of years has not lessened the staff of Sandy Station's horticultural skills.

R. Powell

The view looking towards Bedford at Old North Road with a deserted platform for the Cambridge-bound diesel multiple unit in the sleepy August sunshine of 1966. This was a very interesting working for this unit. The shadow at the back is, in fact, a milk van that was given special clearance to be attached to this train, which was very much the exception for a multiple unit working. The train left Cambridge at 4.24p.m., arriving at Bletchley at 5.50p.m. It then departed from Bletchley at 6.55p.m., arriving back at Cambridge at 8.11p.m. This was a Sunday only working.

John Spencer

Gamlingay, in August 1966, looking little changed from the earlier chapter view, save for the presence of contemporary motive power. The goods shed road is stoutly held from over running any wagons on to the platform, by some very effective timber 'stops' of the LNWR period.

John Spencer

EXTRACTS FROM PASSENGER SERVICES TIMETABLE— 9th SEPT. 1963 TO 14th JUNE 1964

CAMBRIDGE TO BLETCHLEY AND OXFORD

	am	am	am	am	am	am	am	am	am	SX am	SO am	am	SX am	am	am	SO am	pm	pm	pm	ThSO pm	pm
Cambridge								7 30						9 58	1043	1122					
Lord's Bridge								7 39						10 6		1130					
Old North Road								7 47						1015		1139					
Gamlingay								7 56						1022		1146					
Potton								8 0						1027		1151					
Sandy								8 9						1033		1157					
Blunham								8 15						1037		12 1					
Willington								8 19						1042		12 6					
Bedford St. John's arr.								8 27						1051	1124	1215					
Bedford St. John's dep.		6 5			7 0		7 47	8 28		9 20	9 35		1045	11 5	1124	1216		1235			2 0
Kempston Hardwick		6 10			7 5		7 52			9 25	9 40		1050					1240			2 5
Stewartby		6 15			7 10		7 57			9 30	9 45		1055	1113		1225		1245			2 10
Millbrook		6 18			7 13		8 0	8 37		9 34	9 49		1059	1117		1229		1249			2 14
Lidlington		6 22			7 17		8 4	8 41		9 38	9 53		11 3	1121		1233		1253			2 18
Ridgmont		6 27			7 22		8 9	8 46		9 42	9 57		11 7	1126		1237		1257			2 22
Aspley Guise		6 31			7 26		8 13			9 46	10 1		1111					1 1			2 26
Woburn Sands		6 35			7 30		8 16	8 52		9 49	10 4		1114	1131		1243		1 4			2 29
Bow Brickhill		6 39			7 34		8 20			9 53	10 8		1118					1 8			2 33
Fenny Stratford		6 42			7 37		8 23	8 57		9 56	1011		1121	1136		1248		1 11			2 36
Bletchley arr.		6 45			7 40		8 26	9 1		10 0	1015		1125	1140	1147	1251		1 15			2 40
Bletchley dep.	5 30		7 10	7 38		7 55			9 30			1046			1149		1 5		1 48	2 10	
Swanbourne			7 20	7 48		8 4			9 40			1056					1 14		1 58	2 19	
Winslow	5 45		7 24	7 52		8 8			9 44			11 0			12 1		1 18		2 2	2 23	
Verney Junction			7 28	7 56		8 12			9 48			11 4					1 22		2 6	2 27	
			K			K						K					K			K	
Claydon				8 0					9 52										2 10		
Marsh Gibbon and Poundon				8 6					9 58									SO	2 16		
Launton				8 10					10 2									pm	2 20		
Bicester London Road	6 6			8 16					10 8						1219			1 55	2 25		
Islip	6 15			8 25					1017									2 4	2 34		
Oxford	6 27			8 37					1029						1240			2 15	2 46		

	pm	pm	SO pm	SX pm	2 pm	pm	pm	pm	pm	pm	SO pm	SX pm	pm	SX pm	pm	SO pm	SO pm	SX pm	SO pm
Cambridge	2 12							4 47			6 0	6 18	7 1					9 1	9 10
Lord's Bridge	2 20							4 55			6 8	6 26							9 18
Old North Road	2 29							5 4			6 17	6 35							9 27
Gamlingay	2 36							5 11			6 24	6 42							9 34
Potton	2 41							5 16			6 29	6 47							9 39
Sandy	2 47							5 22			6 35	6 53						9 27	9 46
Blunham	2 51							5 26			6 39	6 57							9 51
Willington	2 56							5 31			6 44	7 2							9 56
Bedford St. John's arr.	3 5							5 40			6 53	7 11	7 41					9 43	10 4
Bedford St. John's dep.	3 5		4 5	4 10			5 15	5 41		6 15	6 56	7 14	7 41		8 29			9 43	10 8
Kempston Hardwick			4 10	4 15			5 21			6 20									1013
Stewartby	3 14		4 15	4 20			5 26	5 50		6 25									1018
Millbrook	3 18		4 19	4 24			5 30	5 54		6 29	7 7	7 25							1022
Lidlington	3 22		4 23	4 28			5 34	5 58		6 33	7 11	7 29							1026
Ridgmont	3 26		4 27	4 32			5 38	6 2		6 37	7 16	7 34							1030
Aspley Guise			4 31	4 36			5 42	6 6		6 41									1034
Woburn Sands	3 31		4 34	4 39			5 45	6 9		6 44	7 21	7 39	7 59		8 49				1037
Bow Brickhill			4 38	4 43			5 49			6 48									1041
Fenny Stratford	3 37		4 41	4 46			5 52	6 15		6 51	7 26	7 44							1044
Bletchley arr.	3 40		4 45	4 50			5 56	6 18		6 55	7 30	7 48	8 9		8 57			10 6	1048
Bletchley dep.	3 50	4 0			5 7	5 22			6 46				8 13	8 55		9 15	10 6	10 6	
Swanbourne	4 0	4 9			5 16	5 31			6 55					9 5		9 25	1016	1016	
Winslow	4 4	4 13			5 20	5 35			6 59					9 9		9 29	1020	1020	
Verney Junction	4 8	4 17			5 24	5 39			7 3					9 13		9 33			
		K				K			K										
Claydon	4 12				5 27									9 17		9 37	1026	1026	
Marsh Gibbon and Poundon	4 18				5 33											9 43			
Launton	4 22				5 37											9 47			
Bicester London Road	E4 32				5 41								8 38	9 28		9 53	1037	1037	
Islip	4 41				5 50								8 47	9 37		10 2			
Oxford	4 53				6 4								9 0	9 51		1014	1057	1057	

2—Second Class only. SX—Saturdays excepted. SO—Saturdays only. K—Continues to Buckingham. E—Arrives Bicester London Road 4.27 p.m.

	am	am	am	J am	SX am	SO am	J am	J am	am	SX am	SO am	SO am	SX am	am	J am	SX am	SO am	am	pm	SO pm	SO pm	pm	J pm
Oxford			6 24						7 57			9 37	9 44					1127			1 8		
Islip			6 37						8 10			9 50	9 57					1141			1 19		
Bicester London Road			6 46						8 19			1000	10 7					1150			1 27		
Launton			6 50						8 23									1154					
Marsh Gibbon and Poundon			6 54						8 26									1158					
Claydon			7 2						8 33									12 5					
Verney Junction			7 6	7 22			7 54	8 33	8 38									12 9					1 45
Winslow			7 11	7 27			7 59		8 43						1128			1214					1 50
Swanbourne			7 15	7 31			8 4	8 40	8 47						1132			1218					1 54
Bletchley arr.			7 25	7 40			8 13	8 49	9 4			1036	1033		1141			1228					2 3
Bletchley dep.	6 35	7 14			8 5	8 10			9 6	9 25	9 25	1038	1038	1120		12 7	12 7		1 10	1 42		2 0	
Fenny Stratford	6 37	7 16			8 7	8 12			9 8	9 27	9 27			1122		12 9	12 9		1 12	1 44		2 2	
Bow Brickhill					8 10	8 15				9 30	9 30			1125					1 15	1 47			
Woburn Sands	6 42	7 21			8 15	8 20			9 13	9 35	9 35			1130		1214	1214		1 20	1 52		2 7	
Aspley Guise	6 45				8 18	8 23				9 38	9 38			1133					1 23	1 55			
Ridgmont	6 49	7 26			8 22	8 27			9 18	9 42	9 42			1137		1219	1219		1 27	1 59		2 12	
Lidlington	6 53	7 30			8 26	8 31			9 22	9 46	9 46			1141		1223	1223		1 31	2 3		2 16	
Millbrook	6 56	7 33			8 29	8 34			9 25	9 49	9 49			1144		1226	1226		1 34	2 6		2 19	
Stewartby	6 59	7 36			8 32	8 37			9 28	9 52	9 52			1147		1229	1229		1 37	2 9		2 22	
Kempston Hardwick	7 3				8 36	8 41				9 56	9 56			1151					1 41	2 13			
Bedford St. John's arr.	7 9	7 44			8 42	8 47			9 36	10 2	10 2	1058	1058	1157		1237	1237		1 47	2 19		2 30	
Bedford St. John's dep.		7 46							9 37		10 3	1059	1059			1238	1246					2 34	
Willington		7 54							9 46		1011					1247	1255					2 43	
Blunham		7 59							9 51		1016	1114	1114			1252	1 0					H2 52	
Sandy		8 4							9 56		1021					1257	1 5					2 57	
Potton		8 10							10 2		1027					1 3	1 11					3 3	
Gamlingay		8 15							10 6		1032					1 7	1 15					3 8	
Old North Road		8 23							1014		1040					1 15	1 23					3 16	
Lord's Bridge		8 30							1022		1047					1 23	1 31					3 23	
Cambridge		8 41							1029		1056	1143	1143			1 33	1 42					3 33	

	SO pm	SX pm	J ThSO pm	SX pm	SO pm	pm	J pm	pm	SX pm	SX pm	pm	J pm	SO pm	SX pm	pm	J pm	2 pm	SO pm	SX pm	SX pm	SO pm
Oxford				2 48	2 55						5 18				6 48		7 55			1050	1055
Islip				3 1	3 8						5 31				7 1						11 8
Bicester, London Road				3 10	3 17						5 41				7 11		8 15			1111	1120
Launton				3 14	3 21						5 45				7 15					1115	1124
Marsh Gibbon and Poundon				3 18	3 25						5 49				7 19						1128
Claydon				3 25	3 32						5 56				7 26					1124	1135
Verney Junction			2 53	3 29	3 36		4 43				6 0	6 6			7 30	7 53					
Winslow			2 58	3 34	3 41		4 48				6 5	6 11			7 35	7 58				1131	1142
Swanbourne			3 2	3 38	3 45		4 52				6 9	6 15			7 39	8 2				1136	1146
Bletchley arr.			3 11	3 48	4 0		5 1				6 19	6 24			7 48	8 11	8 37			1145	1156
Bletchley dep.	2 50	3 10		3 53	4 2	4 22		5 11	5 38	6 15			6 46	6 46	7 54			8 47	8 49		
Fenny Stratford	2 52	3 12		3 55	4 4	4 24		5 13	5 40	6 17			6 48	6 48				8 50	8 52		
Bow Brickhill	2 55	3 15				4 27		5 16		6 20			6 51	6 51							
Woburn Sands	3 0	3 20		4 0	4 9	4 32		5 21	5 45	6 25			6 56	6 56				8 56	8 58		
Aspley Guise	3 3	3 23				4 35		5 24		6 28			6 59	6 59							
Ridgmont	3 7	3 27		4 5	4 14	4 39		5 28	5 50	6 32			7 3	7 3				9 1	9 3		
Lidlington	3 11	3 31		4 9	4 18	4 43		5 32	5 54				7 7	7 7				9 5	9 7		
Millbrook	3 14	3 34		4 12	4 21	4 46		5 35	5 57				7 10	7 10				9 8	9 10		
Stewartby	3 17	3 37				4 49		5 38	6 0				7 13	7 13							
Kempston Hardwick	3 21	F3 41				4 53		5 42					7 17	7 17							
Bedford St. John's arr.	3 27	F3 47		4 21	4 30	4 59		5 48	6 8				7 23	7 23	8 14			9 18	9 20		
Bedford St. John's dep.				4 25	4 31			5 52					7 23		8 15			9 20	9 22		
Willington				4 33	4 39			6 1					B7 36					9 28	A9 36		
Blunham				4 38	4 44			6 6					7 41					9 33	9 42		
Sandy				4 45	4 49			C6 17					7 46					9 38	9 47		
Potton				4 51	4 55			6 23					7 52					9 44	9 53		
Gamlingay				4 55	5 0			6 27					7 57					9 49	9 58		
Old North Road				5 3	5 8			6 35										9 57	10 6		
Lord's Bridge				5 11	5 15			6 43										10 6			
Cambridge				5 21	5 23			6 50					8 18		8 56			1015	1022		

2—Second Class only. A—Arrives Willington 9.30 p.m. B—Arrives Willington 7.32 p.m. C—Arrives Sandy 6.11 p.m. F—On Fridays depart Kempston Hardwick 3.42 p.m. arrive Bedford 3.48 p.m. H—Arrives Blunham 2.48 p.m. SX—Saturdays Excepted. SO—Saturdays only. ThSO—Thursdays and Saturdays only. J—Starts from Buckingham.

One hundred and three years on and a modest two-car train runs between Oxford and Cambridge. It is seen here, leaving Sandy, with the 10.43 ex-Cambridge, travelling over a part of the line now consigned to history and the memorable recollections of a cherished cross-country route.

C. F. Burton